PENGUIN BOOKS

IN PATAGONIA

Bruce Chatwin was born in 1940, and was the author of
In Patagonia, *The Viceroy of Ouidah*, *On the Black Hill*,
The Songlines, and *Utz*. The last three he considered
works of fiction. His other books are *What Am I Doing
Here*, *Anatomy of Restlessness*, and *Far Journeys*, a collec-
tion of his photographs which also includes selections
from his travel notebooks. Chatwin died outside Nice,
France, on January 17, 1989.

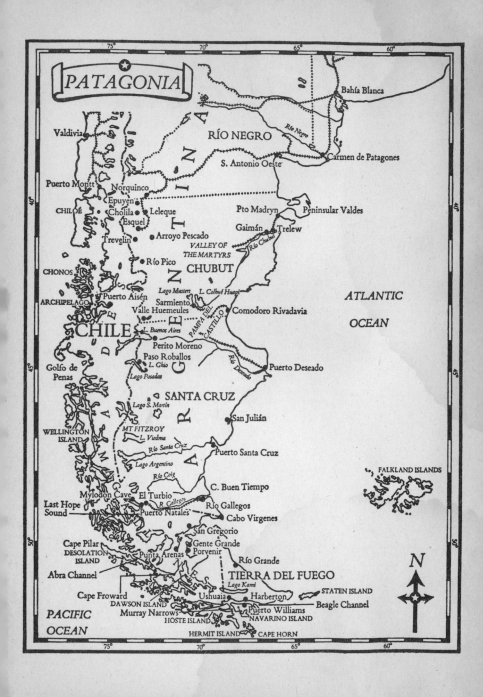

In Patagonia

BRUCE CHATWIN

Il n'y a plus que la Patagonie, la Patagonie,
qui convienne à mon immense tristesse . . .
Blaise Cendrars,
Prose du Transsibérien

PENGUIN BOOKS

PENGUIN BOOKS
Published by the Penguin Group
Penguin Books USA Inc.,
375 Hudson Street, New York, New York 10014, U.S.A.
Penguin Books Ltd, 27 Wrights Lane
London W8 5TZ, England
Penguin Books Australia Ltd, Ringwood,
Victoria, Australia
Penguin Books Canada Limited, 10 Alcorn Avenue,
Toronto, Ontario, Canada M4V 3B2
Penguin Books (N.Z.) Ltd, 182–190 Wairau Road,
Auckland 10, New Zealand

Penguin Books Ltd, Registered Offices:
Harmondsworth, Middlesex, England

First published in Great Britain by Jonathan Cape Ltd 1977
First published in the United States of America by
Summit Books, a division of Simon & Schuster, Inc. 1979
Published in Penguin Books 1988

18

Copyright © Bruce Chatwin, 1977
Sections 73, 75, 86 Copyright © Monica Barnett, 1977
All rights reserved

LIBRARY OF CONGRESS CATALOGING IN PUBLICATION DATA
Chatwin, Bruce, 1942–1989
   In Patagonia.
Reprint. Originally published: New York: Summit
Books, c1977.
1. Patagonia (Argentina and Chile)—Description and
travel.   2. Chatwin, Bruce, 1942–1989—Journeys—
Patagonia   (Argentina and Chile).   I. Title.
[F2936.C47   1988]   918.2'70464   87-38485
ISBN 0 14 01.1291 X

Printed in the United States of America
Set in Garamond No. 3

In Patagonia

I

IN MY grandmother's dining-room there was a glass-fronted cabinet and in the cabinet a piece of skin. It was a small piece only, but thick and leathery, with strands of coarse, reddish hair. It was stuck to a card with a rusty pin. On the card was some writing in faded black ink, but I was too young then to read.

'What's that?'

'A piece of brontosaurus.'

My mother knew the names of two prehistoric animals, the brontosaurus and the mammoth. She knew it was not a mammoth. Mammoths came from Siberia.

The brontosaurus, I learned, was an animal that had drowned in the Flood, being too big for Noah to ship aboard the Ark. I pictured a shaggy lumbering creature with claws and fangs and a malicious green light in its eyes. Sometimes the brontosaurus would crash through the bedroom wall and wake me from my sleep.

This particular brontosaurus had lived in Patagonia, a country in South America, at the far end of the world. Thousands of years before, it had fallen into a glacier, travelled down a mountain in a prison of blue ice, and arrived in perfect condition at the bottom. Here my grandmother's cousin, Charley Milward the Sailor, found it.

Charley Milward was captain of a merchant ship that sank at the entrance to the Strait of Magellan. He survived the wreck and settled nearby, at Punta Arenas, where he ran a ship-repairing yard. The Charley Milward of my imagination was a god among men—tall, silent and strong, with black mutton-chop whiskers and fierce blue eyes. He wore his sailor's cap at an angle and the tops of his sea-boots turned down.

Directly he saw the brontosaurus poking out of the ice, he knew what to do. He had it jointed, salted, packed in barrels, and shipped to the Natural History Museum in South Kensington.

I pictured blood and ice, flesh and salt, gangs of Indian workmen and lines of barrels along a shore—a work of giants and all to no purpose; the brontosaurus went rotten on its voyage through the tropics and arrived in London a putrefied mess; which was why you saw brontosaurus bones in the museum, but no skin.

Fortunately cousin Charley had posted a scrap to my grandmother.

My grandmother lived in a red-brick house set behind a screen of yellow-spattered laurels. It had tall chimneys, pointed gables and a garden of blood-coloured roses. Inside it smelled of church.

I do not remember much about my grandmother except her size. I would clamber over her wide bosom or watch, slyly, to see if she'd be able to rise from her chair. Above her hung paintings of Dutch burghers, their fat buttery faces nesting in white ruffs. On the mantelpiece were two Japanese homunculi with red and white ivory eyes that popped out on stalks. I would play with these, or with a German articulated monkey, but always I pestered her: 'Please can I have the piece of brontosaurus.'

Never in my life have I wanted anything as I wanted that piece of skin. My grandmother said I should have it one day, perhaps. And when she died I said: 'Now I *can* have the piece of brontosaurus,' but my mother said: 'Oh, that thing! I'm afraid we threw it away.'

At school they laughed at the story of the brontosaurus. The science master said I'd mixed it up with the Siberian mammoth. He told the class how Russian scientists had dined off deep-frozen mammoth and told me not to tell lies. Besides, he said, brontosauruses were reptiles. They had no hair, but scaly armoured hide. And he showed us an artist's impression of the beast—so different from that of my imagination—grey-green, with a tiny head and gigantic switchback of vertebrae, placidly eating weed in a lake. I was ashamed of my hairy brontosaurus, but I knew it was not a mammoth.

It took some years to sort the story out. Charley Milward's animal was not a brontosaurus, but the mylodon or Giant Sloth. He never found a whole specimen, or even a whole skeleton, but some skin and bones, preserved by the cold, dryness and salt, in a cave on Last Hope Sound in Chilean Patagonia. He sent the collection to England and sold it to the British Museum. This version was less romantic but had the merit of being true.

My interest in Patagonia survived the loss of the skin; for the Cold War woke in me a passion for geography. In the late 1940s the Cannibal of the Kremlin shadowed our lives; you could mistake his moustaches for teeth. We listened to lectures about the war he was planning. We watched the civil defence lecturer ring the cities of Europe to show the zones of total and partial destruction. We saw the zones bump one against the other leaving no space in between. The instructor wore khaki shorts. His knees were white and knobbly, and we saw it was hopeless. The war was coming and there was nothing we could do.

Next, we read about the cobalt bomb, which was worse than the hydrogen bomb and could smother the planet in an endless chain reaction.

I knew the colour cobalt from my great-aunt's paintbox. She had lived on Capri at the time of Maxim Gorky and painted Capriot boys naked. Later her art became almost entirely religious. She did lots of St Sebastians, always against a cobalt-blue background, always the same beautiful young man, stuck through and through with arrows and still on his feet.

So I pictured the cobalt bomb as a dense blue cloudbank, spitting tongues of flame at the edges. And I saw myself, out alone on a green headland, scanning the horizon for the advance of the cloud.

And yet we hoped to survive the blast. We started an Emigration Committee and made plans to settle in some far corner of the earth. We pored over atlases. We learned the direction of prevailing winds and the likely patterns of fall-out. The war would come in the Northern Hemisphere, so we looked to the Southern. We ruled out Pacific Islands for islands are traps. We ruled out Australia and New Zealand, and we fixed on Patagonia as the safest place on earth.

I pictured a low timber house with a shingled roof, caulked against storms, with blazing log fires inside and the walls lined with the best books, somewhere to live when the rest of the world blew up.

Then Stalin died and we sang hymns of praise in chapel, but I continued to hold Patagonia in reserve.

2

THE HISTORY of Buenos Aires is written in its telephone directory. Pompey Romanov, Emilio Rommel, Crespina D.Z. de Rose, Ladislao Radziwil, and Elizabeta Marta Callman de Rothschild — five names taken at random from among the R's — told a story of exile, disillusion and anxiety behind lace curtains.

It was lovely summery weather the week I was there. The Christmas decorations were in the shops. They had just opened the Perón Mausoleum at Olivos; Eva was in good shape after her tour of European bank-vaults. Some catholics had said a Requiem Mass for the soul of Hitler and they were expecting a military coup.

By day the city quivered in a silvery film of pollution. In the evenings boys and girls walked beside the river. They were hard and sleek and empty-headed, and they walked arm in arm under the trees, laughing cold laughter, separated from the red river by a red granite balustrade.

The rich were closing their apartments for the summer. White dust sheets were spread over gilded furniture and there were piles of leather suitcases in the hall. All summer the rich would play on their estancias. The very rich would go to Punta del Este in Uruguay, where they stood less chance of being kidnapped. Some of the rich, the sporting ones anyway, said summer was a closed season for kidnaps. The guerillas also rented holiday villas, or went to Switzerland to ski.

At a lunch we sat under a painting of one of General Rosas's gauchos, by Raymond Monvoisin, a follower of Delacroix. He lay swathed in a blood-red poncho, a male odalisque, cat-like and passively erotic.

'Trust a Frenchman,' I thought, 'to see through all the cant about the gaucho.'

On my right was a lady novelist. She said the only subject worth tackling was loneliness. She told the story of an international violinist, stuck one night on tour in a Mid-Western motel. The story hinged on the bed, the violin and the violinist's wooden leg.

Some years ago she knew Ernesto Guevara, at that time an untidy young man pushing for a place in society.

'He was very *macho*,' she said, 'like most Argentine boys, but I never thought it would come to *that*.'

The city kept reminding me of Russia—the cars of the secret police bristling with aerials; women with splayed haunches licking ice-cream in dusty parks; the same bullying statues, the pie-crust architecture, the same avenues that were not quite straight, giving the illusion of endless space and leading out into nowhere.

Tsarist rather than Soviet Russia. Bazarov could be an Argentine character, *The Cherry Orchard* is an Argentine situation. The Russia of greedy kulaks, corrupt officials, imported groceries and landowners asquint to Europe.

I said as much to a friend.

'Lots of people say that,' he said. 'Last year an old White *émigrée* came to our place in the country. She got terrifically excited and asked to see every room. We went up to the attics and she said: "Ah! I knew it! The smell of my childhood!"'

3

I TOOK the train to La Plata to see the best Natural History Museum in South America. In the compartment were two everyday victims of *machismo*, a thin woman with a black eye and a sickly teenage girl clinging to her dress. Sitting opposite was a boy with green squiggles on his shirt. I looked again and saw the squiggles were knife blades.

La Plata is a university town. Most of the graffiti were stale imports from May 1968 but some were rather unusual: 'Isabel Perón or Death!' 'If Evita were alive she would have been a *Montonera*.' 'Death to the English Pirates!' 'The Best Intellectual is a Dead Intellectual.'

An alley of gingko trees led past a statue of Benito Juárez to the steps of the museum. The Argentine national colours, the 'blue and white', fluttered from the flagpole, but a red tide of

Guevara dicta sprawled up the classical façade, over the pediment and threatened to engulf the building. A young man stood with his arms folded and said: 'The Museum is shut for various reasons.' A Peruvian Indian who had come specially from Lima stood about looking crestfallen. Together we shamed them into letting us in.

In the first room I saw a big dinosaur found in Patagonia by a Lithuanian immigrant, Casimir Slapelič, and named in his honour. I saw the glyptodons or giant armadillos looking like a parade of armoured cars, each one of their bone plates marked like a Japanese chrysanthemum. I saw the birds of La Plata stuffed beside a portrait of W. H. Hudson; and, finally, I found some remains of the Giant Sloth, *Mylodon Listai*, from the cave on Last Hope Sound—claws, dung, bones with sinews attached, and a piece of skin. It had the same reddish hair I remembered as a child. It was half an inch thick. Nodules of white cartilage were embedded in it and it looked like hairy peanut brittle.

La Plata was the home of Florentino Ameghino, a solitary autodidact, the son of Genoese immigrants, who was born in 1854 and died Director of the National Museum. He started collecting fossils as a boy, and, later, opened a stationery business called *El Gliptodonte* after his favourite. In the end the fossils squeezed out the stationery and took the place over, but by that time Ameghino was world-famous, for his publications were so prolific and his fossils so very strange.

His younger brother, Carlos, spent his time exploring the barrancas of Patagonia, while Florentino sat at home sorting the fossils out. He had wonderful powers of imagination and would reconstruct a colossal beast from the least scrap of tooth or claw. He also had a weakness for colossal names. He called one animal *Florentinoameghinea* and another *Propalaeohoplophorus*. He loved his country with the passion of the second generation immigrant and sometimes his patriotism went to his head. On one issue he took on the entire body of scientific opinion:

About fifty million years ago, when the continents were wandering about, the dinosaurs of Patagonia were much the same as the dinosaurs of Belgium, Wyoming or Mongolia. When they died out, hot-blooded mammals took their place. The scientists who examined this phenomenon proposed an origin for the newcomers in the northern hemisphere, whence they colonized the globe.

The first mammals to reach South America were some odd species now known as the notoungulates and condylarths. Shortly after their arrival, the sea broke through the Isthmus of Panama and exiled them from the rest of Creation. Without carnivores to harass them, the mammals of South America developed odder and odder forms. There were the huge ground-sloths, toxodon, megatherium, and mylodon. There were porcupines, ant-eaters, and armadillos; liptoterns, astrapotheriums, and the macrauchenia (like a camel with a trunk). Then the land-bridge of Panama resurfaced and a host of more efficient, North American mammals, such as the puma and sabre-tooth tiger, rushed south and wiped out many indigenous species.

Dr Ameghino did not like this zoological version of the Monroe Doctrine. A few southerners, it was true, did push against the *Yanqui* invasion. Small sloths got to Central America, the armadillo to Texas, and the porcupine to Canada (which shows there is no invasion without a counter-invasion). But this didn't satisfy Ameghino. He did his duty to his country and up-ended the chronology. He twisted the evidence to show that *all* hot-blooded mammals began in South America and went north. And then he got quite carried away: he published a paper suggesting that Man himself had emerged from the soil of the patria; which is why, in some circles, the name of Ameghino is set beside Plato and Newton.

4

I LEFT the boneyard of La Plata, reeling under the blows of Linnaean Latin, and hurried back to Buenos Aires, to the Patagonia station, to catch the night bus south.

The bus was passing through low hilly country when I woke. The sky was grey and patches of mist hung in the valleys. The wheatfields were turning from green to yellow and in the pastures black cattle were grazing. We kept crossing streams with willows and pampas grass. The houses of the estancias shrank behind screens of poplar and eucalyptus. Some of the houses had pantile roofs, but most were of metal sheet, painted red. The tallest eucalyptus trees had their tops blown out.

At half past nine the bus stopped at the small town where I hoped to find Bill Philips. His grandfather was a pioneer in Patagonia and he still had cousins there. The town was a grid of one-storey brick houses and shops with an overhanging cornice. In the square was a municipal garden and a bronze bust of General San Martín, the Liberator. The streets around the garden were asphalted but the wind blew in sideways and coated the flowers and the bronze with white dust.

Two farmers had parked their pick-ups outside the bar and were drinking *vino rosado*. An old man huddled over his maté kettle. Behind the bar were pictures of Isabelita and Juan Perón, he wearing a blue and white sash and looking old and degenerate; another of Evita and Juan, much younger then and more dangerous; and a third of General Rosas, with sideburns and a down-curved mouth. The iconography of Peronism is extremely complicated.

An old woman gave me a leathery sandwich and coffee. Naturally, she said, I could leave my bag while I tried to find Señor Philips.

'It is far to Señor Philips. He lives up in the sierra.'

'How far?'

'Eight leagues. But you may find him. Often he comes to town in the morning.'

I asked around but no one had seen the gringo Philips that morning. I found a taxi and haggled over the price. The driver was a thin, cheerful type, Italian I guessed. He seemed to enjoy bargaining and went off to buy gasoline. I looked General San Martín over and humped my bag on to the sidewalk. The taxi drove up and the Italian jumped out excitedly and said:

'I've seen the gringo Philips. There, walking this way.'

He didn't mind losing the fare and refused to be paid. I was beginning to like the country.

A shortish, thick-set man in khaki bags was coming down the street. He had a cheerful boyish face, and a tuft of hair stood up on the back of his head.

'Bill Philips?'

'How did you know?'

'I guessed.'

'Come on home,' he said, grinning.

We drove out of town in his old pick-up. The door on the passenger side had jammed and we had to pile out at a rusty shack to let in a wrinkled, sandy-haired Basque, who did odd jobs on the farm and was a bit simple. The road sliced through flat cattle country. Black Aberdeen Angus clustered round the wind-pumps. The fences were in perfect shape. Every five miles or so we passed the pretentious gates of a big estancia.

'Millionaire country down here,' Bill said. 'I'm up in the sheep zone. I can do a few Jerseys, but we don't get the grass or water for a big herd. One bad drought and I'd be wiped clean.'

Bill turned off the main road towards some pale rocky hills. The clouds and mist were breaking up. Beyond the hills I saw a chain of mountains, the same silvery grey as the clouds. The sun caught their flanks and they seemed to be shining.

'Are you here because of Darwin, or to see us?' Bill asked.

'To see you. But Darwin?'

'He was here. You can see the Sierra Ventana, showing up now, far left. Darwin went up it on his way to Buenos Aires. Haven't done it myself. Too much work on a new farm.'

The road climbed and gave out into a bumpy track. Bill opened a gate by a farmhouse and a dog streaked towards us. He nipped back into the cab and the dog crouched, hatefully baring its gums.

'My neighbours are Italian,' Bill said. 'The Its have got the whole region buttoned up. All came from one village in the Marches forty years back. All ardent Perónistas and not to be trusted. They have a simple philosophy: breed like flies, belly-ache about land reform later. They all started off with good-sized lots, but they go on splitting them up. You see that house building over there?'

The track had risen sharply and the whole country was spread out behind, a basin of fields ringed by rocky hills and lit by flashing shafts of sunlight. All the farmhouses were set in clumps of poplars, except the new one, a plain block of white, bare of trees.

'There's a family who've just split up. Old man dies. Two sons quarrel. Elder son gets best land and builds new house. Younger son active in local politics. Wants to lay fingers on gringo's best sheep-pasture. I've got just enough to keep going without frills. And we were Argentine citizens when this lot were holed up in their bloody Italian village.'

'Here's the house coming up now,' he said.

We stopped to let out the Basque, who walked down the hill. The house was a prefabricated cottage of two rooms, stuck on a bare hillside, with big windows and a wonderful view.

'Don't mind Anne-Marie,' Bill said. 'She gets a bit jumpy when we have visitors. Works herself into a state. Seems to think visitors mean housework. Not the domesticated type. But don't take any notice. She loves having visitors really.'

'Darling, we've got a visitor,' he called.

I heard her say, 'Have we?' and the bedroom door slammed shut. Bill looked unhappy. He patted the dog and we talked about dogs. I looked at his bookshelf and saw he had all the best books. He had been reading Turgenev's *Sportsman's Sketches* and we talked about Turgenev.

A boy in blue trousers and a freshly laundered shirt poked his head round the door. He looked at the visitor apprehensively and sucked his thumb.

'Nicky, come and say hullo,' Bill said.

Nicky ran back into the bedroom and the door shut again. Finally, Anne-Marie did come out and shake hands. She was edgy and formal. She couldn't think what had possessed her father to suggest I come.

'We're in chaos here,' she said.

She had a bright open smile when she smiled. She was thin and healthy and had black hair cropped short and a clear tanned skin. I liked her tremendously, but she kept talking about 'us provincials'. She had worked in London and New York. She knew the way things ought to be and apologized for the way they were. 'If only we'd known you were coming we'd have. ... '

It didn't matter, I said. Nothing mattered. But I could see it did matter to her.

'We shall need more meat for lunch,' she said, 'now we've got a visitor. Why don't you both take Nicky down to the farm and I'll clean up.'

Bill and I waited for Nicky to change out of the clothes he'd put on for my benefit. In the first field we saw some brown birds with long tails and crests.

'What's that bird, Nicky?' Bill asked.

'Ouraka.'

'Ugliest bird in the book,' said Bill.

'And that's tero-teros,' Nicky said.

A pair of black and white plovers got up and circled above us, shrieking that the enemy was about.

'And that's the ugliest damned noise. Hates man, that bird. Absolutely hates man.'

The track cut through a patch of bristly grass and came up to some farm buildings in a hollow out of the wind. A wiry kid called Dino ran out of the concrete house and played with Nicky in the yard shouting. There was a sheep-dip full of slimy green liquid, and Bill had to call them away from it.

'Bad business,' he said. 'Two months ago, neighbour's child drowned in the gringo's sheep-dip. Parents drunk after Sunday lunch. Thank God the mother's pregnant again—for the ninth time!'

The boy's father came out, doffed his cap to Bill and Bill asked him to kill a sheep. We looked round the farm, at the Jerseys, some new rams and a McCormick tractor.

'And you can imagine what that bloody thing cost with our exchange rate. Can't afford another thing. Do you know what we pray for down here? Pray for sadistically? Bad winter in Europe. Makes the price of wool go up.'

We walked up to the orchard where Dino's father had strung the carcass to an apple tree and his dog was eating the purple bunch of intestines in the grass. He took his knife to the neck and the head came away in his hand. The carcass swung on the branch. He steadied it and cut off a leg, which he handed to Bill.

Halfway back to the house, Nicky asked if he could hold the visitor's hand.

'I can't think what you've done to Nicky,' Anne-Marie said when we got back. 'Usually he hates visitors.'

5

In the evening Bill drove me down to Bahía Blanca. On the way we went to see a Scot about a bull.

Sonny Urquhart's farm was out on the flat land, about three miles back from the road. It had passed from father to son for four generations, since the time of the Indian raids. We had to open four wire gates along the track. The night was silent but for the teros. We made for a hump of black cypresses with a light shining among them.

The Scot called the dogs off and led the way down a narrow green corridor into a tall, darker green room lit by a single bulb. Round the fire were some Victorian easy chairs with flat wooden armrests. Damp whisky glasses had bitten rings into the french polish. Hung high on the walls were prints of willowy gentlemen and ladies in crinolines.

Sonny Urquhart was a hard stringy man with blond hair swept back and parted in the centre. He had moles on his face and a big Adam's apple. The back of his neck was criss-crossed with lines from working hatless in the sun. His eyes were watery blue, and rather bloodshot.

He finished his business with Bill about the bull. And Bill talked about farm prices and land reform and Sonny shook or nodded his head. He sat on a firestool and sipped his whisky. Of Scotland he preserved a certain pride of blood and a dim memory of kilts and pipes, but those were the festivities of another generation.

His aunt and uncle had come down from Buenos Aires to look after him. The aunt was pleased we had come. She had been baking and brought in a cake, iced with pink sugar and fluffy inside. She cut huge slices and served them on delicate china plates with silver forks. We had eaten earlier but we couldn't refuse. She cut a slice for Sonny.

'You know I don't eat cake,' he said.

Sonny had a sister who was a nurse in Buenos Aires. When their mother died she came back home but she quarrelled with Sonny's peon. He was half-Indian and he slept in the house. She hated his knife. She hated the way he used it at table. She knew the peon was bad for Sonny. They drank most nights. Sometimes they drank all night and slept through the next day. She tried to change the house, to make it more cheerful, but Sonny said: 'The house stays the way it was.'

One night they were both drunk, and the peon insulted her. She panicked and locked herself in her room. She felt something bad was going to happen and went back to her old job.

Sonny and the peon fought after she'd gone. The neighbours said it could have been much worse. The aunt and uncle came down then, but they couldn't take the farm either. Fortunately they had savings enough to buy a bungalow in a Buenos Aires suburb, in a nice neighbourhood, mind you, with other English people.

They chattered on and Sonny sipped his whisky. He wanted the peon back. You could tell from what he did not say that he wanted the peon back.

6

BAHÍA BLANCA is the last big place before the Patagonian desert. Bill dropped me at the hotel near the bus station. The bar-room was green and brightly lit and full of men playing cards. A country boy stood by the bar. He was shaky on his feet but he kept his head up like a gaucho. He was a nice-looking boy with curly black hair and he really was very drunk. The owner's wife showed me a hot airless room, painted purple, with two beds in it. The room had no window and the door gave out on to a glassed-in courtyard. It was very cheap and the woman said nothing about having to share.

I was half asleep when the country boy reeled in, flung himself on the other bed and groaned and sat up and was sick. He was sick on and off for an hour and then he snored. I did not sleep that night for the smell of the sick and the snoring.

So next day, as we drove through the desert, I sleepily watched the rags of silver cloud spinning across the sky, and the sea of grey-green thornscrub lying off in sweeps and rising in terraces and the white dust streaming off the saltpans, and, on the horizon, land and sky dissolving into an absence of colour.

Patagonia begins on the Río Negro. At mid-day the bus crossed an iron bridge over the river and stopped outside a bar. An Indian woman got off with her son. She had filled up two seats with her bulk. She chewed garlic and wore real gold jangly earrings and a hard white hat pinned over her braids. A look of abstract horror passed over the boy's face as she manœuvred herself and her parcels on to the street.

The permanent houses of the village were of brick with black stove pipes and a tangle of electric wires above. Where the brick houses gave out, the shacks of the Indians began. These were patched out of packing cases, sheet plastic and sacking.

A single man was walking up the street, his brown felt hat pulled low over his face. He was carrying a sack and walking into the white dustclouds, out into the country. Some children sheltered in a doorway and tormented a lamb. From one hut came the noise of the radio and sizzling fat. A lumpy arm appeared and threw a dog a bone. The dog took it and slunk off.

The Indians were migrant workers from Southern Chile. They were Araucanian Indians. A hundred years ago the Araucanians were incredibly fierce and brave. They painted their bodies red and flayed their enemies alive and sucked at the hearts of the dead. Their boys' education consisted of hockey, horsemanship, liquor, insolence and sexual athletics, and for three centuries they scared the Spaniards out of their wits. In the sixteenth century Alonso de Ercilla wrote an epic in their honour and called it the *Araucana*. Voltaire read it and through him the Araucanians became candidates for the Noble Savage (tough version). The Araucanians are still very tough and would be a lot tougher if they gave up drink.

Outside the village there were irrigated plantations of maize and squash, and orchards of cherries and apricots. Along the line of the river, the willows were all blown about and showing their silvery undersides. The Indians had been cutting withies and there were fresh white cuts and the smell of sap. The river was swollen with snowmelt from the Andes, fast-running and rustling the reeds. Purple swallows were chasing bugs. When they flew above the cliff, the wind caught them and keeled them over in a fluttering reversal and they dropped again low over the river.

The cliff rose sheer above a ferry-landing. I climbed a path and from the top looked up-stream towards Chile. I could see the river, glinting and sliding through the bone-white cliffs with strips of emerald cultivation either side. Away from the cliffs was the desert. There was no sound but the wind, whirring through thorns and whistling through dead grass, and no other sign of life but a hawk, and a black beetle easing over white stones.

The Patagonian desert is not a desert of sand or gravel, but a low thicket of grey-leaved thorns which give off a bitter smell when crushed. Unlike the deserts of Arabia it has not produced any dramatic excess of the spirit, but it does have a place in the record of human experience. Charles Darwin found its negative qualities irresistible. In summing up *The Voyage of the Beagle*, he tried, unsuccessfully, to explain why, more than any of the wonders he had seen, these 'arid wastes' had taken such firm possession of his mind.

In the 1860s W. H. Hudson came to the Río Negro looking for the migrant birds that wintered around his home in La Plata. Years later he remembered the trip through the filter of his Notting Hill boarding-house and wrote a book so quiet and sane it makes Thoreau seem a ranter. Hudson devotes a whole chapter of *Idle Days in Patagonia* to answering Mr Darwin's question, and he concludes that desert wanderers discover in themselves a primaeval calmness (known also to the simplest savage), which is perhaps the same as the Peace of God.

About the time of Hudson's visit, the Río Negro was the northern frontier of an unusual kingdom which still maintains a court in exile in Paris.

7

ON A drizzling November afternoon, His Royal Highness Prince Philippe of Araucania and Patagonia gave me an audience at his public relations firm on the Faubourg Poissonière.

To get there I had to pass the Marxist daily *L'Humanité*, a cinema showing 'Pinocchio', and a shop that sold fox and skunk skins from Patagonia. Also present was the Court Historian, a young and portly Argentine of French descent with royal buttons on his blazer.

The Prince was a short man in a brown tweed suit who sucked at a briar pipe that curled down his chin. He had just come back from East Berlin on business and disdainfully waved about a copy of *Pravda*. He showed me a long manuscript in search of a publisher; a photo of two Araucanian citizens holding up their tricolour, the Blue, White and Green; a court order allowing M. Philippe Boiry to use his royal title on a French passport; a letter from the Consul of El Salvador in Houston recognizing him as a head of state in exile; and his correspondence with Presidents Perón and Eisenhower (whom he had decorated) and with Prince Montezuma, the pretender to the Aztec throne.

In parting he gave me copies of the *Cahiers des Hautes-Etudes Araucaniennes*, among them Comte Léon M. de Moulin-Peuillet's study, *The Royal Succession of Araucania and the Order of Memphis and Misräim (Egyptian Rite)*.

'Every time I try something,' the Prince said, 'I gain a little.'

8

IN THE spring of 1859 the lawyer Orélie-Antoine de Tounens closed his grey-shuttered office in the Rue Hiéras in Périgueux, looked back at the byzantine profile of the cathedral, and left for England, clutching the valise that held the 25,000 francs he had withdrawn from his family's joint account, thus accelerating their ruin.

He was the eighth son of peasant farmers who lived in a collapsing *gentilhommière* at the hamlet of La Chèze near the hamlet of Las Fount. He was thirty-three (the age when geniuses die), a bachelor and a freemason, who, with a bit of cheating, had traced his descent from a Gallo-Roman senator and added a *de* to his name. He had moonstruck eyes and flowing black hair and beard.

He dressed as a dandy, held himself excessively erect and acted with the unreasoning courage of the visionary.

Through Voltaire he had come on Ercilla's epic of wooden stanzas and learned of the untamed tribes of the Chilean South:

> Robust and beardless,
> Bodies rippling and muscular,
> Hard limbs, nerves of steel,
> Agile, brazen, cheerful,
> Spirited, valiant, daring,
> Toughened by work, patient
> Of mortal cold, hunger and heat.

Murat was a stable boy and he was King of Naples. Bernadotte was a lawyer's clerk from Pau and he was King of Sweden. And Orélie-Antoine got it into his head that the Araucanians would elect him king of a young and vigorous nation.

He boarded an English merchantman, rounded the Horn in mid-winter, and landed at Coquimbo, on the desert shore of Chile, where he lodged with a fellow mason. He soon learned that the Araucanians were heading for their last stand against the Republic, began an encouraging correspondence with their Cacique, Mañil, and in October crossed the River Bio-Bio, the frontier of his designated kingdom.

An interpreter and two Frenchmen went along—MM. Lachaise and Desfontaines, his Minister for Foreign Affairs and Secretary of State for Justice, phantom functionaries, named after La Chèze and Las Fount and contained within the person of His Majesty.

Orélie-Antoine and his two invisible ministers battled through an underscrub of scarlet flowers and fell in with a young horseman. The boy told him Mañil was dead and led the way to his successor, Quilapán. The Frenchman was delighted to hear that the word 'Republic' was as odious to the Indian as to himself. But there was one new fact he did not know: before dying the Cacique Mañil prophesied that eternal delusion of the Amerindian: the end of war and slavery would coincide with the coming of a bearded white stranger.

The Araucanians' welcome encouraged Orélie-Antoine to proclaim a constitutional monarchy with a succession to be established within his own family. He signed the document with his spidery royal signature, endorsed it with the bolder hand of M. Desfontaines, and sent copies to the Chilean President and the Santiago newspapers. Three days later, a horseman, exhausted by two crossings of the Cordillera, brought fresh news: the Patagonians also accepted the kingdom. Orélie-Antoine signed another paper, annexing the whole of South America from Latitude 42° to the Horn.

Staggered by the magnitude of his act, the king retired to a boarding house in Valparaíso and busied himself with the Constitution, the Armed Forces, the steamship line to Bordeaux and the National Anthem (composed by a Sr Guillermo Frick of Valdivia). He wrote an open letter to his home newspaper *Le Périgord* advertising 'La Nouvelle France' as a fertile land bursting with minerals, which would compensate for the loss of Louisiana and Canada, but didn't mention it was full of warrior Indians. Another newspaper, *Le Temps*, jibed that 'La Nouvelle France' inspired about as much confidence as M. de Tounens his former clients.

Nine months later, penniless and stung by indifference, he returned to Araucania with a horse, a mule and a servant called Rosales. (When hiring this individual he made the common tourist's mistake of confusing fifteen for fifty pesos.) At the first village his subjects were drunk, but they revived and passed word for the tribes to muster. The king spoke of Natural and International Law; the Indians replied with *vivas*. He stood within a circle of naked horsemen, in a brown poncho, with a white fillet round his head, saluting with stiff Napoleonic gestures. He unfurled the Tricolour, crying, 'Long live the Unity of the Tribes! Under a single chief! Under a single flag!'

The king was now dreaming of an army of thirty thousand warriors and of imposing his frontier by force. War cries echoed through the forest and the itinerant hooch-sellers scuttled for civilization. Across the river, the white colonists saw smoke signals and signalled their own fears to the military. Meanwhile Rosales scribbled a note to his wife (which she alone could decipher) telling of his plan to kidnap the French adventurer.

Orélie-Antoine moved through the settlements without escort. Stopping one day for lunch, he sat by a riverbank, lost in reverie, ignoring a party of armed men he saw talking to Rosales in the trees. A weight pressed on his shoulders. Hands clamped round his arms. More hands stripped him of his possessions.

The Chilean carabineers forced the king to ride to the provincial capital of Los Angeles and hauled him before the Governor, a patrician landowner, Don Cornelio Saavedra.

'Do you speak French?' the prisoner demanded. He began by asserting his royal rights and ended by offering to return to the bosom of his family.

Saavedra appreciated that Orélie-Antoine could want nothing better. 'But,' he said, 'I am having you tried as a common criminal to discourage others who may imitate your example.'

The jail in Los Angeles was dark and damp. His warders waved lanterns in his face as he slept. He caught dysentery. He writhed on a sodden straw mattress and saw the spectre of the garrotte. In one lucid interval he composed the order of succession: 'We, Orélie-Antoine Ier, bachelor, by the Grace of God and the National Will, Sovereign etc. etc. ... ' The throne would pass to his old father, at that season gathering in his walnuts — then to his brothers and their issue.

And then his hair fell out and with it went the will to rule.

Orélie-Antoine renounced the throne (under duress) and M. Cazotte, the French Consul, managed to get him out of prison and shipped him home aboard a French warship. He was put on short rations but the cadets asked him over to dine at their table.

Exiled in Paris, his hair grew back longer and blacker than before, and his appetite for rule swelled to megalomaniac proportions. 'Louis XI after Péronne,' he concluded his memoirs, 'François Ier after Pavia were no less Kings of France than before.' And yet his career followed that of other dislocated monarchs; the picaresque attempts to return; the solemn ceremonial in shabby hotels; the bestowal of titles as the price of a meal ticket (at one point his Court Chamberlain was Antoine Jimenez de la Rosa, Duc de Saint-Valentin, Member of the University of Smyrna and other scientific institutions etc.); a certain success in attracting parvenu financiers and *anciens combattants de guerre*; and an unwavering conviction that the hierarchic principle of God is incarnate in a King.

He tried to get back three times. Three times he appeared on the Río Negro and set off up-river to cross the Cordillera. All three times he was thwarted and sent packing to France, once through Indian treachery, next through the vigilance of an Argentine governor (who saw through his disguise of short hair, dark glasses and the pseudonym of M. Jean Prat). The third attempt is open to different interpretations: either the gauchos' unrelieved diet of meat caused an intestinal blockage, or some freemasons poisoned him for renouncing his vows. The fact is, in 1877 he appeared half-dead on the operating theatre of a Buenos Aires hospital. A Messageries-Maritimes steamer landed him at Bordeaux. He went to Tourtoirac, to the house of his nephew Jean, a butcher. For one painful year he worked as the village lamplighter, and then he died, on September 19th 1878.

The later history of the Kingdom of Araucania and Patagonia belongs rather to the obsessions of bourgeois France than to the politics of South America. In default of a successor from the Tounens family, a M. Gustave Achille Laviarde interposed himself and reigned as Achille Ier. He was a native of Rheims where his mother ran a wash-house known locally as 'The Castle of Green Frogs'. He was a Bonapartist, a freemason, an 'actionnaire' of Möet and Chandon, an expert on barrage balloons (which he somewhat resembled) and an acquaintance of Verlaine. He financed his receptions with his commercial enterprise known as the Royal Society of the Constellation of the South, never removed his court from Paris, but did open consulates in Mauritius, Haiti, Nicaragua and Port-Vendres. When he made overtures to the Vatican, a Chilean prelate said: 'This kingdom exists only in the minds of drunken idiots.'

The third king, Dr Antoine Cros (Antoine II) had been physician to the Emperor Dom Pedro of Brazil and died at Asnières after reigning a year and a half. He was an amateur lithographer in the style of Hieronymus Bosch and brother of Charles Cros, the inventor and poet of *Le Coffret de Santal*.

Dr Cros's daughter succeeded and passed the crown to her son, M. Jacques Bernard. For a second time a monarch of Araucania went behind bars, for services to the Pétain Government.

M. Philippe Boiry, his successor, reigns modestly with the title of hereditary prince and has restored the house at La Chèze for use as a holiday home.

I asked him if he knew Kipling's story *The Man who would be King*.

'Certainly.'

'Don't you think it's odd that Kipling's heroes, Peachey and Dravot, should also have been freemasons?'

'Purely a coincidence,' the Prince said.

9

I LEFT the Río Negro and went on south to Port Madryn.

A hundred and fifty-three Welsh colonists landed here off the brig *Mimosa* in 1865. They were poor people in search of a New Wales, refugees from cramped coal mining valleys, from a failed independence movement, and from Parliament's ban on Welsh in schools. Their leaders had combed the earth for a stretch of open country uncontaminated by Englishmen. They chose Patagonia for its absolute remoteness and foul climate; they did not want to get rich.

The Argentine Government gave them land along the Chubut River. From Madryn it was a march of forty miles over the thorn desert. And when they did reach the valley, they had the impression that God, and not the Government, had given them the land.

Port Madryn was a town of shabby concrete buildings, tin bungalows, tin warehouses and a wind-flattened garden. There was a cemetery of black cypresses and shiny black marble tombstones. The Calle Saint-Exupéry was a reminder that the storm in *Vol de Nuit* was somewhere in these parts.

I walked along the esplanade and looked out at the even line of cliffs spreading round the bay. The cliffs were a lighter grey than the grey of the sea and sky. The beach was grey and littered with dead penguins. Halfway along was a concrete monument in memory of the Welsh. It looked like the entrance to a bunker. Let into its sides were bronze reliefs representing Barbarism and

Civilization. Barbarism showed a group of Tehuelche Indians, naked, with slabby back muscles in the Soviet style. The Welsh were on the side of Civilization—greybeards, young men with scythes, and big-breasted girls with babies.

At dinner the waiter wore white gloves and served a lump of burnt lamb that bounced on the plate. Spread over the restaurant wall was an immense canvas of gauchos herding cattle into an orange sunset. An old-fashioned blonde gave up on the lamb and sat painting her nails. An Indian came in drunk and drank through three jugs of wine. His eyes were glittering slits in the red leather shield of his face. The jugs were of green plastic in the shape of penguins.

10

I TOOK the night bus on to the Chubut Valley. By next morning I was in the village of Gaimán, the centre of Welsh Patagonia today. The valley was about five miles wide, a net of irrigated fields and poplar windbreaks, set between the white cliffs of the barranca—a Nile Valley in miniature.

The older houses in Gaimán were of red brick, with sash windows and neat vegetable gardens and ivy trained to grow over the porches. The name of one house was *Nith-y-dryw*, the Wren's Nest. Inside, the rooms were whitewashed and had brown painted doors, polished brass handles and grandfather clocks. The colonists came with few possessions but they clung to their family clocks.

Mrs Jones's teashop lay at the far end of the village where the bridge crossed over to the Bethel. Her plums were ripe and her garden full of roses.

'I can't move, my dear,' she called through. 'You'll have to come and talk to me in the kitchen.'

She was a squat old lady in her eighties. She sat propped up at a scrubbed deal table filling lemon-curd tarts.

'I can't move an inch, my darling. I'm crippled. I've had arthritis since the flood and have to be carried everywhere.'

Mrs Jones pointed to the line where the floodwater came, above the blue-painted dado, on the kitchen wall.

'Stuck in here I was, with the water up to my neck.'

She came out nearly sixty years ago from Bangor in North Wales. She had not left the valley since. She remembered a family I knew in Bangor and said: 'Fancy, it's a small world.'

'You won't believe it,' she said. 'Not to look at me now you won't. But I was a beauty in my day.' And she talked about a laddie from Manchester and his bouquet of flowers and the quarrel and the parting and the ship.

'And how are the morals back home?' she asked. 'Down?' 'Down.'

'And they're down here too. All this killing. You can't tell where it'll end.'

Mrs Jones's grandson helped run the teashop. He ate too much cake for his own good. He called his grandmother 'Granny' but otherwise he did not speak English or Welsh.

I slept in the Draigoch Guest House. It was owned by Italians who played Neapolitan songs on the juke box late into the night.

II

IN THE morning I walked to Bethesda along a white road lined with poplars. A farmer was walking in my direction and he took me to call on his brother Alun Powell. We turned up a track into a farmyard shaded by willows. A Welsh sheepdog barked and then licked our faces. There was a low mudbrick house with sash windows and a tin roof, and in the yard a horse-drawn buggy and some old machinery.

Alun Powell was a small man, crinkled by the sun and wind. His wife had shiny cheeks and was always laughing. Their living room was blue and had a Welsh dresser with postcards from Wales on it. Mrs Powell's first cousin had left Patagonia and gone back home to Wales.

'He *has* done well,' she said. 'He's now the Archdruid.'

Their grandfather came out from Caernarvon but she couldn't

say where that was. Caernarvon wasn't marked on her map of Wales.

'You can't expect much,' she said, 'when it's printed on a tea-towel.'

I pointed out where Caernarvon should be. She had always wanted to know.

The Powells had a boy called Eddy and a girl. They had five cows, a small herd of sheep, a field of potatoes, squashes, maize and sunflowers; and a vegetable garden, an orchard and a spinney. They had a mare in foal, hens, ducks, and the dog. Behind the spinney was a row of pigsties. One pig had scab and we doused it with medicament.

The day was hot. Mrs Powell said: 'It's better to talk than work. Let's have an *asado*.' She went to the barn and set a table with a red and white check cloth. Eddy lit the fire and his father went to an underground larder. He cut a side of mutton from a hanging carcass, stripped off the fat and gave it to the dog. He fixed the meat to an *asador*, which is an iron spit in the shape of a cross, and stuck it in the ground slanting over the fire. Later we ate the *asado* with a sauce called *salmuera*, made of vinegar, garlic, chillies and oregano.

'It takes the fattiness off the meat,' Mrs Powell said.

We drank thin *vino rosado* and Alun Powell talked about the herbs that grew in the desert.

'You can cure every kind of sickness with them,' he said. His grandparents learned them from the Indians. But it had all changed now.

'Not even the birds are the same. The ouraka came down from Buenos Aires thirty years back. That just shows you. Things change with the birds, just as they do with us.'

The wine made us drowsy. After lunch Eddy gave me his room for a siesta. The walls were whitewashed. There was a white painted bed and a grey chest for clothes. The only other things in the room were spurs and stirrups arranged symmetrically on a shelf.

12

IN GAIMÁN the schoolmaster's wife introduced me to the pianist. He was a thin nervous boy with a drained face and eyes that watered in the wind. His hands were strong and red. The ladies of the Welsh choir had adopted him and taught him their songs. He had taken piano lessons and now he was leaving for Buenos Aires to study at the Conservatoire.

Anselmo lived with his parents behind their grocery shop. The mother made the pasta herself. She was a big German woman and she cried a lot. She cried when her Italian husband lost his temper and she cried at the thought of Anselmo going away. She had spent all her savings on the piano and now he was going away. The husband wouldn't have the piano played when he was in the house. And now the piano would be silent and her tears would water the pasta. Secretly, however, she was pleased about him going. Already she saw the white tie and heard the standing ovation.

Over the Christmas holiday Anselmo's parents went to the seaside with his elder brother, leaving him alone to practise. The brother was a garage mechanic, married to a solid Indian girl, who stared at people as if they were mad.

Anselmo had a passion for the culture of Europe, the authentic, blinkered passion of the exile. When his father stopped him playing he would lock himself in his room and read sheet music or the lives of great composers from a musical encyclopædia. He was learning to play Liszt and asked complicated questions about Villa d'Este and the friendship with Wagner. I couldn't help him.

The Welsh showered him with attentions. The leading soprano had sent him a fruit cake for Christmas. And the tenor, the young farmer he'd accompanied at the Eisteddfod, had sent a plate painted with a penguin, a sea-lion and an ostrich. He was very pleased with these presents.

'It is for what I do for them,' he said. 'And now I will play the *Pathétique*. Yes?'

The room was bare, in the German way, white with lace curtains. Outside the wind kicked up dust clouds in the street and tilted the poplars. Anselmo went to a cupboard and took out a small white plaster bust of Beethoven. He put it on the piano and began.

The playing was remarkable. I could not imagine a finer *Pathétique* further South. When he finished he said: 'Now I play Chopin. Yes?' and he replaced the bust of Beethoven with one of Chopin. 'Do you wish waltzes or mazurkas?'

'Mazurkas.'

'I shall play my best favourite. It is the last music Chopin is writing.'

And he played the mazurka that Chopin dictated on his death-bed. The wind whistled in the street and the music ghosted from the piano as leaves over a headstone and you could imagine you were in the presence of genius.

13

CHRISTMAS DAY began badly when Mr Caradog Williams, the station master for twenty years, went to the Old Bethel and got out the cauldron to boil water for the children's tea-party. He happened to look in the river and saw the corpse of a naked man, all bloated up and caught against the trunk of a fallen willow. It was not a Welshman.

'Probably a tourist,' the policeman said.

Anselmo and I went to spend the day with the Davies family on their farm, Ty-Ysaf, one of the original hundred-acre lots. The Davieses were cousins of the Powells but better off. The farm supported six people, not counting the Chilean peon: Mrs Davies Senior, her son Ivor, his wife and their two boys, and Ivor's bachelor brother Euan.

Old Mrs Davies lived in the big house of five rooms. She was a shrunken old lady with the nicest smile and her hair worn up in braids. You could tell she was very tough underneath. In the afternoons she sat on the east porch, out of the wind, and watched the hollyhocks and peonies changing day by day. The living-room hadn't changed since she came here as a young bride in

1913. The pink walls were the same. The two Sheffield-plate trays—they were wedding presents—were on the mantelpiece, and the two pottery pug-dogs. On either side of the dresser were tinted photographs of her husband's parents, who came out from Ffestiniog. They had always hung there and they'd hang there when she'd gone.

Old Mr Davies passed on last year. He was eighty-three. But she always had Euan for company. He was a brawny man with hazel eyes and dark red hair and a cheerful, freckled face.

'No,' Mrs Davies said. 'Euan hasn't married yet, but he sings instead. He's a wonderful tenor. He made them all cry at the Eisteddfod when he carried off the prize. Anselmo was the accompanist and they made a fine pair. Oh, how that boy plays the piano. I'm so pleased Euan gave him the nice plate for Christmas. The poor thing looks so lost and lonely and it's no fun living in Chubut if your family doesn't help.

'Yes. Euan must get married one day, but who to? There's a shortage of young ladies and she has to be the right one. Suppose she quarrelled with the others? Suppose the farm couldn't support two families? They'd have to split and that would be terrible. One lot would have to go away and start somewhere else.'

Mrs Davies hoped that would not happen as long as she were alive.

Ivor Davies lived with his family in the smaller mudbrick house of three rooms. He was a tall upright man, balding, with eyes set well back into the skull. He was a religious man himself, and on his dresser were pamphlets from the Welsh Bible Society. Ivor Davies could not believe the world was as bad as everyone said.

Ivor and Euan did all the work on the farm. The hardest work was digging out the irrigation ditches. The peon hardly did a thing. He had lived in the tool shed for five years. He planted his own patch of beans and did enough odd jobs to keep him in maté and sugar. He never went back to Chile and they wondered if he'd killed a man.

Mrs Ivor Davies was an Italian woman of the happiest disposition. Both her parents were Genoese. She had black hair and blue eyes and a rose-pink complexion you somehow didn't associate with the climate. She kept saying how beautiful every-thing was — '*Qué linda familia!*' even if the children were ugly. '*Qué lindo dia!*' if it poured with rain. Whatever was not beautiful she made it seem so. She thought the Welsh community especially beautiful. She spoke Welsh and sang in Welsh. But, as an Italian, she couldn't make the boys Welsh. They were bored with the community and wanted to go to the States.

'That's the trouble,' said Gwynneth Morgan, who was a fine Celtic woman with golden hair tied in a bun. 'When Welshmen marry foreigners, they lose the tradition.' Gwynneth Morgan was unmarried. She wanted to keep the valley Welsh, the way it was. 'But it's all going to pieces,' she said.

For Mrs Ivor Davies was dreaming of Italy, and of Venice in particular. She had once seen Venice and the Bridge of Sighs. And when she said the word *sospiri*, she said it so loudly and insistently that you knew she was pining for Italy. Chubut was so very far from Venice and Venice was far more beautiful than anything else she knew.

After tea we all went to the hymn-singing at Bryn-Crwn Chapel. Ivor took his wife and mother in the pick-up, and the rest of us went in the Dodge. Ivor's father bought the Dodge in the 1920s and it hadn't broken down yet, but machinery was better then than now.

Bryn-Crwn Chapel was built in 1896 and sat in the middle of a field. Six Welshmen in dark suits and flat caps stood in line against the red brick wall. Inside the annexe the women were laying the table for tea.

Anselmo played the harmonium and the wind howled and the rain beat on the windows and the teros screamed. The Welsh sang John Wesley's hymns and the sad songs of God's promise to Cymry, the high-pitched trebles and sopranos, and the old men growling at the back. There was old Mr Hubert Lloyd-Jones, who could hardly walk; and Mrs Lloyd-Jones in a straw-flowered hat; and Mrs Cledwyn Hughes, the one they call Fattie; and Nan Hammond and Dai Morgan. All the Davies and Powell families were present, even Oscar Powell 'the wild boy', who wore a T-shirt with Llanfairpwllgwyngyllgogerychwyrndrobwllllantysilio-gogogoch in red letters around a Welsh dragon.

The service ended. The old people chatted and the children

played hide-and-seek among the pews. Then we all trooped in to tea. It was the second tea of the day, but Christmas was a day of teas. The women poured tea from black pottery teapots. Mrs Davies had brought a pizza and the Welsh tried a little of that. Anselmo was talking and laughing with Euan. They were close friends. He was full of vitality, but it was a borrowed vitality, for the Welshmen cheered up all who saw their bright and weather-beaten faces.

14

ANSELMO TOLD me to go and see the poet. 'The Maestro,' he said.

The poet lived along a lonely stretch of river, in overgrown orchards of apricots, alone in a two-roomed hut. He had been a teacher of literature in Buenos Aires. He came down to Patagonia forty years back and stayed.

I knocked on the door and he woke. It was drizzling and while he dressed I sheltered under the porch and watched his colony of pet toads.

His fingers gripped my arm. He fixed me with an intense and luminous stare.

'Patagonia!' he cried. 'She is a hard mistress. She casts her spell. An enchantress! She folds you in her arms and never lets go.'

The rain drummed on the tin roof. For the next two hours he was my Patagonia.

The room was dark and dusty. At the back, shelves made of planks and packing cases bent under the weight of books, mineral specimens, Indian artefacts and fossil oysters. On the walls were a cuckoo clock, a lithograph of Pampas Indians, and another of the Gaucho Martín Fierro.

'The Indians rode better than the gauchos,' he said. 'Brown limbs! Naked on horseback! Their children learned to ride before they walked. They were one with their horses. *Ah! Mi Indio!*'

His desk was littered with broken almond shells and his

favourite books; Ovid's *Tristia*, *The Georgics*, *Walden*, Pigafetta's *Voyage of Magellan*, *Leaves of Grass*, *The Poem of Martín Fierro*, *The Purple Land* and Blake's *Songs of Innocence*, of which he was especially fond.

Smacking it free of dust, he gave me a copy of his *Canto on the Last Flooding of the Chubut River*, privately printed in Trelew, which combined, in Alexandrines, his vision of the Deluge and a paean of praise for the engineers of the new dam. He had published two volumes of poetry in his life, *Voices of the Earth* and *Rolling Stones*, the last named after the layer of glacier-rolled pebbles that cover the Patagonian pampas. The scope of his verse was cosmic; technically it was astonishing. He managed to squeeze the extinction of the dinosaurs into rhymed couplets using Spanish and Linnaean Latin.

He gave me a sticky apéritif of his own manufacture, sat me in a chair, and read, with gestures and clattering of false teeth, weighty stanzas that described the geological transformations of Patagonia.

I asked him what he was writing at present. He cackled humorously.

'My production is limited. As T. S. Eliot once said: "The poem can wait." '

It stopped raining and I came to leave. Bees hummed around the poet's hives. His apricots were ripening the colour of a pale sun. Clouds of thistledown drifted across the view and in a field there were some fleecy white sheep.

15

WAVING TO the poet, I walked towards the road that goes westwards up the Chubut River and on to the Cordillera. A truck stopped with three men in the cab. They were going to get a load of hay from the mountains. All night I bounced in the back, and at dawn, covered in dust, I watched the sun strike the Ice-caps and saw the high slopes, far off, streaked white with snow and black with forests of southern beech.

As we drove into Esquel, a bush fire was burning on one of the tight brown hills that hemmed in the town. I ate at a green restaurant on the main street. A zinc counter ran the length of the room. At one end a glass vitrine displayed steaks and kidneys and racks of lamb and sausages. The wine was acid and came in pottery penguins. There were hard black hats at every table. The gauchos wore boots creased like concertinas and black bombachas. (Bombachas are baggy pants, once French ex-army surplus from Zouave regiments in the Crimean War.)

A man with bloodshot eyes left his friends and came over.

'Can I speak with you, Señor?'

'Sit down and have a glass.'

'You are English?'

'How did you know?'

'I know my people,' he said. 'Same blood as my employer.'

'Why not Welsh?'

'I know Welsh from English and you are English.'

'Yes.'

He was very pleased and shouted over to his friends: 'You see, I know my people.'

The man directed me to the stud farm of an Englishman about twenty miles into the country. 'A *tipo macanudo*,' he said, a good fellow, the perfect English gentleman.

Jim Ponsonby's place was a hill farm, with winter grazing in the valley and summer pasture on the mountain. There were Hereford bulls in his meadow and among them yellow-fronted ibises, big birds with bright pink feet that made a melancholy honking sound.

The house was low and white and stood in a planting of silver birches. A Spanish woman came to the door.

'My husband's helping the *patrón* with the rams,' she said. 'They're choosing rams for the show. You'll find them in the shearing shed.'

He was, certainly, the perfect English gentleman, of middle height, with thick grey hair and a close-clipped moustache. His eyes were a particularly cold shade of blue. His face was netted with a regular pattern of burst blood vessels and his stomach showed signs of indulgence in food and drink. His dress was the result of meticulous planning: the Norfolk jacket in brown herring-bone tweed, the hardwood buttons, the open-necked khaki shirt, the worsted trousers, tortoiseshell bifocals and spit-and-polished shoes.

He was making notes in his stud book. His man Antonio was got up in full gaucho rig, with a knife or *facón* thrust diagonally across the small of his back. He was parading a group of Australian Merinos before his employer.

The rams panted under the weight of their own fleece and virility, mouthing a little alfalfa with the resignation of obese invalids on a diet. The best animals wore a cotton oversheet to protect them from dirt. Antonio had to undress them, and the Englishman would plunge his hand in and splay out his fingers, laying bare five inches of creamy yellow fleece.

'And what part of the old country d'you come from?' he asked.

'Gloucestershire.'

'Gloucestershire, eh! Gloucestershire! In the North, what?'

'In the West.'

'Damn me, so it is. The West. Yes. Our place was in Chippenham. Probably never heard of it. That's in Wiltshire.'

'About fifteen miles from me.'

'Probably a different Chippenham. And how is the old country getting along?' He changed the subject to avoid our geographical conversation. 'Thing's aren't going too well, are they? Damned shame!'

16

I SLEPT in the peons' quarters. The night was cold. They gave me a cot bed and a black winter poncho as a coverlet. Apart from these ponchos, their maté equipment and their knives, the peons were free of possessions.

In the morning there was a heavy dew on the white clover. I walked down the track to the Welsh village of Trevelin, the Place of the Mill. Far below in the valley, tin roofs were glinting. I saw the mill, an ordinary Victorian mill, but on the edge of the

village were some strange timber buildings with roofs sloping at
all angles. Coming up close I saw that one was a water-tower.
A banner floated from it, reading *'Instituto Bahai'*.

A black face popped over the bank.

'¿Qué tal?'

'Walking.'

'Come in.'

The Bahai Institute of Trevelin consisted of one short, very
black and very muscular negro from Bolivia and six ex-students
from the University of Teheran, only one of whom was present.

'All men,' the Bolivian sniggered. 'All very religious.'

He was making a makeshift spinner from a tin can and wanted
to go fishing in the lake. The Persian was dousing himself in
the shower.

The Persians had come to Patagonia as missionaries for their
world religion. They had plenty of money and had stuffed the
place with the trappings of middle-class Teheran—wine-red
Bokhara rugs, fancy cushions, brass trays, and cigarette boxes
painted with scenes from the Shahnama.

The Persian, whose name was Ali, swanned out of the shower
in a sarong. Black hairs rippled over his unhealthy white body.
He had enormous syrupy eyes and a drooping moustache. He
sank back on a pile of cushions, ordered the negro to do the
washing up and discussed the world situation.

'Persia is a very poor country,' he said.

'Persia is a bloody rich country,' I said.

'Persia could be a rich country but the Americans have robbed
her wealth.' Ali smiled showing a set of swollen gums.

He offered to show me over the Institute. In their library the
books were all Bahai literature. I noted down two titles—*The
Wrath of God* and *Epistle to the Son of the Wolf, Bahai Ullah*. There
was also a *Guide to Better Writing*.

'Which religion have you?' Ali asked. 'Christian?'

'I haven't got any special religion this morning. My God is
the God of Walkers. If you walk hard enough, you probably
don't need any other God.'

The negro was delighted to hear this. He wanted to walk to
the lake and go fishing.

'How you like my friend?' asked Ali.

'I like him. He's a nice friend.'

'He is *my friend*.'

'I'm sure.'

'He is my very good friend.' He pushed his face up to mine. 'And this is *our room*.' He opened a door. There was a double-bed with a stuffed doll perched on the pillow. On the wall, strung up on a leather thong, was a big steel machete, which Ali waved in my face.

'Ha! I kill the ungodly.'

'Put that thing down.'

'English is infidel.'

'I said put that thing down.'

'I only joke,' he said and strung the machete back on its hook. 'Is very dangerous here. Argentine is very dangerous people. I have revolver also.'

'I don't want to see it.'

Ali then showed me the garden and admired it. The Bahais had set their hand to sculpture and garden furniture, and the Bolivian had made a crazy-paving path.

'And now you must go,' Ali said. 'I am tired yet and we must sleep.'

The Bolivian did not want me to go. It was a lovely day. He did want to go fishing. Going to bed that morning was the last thing he wanted to do.

17

MILTON EVANS was the principal resident of Trevelin and son of its founder. He was a round moustachioed gentleman of sixty-one, who prided himself on his English. His favourite expression was 'Gimme another horse piss!' And his daughter, who did not speak English, would bring a beer and he'd say, 'Aah! Horse piss!' and drain the bottle.

His father, John Evans, came out on the *Mimosa* as a baby. He was the first of his generation to ride like an Indian. Not for him the inflexible round of field-work, chapel and tea. He settled up-country in the Cordillera, made money and built the mill. Once established he took his family to Wales on a year's visit. Milton went to school in Ffestiniog and had a long story about fishing from a bridge.

He directed me to the grave of his father's horse. Inside a white fence was a boulder set in a plantation of marigolds and Christmas trees. The inscription read:

HERE LIE THE REMAINS OF MY HORSE EL-MALACARA
WHICH SAVED MY LIFE FROM THE INDIANS ON THE
14TH OF MARCH 1883 ON MY RETURN FROM THE
CORDILLERA.

At the beginning of that month, John Evans, with three companions, Hughes, Parry and Davies, rode west up the Chubut Valley. There was an old legend of a city and a new rumour of gold. They stayed in the tents of a friendly Cacique and saw the grass country beginning and the peaks of the Cordillera, but having no food they decided to return. The horses' hooves splintered on sharp stones and set them limping. They were thirty-six hours in the saddle. Parry and Hughes hung their heads and let the reins go limp. But Evans was tougher and shot two hares, so the four did eat that night.

Next afternoon they were crossing a valley of blinding white dust and heard the thud of hooves behind. John Evans spurred El-Malacara clear of the Indian lances, but, looking back, saw Parry and Hughes fall and Davies clinging to the saddle with a spear in his side. The horse outpaced the Indians', but stopped dead before a gulch, where the desert floor split wide. With the Indians on him, Evans spurred again and El-Malacara took a clean jump of twenty feet, sheer over the precipice, slid down the screes and made the farther side. The Indians, who recognized a brave man, did not attempt to follow.

Forty hours later, Evans rode into the Welsh colony and reported the deaths to the leader Lewis Jones.

'But, John,' he said, 'the Indians are our friends. They'd never kill a Welshman.'

Then Lewis Jones learned of an Argentine patrol that had trespassed on Indian land and he knew that it was true. Evans led a party of forty Welshmen to the place. Hawks flew off as they came near. The bodies were not yet picked clean and their sexual organs were in their mouths. Lewis Jones said to John Evans: 'Heaven hath saved thee, John, from a horrible death.'

They took up the remains and buried them. A marble monument marks the spot. Its name is *Biddmyrd os syrfeddod* 'There will be a myriad wonders ... '—a line from the hymn of Anne Griffith, the mystic girl from Montgomery who lived on a remote hill-farm and also died young.

'You're not looking for a job, I suppose?' Milton Evans asked. It was lunch time and he presented me with a slab of meat on the end of a small sword.

'Not particularly.'

'Funny, you remind me of Bobby Dawes. Young Englishman, same as yourself, wandering about Patagonia. One day he walks up to an estancia and says to the owner: "If you give me work, you're a saint, and your wife's a saint, and your children are angels, and that dog's the best dog in the world." But the owner says, "There is no work." "In which case," Bobby says, "you're the son of a whore, your wife *is* a whore, your children are monkeys, and if I catch that dog, I'll kick its arse till its nose bleeds." '

Milton laughed a lot as he told this story. Then he told another he once heard from the Cooper sheep-dip man. The second story was about a cure for scab. The punch line was 'Put a lump of sugar in the sheep's mouth and suck its arse till it tastes sweet.' He repeated the story twice to make sure I'd get the point. I lied. I couldn't face it a third time.

I left Milton to his hay-making and went north of Esquel to a small settlement called Epuyen.

18

THE NIGHT was hot and it was getting late and the owner of the one shop in Epuyen was swabbing down the counter which also served as a bar. Señor Naitane was a small creased man with unusually white skin. He eyed his customers nervously and wished they would go. His wife was waiting for him in bed. The rooms around the courtyard were in darkness. Only in the shop a single electric bulb smeared its thin yellow light over the green walls and the lines of bottles and packets of maté. From the roof-beams hung strings of peppers, garlic, saddle-trees, bits and spurs, which cast jagged shadows on the ceiling.

Earlier, the eight gauchos present had shown signs of leaving. Their horses, tied to the fence, were chomping and stamping. But whenever Naitane swabbed the counter clean, one of them slammed down a wet glass or bottle and called for another round. Naitane let his boy serve. He took a duster of ostrich feathers and flicked, agitatedly, at the things on the shelves.

Once you get a drunk gaucho in the saddle, he won't fall off and his horse will get him home. But this presupposes a dangerous moment while you seat him. Naitane thought this moment was approaching. The youngest gaucho was bright red in the face, propping himself against the bar on his elbows. His friends watched to see if his legs would hold. All had knives stuck into their waistbands.

Their leader was a scrawny rough in black bombachas and a black shirt open to his navel. His chest was covered with a fuzz of ginger hair and the same ginger bristles sprouted all over his face. He had a few long, sharp, brown teeth and a shark's fin of a nose. He moved with the grace of a well-oiled piece of machinery and leered at Naitane with a teasing smile.

Then he crunched my hand and introduced himself as Teófilo Breide. The words slurred through his teeth and he was hard to follow, but from something he did say, I realized he was an Arab; the nose had explained itself. Epuyen, in fact, was a colony of Arabs, Christian Arabs, but whereas I could picture Naitane as a shopkeeper in Palestine, Teófilo Breide belonged in the black tents.

'And what,' he asked, 'is a gringito doing in Epuyen?'

'I want to know about an American called Martin Sheffield who lived here forty years back.'

'Bah!' said Teófilo Breide. 'Sheffield! *Fantasista! Cuentero! Artista!* You know the story of the plesiosaurus?'

'I do.'

'*Fantasía!*' he roared and launched into an anecdote that made the gauchos laugh.

'Funny you should mention him. You see this?' He handed me a *rebenque*, the Argentine riding whip, with a silver-sheathed handle and leather strap. 'This was Martin Sheffield's.'

He directed me to the *lagunita* where the American once had his camp. Then he smacked the *rebenque* on the counter. The young man's knees did hold. The gauchos drained their glasses and filed out.

Señor Naitane, in whose house I had hoped to pass the night, pushed me out into the street and bolted the door. The generator cut out. From all directions I heard the sound of hooves dwindling into the night. I slept behind a bush.

19

THE *lagunita* lay under a mountain of red screes. It was little bigger than a pond and not more than a metre deep. Its unruffled surface reflected the black conifers that grew round the edge. Coots were swimming in the reeds. It was hardly a place to attract world headlines.

On a January morning in 1922, Dr Clemente Onelli, the Director of the National Zoological Gardens in La Plata, found this letter on his desk:

Dear Sir,
    Knowing of your concern to keep the Zoo in the public eye, I would like to draw your attention to a phenomenon, which is certainly of great interest and could lead to your acquiring an animal unknown to science. Here are the facts: Some nights ago I noticed some tracks on a pasture near the lake where I pitched my hunting camp. The tracks resembled those left by a heavy cart. The grass was completely flattened and hasn't stood up yet. Then, in the middle of the lake, I saw the head of an animal. At first sight it was like some unknown species of swan, but swirls in the water made me think its body must resemble a crocodile's.

The purpose of this letter is to request your material aid for an expedition i.e. boat, harpoons, etc. (The boat we could build here.) Furthermore, in case it proves impossible to capture the beast alive, you should send embalming fluid. If you are interested, please send to the house of Perez Gabito funds to realize the expedition.

I hope for a reply as soon as possible,

With my kindest regards,

Martin Sheffield.

The writer was an adventurer from Tom Green County, Texas, who styled himself sheriff and wore a star and sheriff's hat to prove it. Around 1900 he appeared in Patagonia looking rather like Ernest Hemingway, roaming the mountains 'poorer than Job' with a white mare and an Alsatian for company. He persisted in the illusion that Patagonia was an extension of the Old West. He panned the streams for gold. Some winters he stayed with John Evans at Trevelin and swapped dirty nuggets for flour. He was a crack shot. He shot trout from the rivers; a cigarette packet from the police commissioner's mouth; and had the habit of picking off ladies' high-heels.

Sheffield offered his services, as fellow drinker and guide, to any explorer who appeared in this part of the Andes. On one expedition he helped unearth the fossilized skeleton of a plesiosaurus, a small dinosaur related to the modern turtle, which had indeed a neck like a swan. Now he was proposing a live specimen.

Onelli called a press conference and announced the forthcoming plesiosaurus hunt. An upper-class lady subscribed 1,500 dollars for the purchase of equipment. Two old age pensioners escaped from the Hospital de la Mercedes to fight the monster. The plesiosaurus also lent its name to a tango and a brand of cigarettes. When Onelli suggested it might have to be embalmed, the Jockey Club hoped to have the privilege of exhibiting, but this brought a denunciation from Don Ignacio Albarracín, of the Society for the Protection for Animals.

Meanwhile the country was paralysed by a general election which would decide whether to unseat its Radical President, Dr Hipólito Yrigoyen, and somehow the plesiosaurus managed to insert itself into the campaign as emblematic beast of the Right. Two newspapers whose policy was to welcome foreign capital adopted the plesiosaurus. *La Nación* confirmed preparations for the hunt and wished it well. In *La Prensa* enthusiasm was even greater: 'The existence of this unusual animal, which has roused the attention of foreigners, is a scientific event, which will bring to Patagonia the definitive prestige of possessing so unsuspected a creature.'

Foreign cables buzzed into Buenos Aires. Mr Edmund Heller, Teddy Roosevelt's hunting companion, wrote asking for a piece of skin for the American Museum of Natural History in memory of his old friend. The University of Pennsylvania said a team of zoologists was ready to leave for Patagonia at once, adding that if the animal were caught, the proper place for it was the United States. 'It is clear,' commented the *Diario del Plata*, 'that this world has been created for the greater glory of the North Americans, viz. The Monroe Doctrine.'

The plesiosaurus was an electoral gift to the Left. Clemente Onelli, the Beast-Slayer, was presented as a new Parsifal, a Lohengrin or a Siegfried. The journal *La Montaña* said that, domesticated, the animal might prove of service to the blighted inhabitants of the *Tierra del Diablo*, a reference to the revolt of the peons in Southern Patagonia, whom the Argentine Army had brutally massacred the month before. Another article bore the title 'The Cappadocian Dragon'; and the nationalistic *La Fronda* wrote: 'This millenarian, pyramidal, apocalyptic animal makes a noise like a Madonna and usually appears in the opaline stupors of drunken gringos.'

There is a difference of opinion as to whether the expedition, equipped with an enormous hypodermic, actually reached the lake. But the animal's non-existence must have been evident to whoever stood on its bank. And with the plesiosaurus died the hope of finding, in Patagonia, live dinosaurs like those described by Conan Doyle, stranded on their plateau in *The Lost World*.

Martin Sheffield died in 1936 in Arroyo Norquinco, a place he believed was his personal Klondike, of gold-fever, starvation, and D.T.s. A wooden cross with the initials M.S. marked the grave, but a souvenir hunter from Buenos Aires stole it. His son, by an Indian woman, lives drunkenly at El Bolsón, believing himself a Texas sheriff by inheritance and wearing his father's star.

From Epuyen, I walked to Cholila, a settlement close to the Chilean frontier.

20

'FEEL IT,' she said. 'Feel the wind coming through.'

I put my hand to the wall. The draught blew through the chinks where the mortar had fallen out. The log cabin was the North American kind. In Patagonia they made cabins differently and did not chink them with mortar.

The owner of the cabin was a Chilean Indian woman called Sepúlveda.

'In winter it's terrible,' she said. 'I covered the wall with *materia plastica* but it blew away. The house is rotten, Señor, old and rotten. I would sell it tomorrow. I would have a concrete house which the wind cannot enter.'

Señora Sepúlveda had boarded up the living-room windows when the glass fell out. She had pasted newspapers over the cracks, but you could still see scraps of the old flowered wallpaper. She was a hard-working, covetous woman. She was short and stout and had a bad time with her husband and the rotten cabin.

Señor Sepúlveda was grogged out of his mind, half-sitting, half-lying by the kitchen stove.

'Would you buy the house?' she asked.

'No,' I said, 'but don't sell it for nothing. There are North American gentlemen who would pay good money to take it away piece by piece.'

'This table comes from the *Norteamericanos*,' she said, 'and the cupboard, and the stove.'

She knew the cabin had a certain distinction for being North American. 'It must have been a beautiful place once,' she said.

As well as show me round, she was trying to get her eldest daughter off with a young road engineer. He drove a new pick-up and might be good for some cash. He and the girl were in the yard holding hands and laughing at the old nag tied to a willow. Next day, I passed her walking home to Cholila, alone across the pampas, crying.

21

THE BUILDER of the cabin was a sandy-haired and rather thick-set American, no longer young in 1902, with tapering fingers and a short roman nose. He had likable easy-going manners and a mischievous grin. He must have felt at home here, the country round Cholila is identical to parts of his home state, Utah—a country of clean air and open spaces; of black mesas and blue mountains; of grey scrub breaking into yellow flowers, a country of bones picked clean by hawks, stripped by the wind, stripping men to the raw.

He was alone that first winter. But he liked reading and borrowed books from an English neighbour. Sometimes in Utah he would hole up in the ranch of a retired teacher. He especially liked reading English mediaeval history and the stories of the Scots clans. Writing did not come easily to him, yet he did find time to write this letter to a friend back home:

> Cholila, Ten Chubut
> Argentine Republic, S.Am.
> August 10 1902

Mrs Davies
  Ashley, Utah
My Dear Friend,

I suppose you have thought long before that I had forgotten you (or was dead) but my dear friend, I am still alive, and when I think of my Old friends you are always the first to come to mind. It will probably surprise you to hear from me away down in this country but U.S. was too small for me the last two years I was there. I was restless. I wanted to see more of the world. I had seen all of the U.S. that I thought was good. And a few months after I sent A— over to see you, and get the Photo of the rope jumping ... another of my Uncles died and left $30,000 to our little family of 3 so I took my $10,000 and started to see a little more of the world. I visited the best cities and best parts of South A. till I got here. And this part of the country looked so good that I located, and I think for good, for I like the place better every day. I have 300 cattle, 1500 sheep, and 28 good saddle horses, 2 men to do my work, also a good 4 room house, wearhouse, stable, chicken house and some chickens. The only thing lacking is a cook, for I am still living in Single Cussideness and sometimes I feel very lonely for I am alone all day, and my neighbours don't amount to anything, besides the only language spoken in this country is Spanish, and I don't speak it well enough to converse on the latest scandals so dear to the hearts of all nations, and without which conversations are very stale, but the country is first class. The only industry at present is stockraising (that is in this part) and it can't be beat for that purpose, for I have never seen finer grass country, and lots of it hundreds and hundreds of miles that is unsettled and comparatively unknown, and where I am is good agricultural country, all kinds of small grain and vegetables grow without Irrigation but I am at the foot of the Andes Mountains. And all the land east of here is prairie and deserts, very good for stock, but for farming it would have to be irrigated, but there is plenty of good land along the mountains for all the people that will be here for the next hundred years, for I am a long way from civilization. It is 16 hundred miles to Buenos Aires the Capital of the Argentine, and over 400 miles to the nearest RailRoad or Sea Port but only about 150 miles to the Pacific Coast. To get to Chile we have to cross the mountains which was thought impossible until last summer when it was found that the Chilean Gov. had cut a road almost across so that next summer we will be able to go to Port Mont, Chile in about 4 days, where it used to take 2 months around the old trail. and it will be a great benefit to us for Chile is our Beef market and we can get our cattle there in 1/10th the time and have them fat. Also we can get supplies in Chile for one third what they cost here. The climate here is a great deal milder than Ashley valley. The summers are beautiful, never as warm as there. And grass knee high everywhere and lots of good cold mountain water. but the winters are very wet and disagreeable, for it rains most of the time, but sometimes we have lots of snow, but it don't last long, for it never gets cold enough to freeze much. I have never seen Ice one inch thick ...

The dead Uncle was the Wild Bunch Gang's robbery of the First National Bank at Winnemucca, Nevada, on September 10th 1900. The writer was Robert Leroy Parker, better known as Butch Cassidy, at that time heading the Pinkerton Agency's list of most wanted criminals. The 'little family of 3' was a *ménage à trois* consisting of himself, Harry Longabaugh the Sundance Kid, and the beautiful gun-moll Etta Place. Mrs Davies was the mother-in-law of Butch's greatest friend, Elza Lay, who was languishing in the pen.

22

HE WAS a nice boy, a lively friendly-faced boy, who loved his Mormon family and the cabin in the cottonwoods. Both his parents came out from England as children and trekked the Plains, with Brigham Young's handcart companies, from Iowa City to the Salt Lake. Anne Parker was a nervous and highly strung Scotswoman; her husband, Max, a simple soul, who had a hard time squeezing a living from the homestead and made a little extra in timber haulage.

The two-room cabin is still standing at Circleville, Utah. The corrals are there, and the paddock where Robert Leroy rode his first calf. The poplars he planted still line the irrigation ditch between the orchard and the sage. He was the oldest of eleven children, a boy of precise loyalties and a sense of fair play. He chafed under the straitjacket of Mormonism (and smelled corruption there). He dreamed of being a cowboy and, in dime novels, read the ongoing saga of Jessie James.

At eighteen he identified as his natural enemies the cattle companies, the railroads and the banks, and convinced himself that right lay the wrong side of the law. One June morning in 1884, awkwardly and ashamed, he told his mother he was going to work in a mine at Telluride. She gave him her father's blue travelling blanket and a pot of blueberry preserves. He kissed his baby sister, Lula, crying in her cradle, and rode out of their lives. The truth came out when Max Parker returned to the homestead. His son had rustled some cattle with a young outlaw called Mike Cassidy. The law was after them both.

Bob Parker took the name Cassidy and rode into a new life of wide horizons and the scent of horse leather. (Butch was the name of a borrowed gun.) His apprentice years, the 1880s, were years of the Beef Bonanza; of Texas longhorns peppering the range; of cowboys 'livin' the life of a buck nun' (one woman to ten men); of the Cattle Barons who paid miserly wages and dividends of 40 per cent to their shareholders; of champagne breakfasts at the Cheyenne Club and the English dukes who called their cowboys 'cow-servants' and whose cowboys called them 'dudes'. There were plenty of Englishmen knocking round the West: one cowboy wrote to his Yankee employer: 'That Inglishman yu lef in charge at the other ranch got to fresh and we had to kil the son of a bitch. Nothing much has hapened since yu lef ... '

Then the great white winter of 1886–7 wiped out three-quarters of the stock. Greed combined with natural catastrophe to breed a new type, the cowboy-outlaw, men driven by unemployment and blacklisting into criminal hideouts and the rustling game. At Brown's Hole or Hole-in-the-Wall they joined up with professional desperadoes; men like Black Jack Ketchum, or the psychopath Harry Tracy, or Flat-Nose George Curry, or Harvey Logan, the diarist of his own murders.

Butch Cassidy, in those years, was drover, horse-wrangler, mavericker, part-time bank-robber, and leader of men; the sheriffs feared him most for the last of these accomplishments. In 1894 they gave him two years in the Wyoming State Penitentiary for stealing a horse he hadn't stolen, valued at five dollars. The sentence soured him to any further dealing with the law. And, from 1896 to 1901, his Train Robbers' Syndicate, better known as

The Wild Bunch, performed the string of perfect hold-ups that kept lawmen, Pinkerton detectives and the railroad in perpetual jitters. The stories of his antics are endless; breathless rides along the Outlaw Trail; shooting glass conductors from telegraph poles; or paying a poor widow's rent by robbing the rent man. The homesteaders loved him. Many were Mormons, outlawed themselves for polygamy. They gave him food, shelter, alibis, and occasionally their daughters. Today, he would be classed as a revolutionary. But he had no sense of political organization.

Butch Cassidy never killed a man. Yet his friends were seasoned killers; their murders drove him to fits of remorse. He hated having to rely on the deadly aim of Harry Longabaugh, the Pennsylvania German with evil blue eyes and a foul temper. He tried to go straight, but there was too much on his Pinkerton card and his pleas for amnesty went unheard. Each new robbery spawned another and added years to his sentence. The costs of operating became unbearable. The story goes that the Wild Bunch frittered their hauls on women and the gaming table, but this is only half true. They had another, far greater expense: horseflesh.

The art of the hold-up depends on a quick getaway and Butch Cassidy's hold-ups depended on relays of fine thoroughbreds. His horse dealer was a man called Cleophas Dowd, the son of Irish immigrants to San Francisco, dedicated to the Jesuit priesthood, and forced as a boy to grovel to altar and confessional. Immediately after his ordination, Dowd startled his parents and the Fathers by riding past on his new racehorse, a brace of six-shooters strapped over his cassock. That night, in Sausalito, he had the pleasure—a pleasure he had long savoured—of giving last rites to the first man he shot. Dowd fled from California and settled at Sheep Creek Canyon, Utah, where he raised horses for outlaws. A Dowd horse was ready for sale when its rider could balance a gun between its ears and fire. The necessary speed he purchased from the Cavendish Stud at Nashville, Tennessee, and relayed the cost to his clients.

Around 1900 law and order settled in on the last American frontier. The lawmen bought their own fine bloodstock, solved the problem of outpacing the outlaws, and organized crime hid in the cities. Posses flushed out Brown's Hole; the Pinkertons put mounted rangers in box cars, and Butch saw his friends die in saloon brawls, picked off by hired gunmen, or disappear behind bars. Some of the gang signed on in the U.S. Armed Forces and exported their talents to Cuba and the Philippines. But for him the choices were a stiff sentence — or Argentina.

Word was out among the cowboys that the land of the gaucho offered the lawless freedom of Wyoming in the 1870s. The artist-cowboy Will Rogers wrote: 'They wanted North American riders for foremen over the natives. The natives was too slow.' Butch believed he was safe from extradition there, and his last two hold-ups were to raise funds for the journey. After the Winnemucca raid, the five ringleaders, in a mood of high spirits, had their group portrait taken in Fort Worth and sent a copy to the manager. (The photo is still in the office.)

In the fall of 1901 Butch met the Sundance Kid and his girl, Etta Place, in New York. She was young, beautiful and intelligent, and she kept her men to heel. Her Pinkerton card says she was a school teacher in Denver; one rumour has it she was the daughter of an English remittance man called George Capel, hence Place. Under the names of James Ryan and Mr and Mrs Harry A. Place, the 'family of 3' went to operas and theatres. (The Sundance Kid was a keen Wagnerian.) They bought Etta a gold watch at Tiffany's and sailed for Buenos Aires on S.S. *Soldier Prince*. On landing they stayed at the Hotel Europa, called on the Director of the Land Department, and secured 12,000 acres of rough camp in Chubut.

'Are there any bandits?' they asked. They were glad to hear there were none.

A few weeks later, Milton Roberts, the Welsh police commissioner from Esquel, found them under canvas at Cholila; their fine light thoroughbreds, all ready saddled up, struck him as rather odd. Butch, as we know from the letter, was alone the first winter. He stocked the farm with sheep bought from an English neighbour. The cabin, modelled on Circleville but bigger, was up by June.

In the following year, a Pinkerton detective, Frank Dimaio, tracked them to Cholila with the Winnemucca photograph, but was put off going to Patagonia by stories of snakes and jungles, perhaps invented for his benefit. The 'family of 3' used Cholila as a base for five years without interference. They built a brick house and a country store (now owned by an Arab trader) and put 'another North American' in charge.

The locals thought they were peaceable citizens. At Cholila I met the grandchildren of their neighbour, Señora Blanca de Gérez, who left this note when she died three years ago:

> They were not good mixers, but whatever they did was correct. They often slept in our house. Ryan was more sociable than Place and joined in the festivities of the settlement. On the first visit of Governor Lezana, Place played the samba on his guitar and Ryan danced with the daughter of Don Ventura Solís. No one suspected they were criminals.

The Pinkerton Agency wrote to the Chief of Police in Buenos Aires: 'It is only a question of time until these men commit some desperate robbery in the Argentine Republic.' They were right. Apart from running low in funds, 'the family of 3' were addicted to the art of the hold-up, without which life itself became a bore. Perhaps they were spurred on by the arrival of their friend Harvey Logan. In 1903 he had wormed his way out of jail in Knoxville, Tennessee, after all but throttling his warder with the coil of wire he kept hidden in his boot. He turned up in Patagonia under the name of Andrew Duffy, an alias he had already used in Montana.

In 1905 the reconstituted Wild Bunch broke out and robbed a bank in Southern Santa Cruz. They repeated the performance on the *Banco de la Nación* at Villa Mercedes in San Luis in the summer of 1907. It seems that Harvey Logan shot the manager through the head. Etta was there, dressed as a man—a fact obliquely confirmed by Blanca de Gérez: 'The Señora cropped her hair short and wore a wig.'

In December 1907 they sold Cholila, in a hurry, to a beef syndicate, and scattered into the Cordillera. None of their neighbours ever heard of them again. I have heard a number of reasons for their departure. But the most usual explanation is that Etta was bored, had a grumbling appendix and insisted on going to Denver for the operation. There is another possibility: that appendix was a euphemism for baby and that the father was a young Englishman, John Gardner, who was ranching in Patagonia for his health. The story goes that Harvey Logan had to get him out of the Kid's way, back to his family estate in Ireland.

Etta was apparently living in Denver in 1924. (Her daughter may have been a competitive girl called Betty Weaver, who pulled fifteen spectacular bank robberies before her arrest and jail-sentence at Belleplaine, Kansas, in 1932.) In the Ashley Valley in Utah, I met an old man, rocking on his porch, who remembered Butch Cassidy in 1908. But if they did come back that summer, the pace was too hot; for by December both outlaws were in Bolivia working for a man called Siebert at the Concordia tin mine.

The classic account of their death, at San Vicente, Bolivia, in December 1909, following their theft of a mine payroll, was first set down in *Elk's Magazine* for 1930 by the Western poet, Arthur Chapman. It was an ideal scenario for the movie-makers; the brave cavalry captain shot while trying to arrest the gringos; the mud-walled courtyard full of dead mules; the impossible odds; the Kid first wounded, then shot through the head by Butch, who, having now killed a man, reserves the last bullet for himself. The episode ends with the Bolivian soldiers finding Etta's Tiffany watch on one of the bodies.

No one knows where Chapman got the story: Butch Cassidy could have invented it himself. His aim, after all, was to 'die' in South America and re-emerge under a new name. The shooting at San Vicente was investigated by the late President René Barrientos, Ché Guevara's killer, himself an ardent Western history buff. He put a team on to solving the mystery, grilled the villagers personally, exhumed corpses in the cemetery, checked the army and police files, and concluded that the whole thing was a fabrication. Nor did Pinkertons believe it. They have their own version, based on the skimpiest evidence, that the 'family of 3' died together in a shoot-out with the Uruguayan police in 1911. Three years later they assumed Butch Cassidy dead— which, if he were alive, was exactly what he wanted.

'Bunkum!' his friends said when they heard the stories coming out of South America. Butch didn't go in for shoot-outs. And from 1915 on, hundreds of people saw—or thought they saw—

him; running guns for Pancho Villa in Mexico; prospecting with Wyatt Earp in Alaska; touring the West in a Model T Ford; calling on old girlfriends (who remember him as gotten rather fat); or turning up at a Wild West Show in San Francisco.

I went to see the star witness to his return; his sister, Mrs Lula Parker Betenson, a forthright and energetic woman in her nineties, with a lifetime of service to the Democratic Party. She has no doubts: her brother came back and ate blueberry pie with the family at Circleville in the fall of 1925. She believes he died of pneumonia in Washington State in the late 1930s. Another version puts his death in an Eastern city, a retired railroad engineer with two married daughters.

23

NOT FAR from Cholila there was a narrow gauge railway back to Esquel. The station was a toy station. The ticket salesman had the face of a private drinker. In his office was the photo of a soft middle-class boy with slicked-down hair, wanted for murdering the Fiat executive. The railway officials wore uniforms of pale grey with gold braid. On the platform was a shrine to the Virgin of Luján, the protector of travellers.

The engine was about eighty years old, made in Germany, with a tall funnel and red wheels. In the First Class, food had worked into the upholstery and filled the carriage with the smell of yesterday's picnic. The Second Class was clean and bright, with slat seats, painted pea-green, and a wood stove in the middle.

A man was boiling his blue enamel maté kettle. An old lady talked to her favourite geranium, and two mountaineers from Buenos Aires sat among a heap of equipment. They were intelligent, intolerant, earned pitiful salaries and thought the absolute worst of the U.S.A. The other passengers were Araucanian Indians.

The train started with two whistles and a jerk. Ostriches bounded off the track as we passed, their feathers billowing like smoke. The mountains were grey, flickering in the heat haze. Sometimes a truck smeared a dust-cloud along the horizon.

An Indian eyed the mountaineers and came over to pick a quarrel. He was very drunk. I sat back and watched the history of South America in miniature. The boy from Buenos Aires took his insults for half an hour, then he stood up, exploded and pointed the Indian back to his seat.

The Indian bowed his head and said: '*Si, Señor. Si, Señor.*'

The Indian settlements were strung out along the railway line on the principle that a drunk could always get home. The Indian came to his station and stumbled off the train clutching the last of his gin. Round the shacks broken bottles glinted in the watery sun. A boy in a yellow wind-cheater got off as well and helped the drunk walk. A dog, which had been lying in a doorway, ran up and licked him all over the face.

24

ALL ALONG the Southern Andes you hear stories of the *bandoleros norteamericanos*. I have taken this one from the second volume of *Memorias de un Carrero Patagónico* (*Memoirs of a Patagonian Carter*) by Asencio Abeijón:

In January 1908 [that is, a month after Butch Cassidy sold Cholila], a man riding over the Pampa de Castillo passed four horsemen with a string of hot-blooded horses. They were three gringos and a Chilean peon. They carried Winchesters with wooden handles. One of them was a woman dressed as a man. The traveller thought nothing of it. All gringos dressed in a strange fashion.

The same evening three horsemen stopped at the hotel of Cruz Abeijón at La Mata. There was no woman with them. They were two *norteamericanos* and a Chilean. They said they were looking for land. The shorter one was cheerful and talkative, by the name of Bob Evans. He spoke good Spanish and played with Abeijón's children. The other was tall and fair and silent and sinister. His name was Willie Wilson.

After breakfast the gringos asked Abeijón the name of the best hotel in Comodoro Rivadavia. They left the Chilean in charge of the horses and rode the remaining three leagues into town. Comodoro, in the days before the oil boom, was a tiny place sandwiched between the cliff and the sea. Along its one street were the Salesian Church, the Hotel Vascongada and the Casa Lahusen, a general store which also served as a bank. The Americans drank with the leading citizens and pursued their enquiries about land. They stayed a week. One morning a policeman found them shooting on the beach. 'Just practising,' they joked it off with the commissioner, Don Pedro Barros, who examined their Winchesters and handed them back smiling.

The Americans rode back to La Mata. Bob Evans distributed toffees among Abeijón's children. They were off again in the morning, this time with the horses and the peon. Abeijón found that his telephone wire had been cut.

At one p.m. on February 3rd it was hot and windy and the people of Comodoro were at lunch. Wilson and Evans tied their spare horses to a hitching post on the edge of town and rode down to the Casa Lahusen. Evans stationed himself by the main door. Wilson and the peon made for the goods entrance. They dismounted and the Chilean held the two horses. A bystander heard the two men arguing, then saw the peon hopping about and dodging behind his horse, and Wilson shoot him through the hand. The bullet went up his arm and through his shoulder and he fell back among a pile of wool-bales.

Commissioner Barros heard the shot and found Wilson doubled up with one hand over his chest. 'The pig shot me,' he said. Barros told him to come to the station and explain. Wilson said 'no', and drew a gun, 'his blue eyes shining diabolically'. Evans shouted 'Stop, you fool!' and spurred his horse between the two men, giving Barros a shove that toppled him among the wool-bales as well.

The Americans mounted, unhitched their spare horses, and trotted out of town. The whole business took five minutes. Barros ran to the station and began firing wildly with a sub-machine gun. Four mounted police followed but gave up. That night a Basque heard them singing to an accordion round their campfire.

Back in Comodoro, the peon was behind bars; at the last minute he had asked Wilson for a bigger cut.

From Esquel I went on south to follow up a second Wilson and Evans story:

25

THE OLD track to Arroyo Pescado cut across the thornscrub and headed for the green line where the river came out of the hills and spread into a reedy lagoon. A flock of flamingos took off, flashing orange and black and striping the blue water white as their legs lifted clear. Near the bank a patch of rocky ground was littered with old bottles and tin cans, all that remained of the Welsh *Compania Mercantil de Chubut*'s store.

On the afternoon of December 29th 1909, the manager, a strong ex-athlete from Bala called Llwyd ApIwan, left the shop and went across to his house for tea. Both his arms were bandaged to the elbows as he had put out an unexplained night fire with his bare hands. Some minutes later his assistant, Bobby Roberts, a soft-headed religious maniac, called over that Wilson and Evans had come to buy tack. They were regular customers and were well known in the Cordillera as carters and crack shots.

ApIwan walked back and found Evans covering Bobby Roberts, who was blubbing. Wilson then led him at gunpoint to the office and ordered him to open the safe.

'There's nothing in the safe,' ApIwan said.

But Wilson knew better. The Company was expecting a consignment of gold sovereigns to pay for the wool-clip. ApIwan opened up and showed a few Argentine banknotes.

'And they belong to the Indians,' he said. 'You're out of luck. The sovereigns haven't come.'

Wilson agreed not to take the Indians' money and shouted through to Evans. But as he backed out of the office, his spur caught in an Indian rug. He tripped and the Welshman jumped him as he fell. Even with his bandaged hands he got hold of the revolver and fired. But there was no trigger. Wilson had taken the trigger off and feathered the mechanism. He reached for a miniature revolver strung round his neck and shot ApIwan through the heart.

The outlaws rode off south to their camp at Río Pico. Following the scent of a story, I followed and cut back to the main road. The driver of a wool truck stopped and picked me up. He wore a black shirt embroidered with pink roses and played Beethoven's Fifth on his tape deck. The landscape was empty. The hills went gold and purple in the setting sun. At the foot of a telegraph pole we saw a single standing figure:

26

HE HAD blond hair and was travelling south. The hair flopped over his face and he flipped it back with a shake of his head. His body was soft and girlish. He held back his smile to hide a set of discoloured teeth. He was a miner, he said. He was looking for work in a mine.

He had torn a page from an old copy of the *National Encyclopaedia*. The page had a map showing various mines in Argentina. There was a gold mine at Río Pico.

He had been one of the original Flower Children in the Haight–Ashbury district of San Francisco. Once, when he was hungry, he had picked up a half-eaten Hershey bar off the sidewalk on Haight Street. This incident had printed itself on his memory and he mentioned it a number of times.

In San Francisco he had signed up on methadone, but managed to get detoxicated when he first found work in a mine. There was something elemental, he said, about mining. Mines gave him a feeling of security. Working in a mine in Arizona he had himself a house and a fine living wage, that is, until they came after him for taxes. Those darned taxes, and he'd said: 'I'm through. I'm goin' down South America, find myself another mine.'

We helped the driver change a wheel and he stood us drinks at Gobernador Costa. I asked a Welsh shopkeeper about the mine in Río Pico. He said it had closed fifty years back. The nearest was a kaolin mine at Apeleg.

'What's kaolin?'

'White china clay.'

'White what? D'ye say white? White? Cheesus! A white mine! Where d'ye say that mine was?'

'Apeleg.'

'Where's Apeleg?'

'A hundred kilometres on south,' the Welshman said. 'After that there's the coal mine at Río Turbio, but it's soft coal and you wouldn't want to work there.'

The miner had no money and his passport was stolen. He had dinner on me. In the morning, he said he'd be heading on south. Man, he'd be all right. It was simply a question of finding the right mine.

27

THE HOTEL in Río Pico was painted a pale turquoise and run by a Jewish family who lacked even the most elementary notions of profit. The rooms shambled round a courtyard with a water-tower and flower-beds edged with upturned bottles and full of fierce orange lilies. The owner was a brave and sorrowful woman in black, with heavy-lidded eyes, mourning with a Jewish mother's passion the death of her first-born son. He had been a saxophonist. He had gone to Comodoro Rivadavia and died there, of stomach cancer. She picked her teeth with a thorn and laughed at the futility of existence.

Her second son, Carlos Rubén, was an olive-skinned boy with the flickering eyes of a Semite. He ached for the outside world and would soon disappear into it. Her daughters padded the bare scrubbed rooms in carpet slippers. She ordered a towel and a pink geranium to be put in my room.

In the morning I had a tremendous row about the bill.

'How much was the room?'

'Nothing. If you hadn't slept in it, nobody else would.'

'How much was dinner?'

'Nothing. How could we know you were coming? We cooked for ourselves.'

'Then how much was the wine?'

'We always give wine to visitors.'

'What about the maté?'

'Nobody pays for maté.'

'What can I pay for then? There's only bread and coffee left.'

'I can't charge you for bread, but café au lait is a gringo drink and I shall make you pay.'

The sun was up. Spouts of wood-smoke rose vertically from the chimneys. Río Pico was once the German colony of Nueva Alemania, and the houses had a German look. Elderflowers rubbed their heads against the planked walls. Beside the bar was a logging truck, off up into the mountains.

28

LAS PAMPAS was twenty miles on from Río Pico, the last settlement before the frontier. To the north towered El Cono, an extinct volcano of bone-white screes and brighter snows. In the valley the river ran fast and green over white stones. Each log cabin had a potato patch, barricaded from cattle by stakes and thorns.

There were two families at Las Pampas, Patrocinio and Solís. Each accused the other of cattle-stealing, but both hated the State logging company and in their hatred they were friends.

It was a Sunday. God had given a son to the Patrocinio who owned the bar and he was celebrating the event with an *asado*. Riders had been coming in for two days. Their horses were hitched in the stable, their lariats and boleadoras tucked into the girths. The men lay in white clover, drinking wine from skins and warming themselves by the fire. The sun dispersed the milky haze that hung in patches over the valley.

Rolf Mayer, a gaucho with German and Indian blood, did the butchery. He was lean and silent with mighty scarlet hands. He was dressed all over in chocolate brown and never took off his hat. He had a knife made from a bayonet with a yellowing ivory pommel. He laid each sheep on a trestle and began undressing the carcass until it lay, pink and sheeny, legs in the air on the white inner lining of its own fleece. Then he slipped the knife point in where the skin stretches tight over the belly and the hot blood spurted over his hands. He enjoyed that. You could tell he enjoyed it by the way he lowered his eyelids and stuck out his lower lip and sucked the air in through his teeth. He pulled out the guts, skimmed them of liver and kidneys and threw the rest to the dogs.

He carried the five carcasses to the fire and crucified each one to its iron cross, set on an incline to the flame.

In the afternoon the wind and snow flurries sliced out of the Cordillera, while a tow-haired dreamer stoked the fire and the men played *taba*. The *taba* is the astragalus bone of a cow. The player throws it ten paces on to a prepared circle of mud or sand. If it falls on its concave side, this is *suerte* (good luck) and he wins; on its rounded side, this is *culo* (arse) and he loses; and if it falls on its edge there is no play. A good player knows how much backspin to give so that it lands *suerte*. Naturally there are a number of jokes about *culo*. I was *culo* many times and lost a lot of money.

After dark Patrocinio played the accordion and the dreamer sang in a nasal voice. The girls wore cretonne dresses and the boys held their partners far away from them.

29

A MAN called Florentino Solís offered to ride with me up the mountain. His face was burned a bright even red, and when he took off his hat, there was a sharp line where the red ended and the white began. He was a wanderer, without wife or house, owning nothing but two sleek *criollo* ponies, their saddles and a dog.

A few cattle, stamped with his brand, roamed the rough camps

along the frontier, but usually he let them be. He had come down
to exchange a cow for groceries and stayed for the *asado*. He was
awkward in company. All day he did not drink but sat by the
stream, alone, picking his teeth with grass stems.

The morning was cold. Cumulus clouds were piling up over
the peaks. Solís put on sheepskin chaps and mounted his piebald.
Patrocinio lent me a black gelding and we forded the river. The
ponies went in up to the girth but their feet held. For an hour we
rode up a steep valley, the track zig-zagging over a ridge of red
rocks, then plunging in among the big trees. Another hour and
we came to a sheer cliff. Solís pointed to a pile of hewn timbers
rotting into humus and said: 'This was the prison of Ramos
Otero':

Ramos Luis Otero was a troubled young man, the son of a
patrician family, who dressed in good clothes gone to rags and
liked washing up dirty mess-cans. He hated women. He hated
the salon atmosphere of Buenos Aires, and worked in Patagonia
as a backwoodsman. One year he worked for a government
surveying team, but, when his disguise fell through, he bought
the Estancia Pampa Chica, at Corcovado, mid-way from the
mountain to the plain.

In the last week of March 1911 Otero and his peon, Quintanilla,
were driving a buckboard and two horses to the estancia. Crossing the Cañadón del Tiro they saw two riders trotting in the
opposite direction. One of them, smiling, waved Otero on. The
other grabbed his reins as he passed. The riders were North
Americans.

They unhitched the horses and forced Otero and the peon to
ride with them into the mountains. On coming to the cliff, the
Americans felled some trees and constructed a prison cell, of
trunks lashed together with rawhide. Otero took a special dislike
to the tall blond one called Wilson, who left the heavy work to
his friend.

Cooped up in the prison Otero went suicidal, and Quintanilla
yellow with fear. Their jailers let them out twice a day for food
and the functions of the body. There were several members of the
gang, all gringos, North American or English. After two weeks
one of the guards accidentally dropped a match. Otero picked it
up, lit a fire on the floor and used the embers to burn through the

rawhide. In the evening he heaved a trunk aside and the two men escaped.

Once free, Otero was full of hysterical denunciations. His brothers had come down with the ransom and he accused them of setting up the kidnap to make him leave Patagonia. He was not a balanced young man. Nor did the police believe his story until he led them to the cliff—and then it was a national sensation.

The Minister of the Interior ordered a manhunt to clear the Cordillera of outlaws. In December 1911 Wilson and Evans came down to Río Pico to buy stores from two German brothers called Hahn. The Hahns were founders of the colony and warned their American friends that the Frontier Police were patrolling the area. Wilson's hand was septic and swollen. He had been re-packing a cartridge and it had exploded. Dona Guillermina Hahn dressed the wound and they rode back into the cover of the mountains.

But Evans had been tampering with the wife of one of the Solís family. This man knew the outlaws' camp and led the patrol to it. Evans was under a tree eating lunch. Wilson, feverish from his hand, was lying in the tent. The officer, a Lt Blanco, shouted *'Arriba las manós!'* from behind a tree. Evans fired, killing one soldier and wounding another, Private Pedro Peñas (alive to give an interview in Rawson in 1970 aged 104). The troops returned fire and shot Evans dead. Wilson broke out of the tent and ran, barefoot, among the trees, but the soldiers soon laid him out alongside his friend. On the bodies they found two gold watches and the photograph of *'una mujer hermosísima'*. (Testimony of Pedro Peñas.)

Cantering back to Las Pampas and dodging the low branches across the track, my saddle-girth snapped and the horse pitched me in among sharp rocks below. I looked up through the bushes and saw the sad mask of Solís break into a smile.

'Feet!' he said later to Patrocinio. 'All I could see were the gringo's feet.'

My hand was cut to the bone and we rode down to Río Pico to have it dressed.

30

THE DOCTOR pushed through a swing door. There was something the matter with her legs. She had small white hands and a mane of greying yellow hair. She growled at me in English but I knew she was Russian. She moved with the slow fluidity that saves Russian women of bulk from ungainliness. She screwed up her eyes as if trying not to see.

In her room there were red cushions and red tapestry rugs, and, on the walls, two paintings of Russian subjects, daubed landscapes dimly remembered by a fellow exile: black pines and an orange river; light fluttering through birches on the white planks of a dacha.

She spent every spare peso ordering books from the Y.M.C.A. Press in Paris. Mandelstam, Tsvetayeva, Pasternak, Gumilev, Akhmatova, Solzhenitsyn—the names rolled off her tongue with the reverberation of a litany. She followed from *samizdat* reprints the fluctuations of Soviet dissent. Greedily she reached out for news of the new exiles. What had happened to Sinyavsky in Paris? What would become of Solzhenitsyn in the West?

Her sister was a school-teacher in the Ukraine. The doctor wrote to her often, but for years she had had no word.

I said Patagonia reminded me of Russia. Surely Río Pico was a bit like the Urals? She scowled. Río Pico did not remind *her* of Russia. In Argentina there was nothing—sheep and cows and human sheep and cows. And in Western Europe also nothing.

'Total decadence,' she said. 'The West deserves to be eaten. Take England for example. Tolerating homosexuality. Disgusting! One thing I feel ... One thing I know for a fact ... The future of civilization is in the hands of the Slavs.'

In conversation I made some slight reservation about Solzhenitsyn.

'What can you know about it?' she snapped back. I had spoken a heresy. Every word Solzhenitsyn wrote was the truth, the absolute, blinding truth.

I asked how she came to Argentina.

'I was a nurse in the war. I was captured by the Nazis. When it was over I found myself in West Germany. I married a Pole. He had family here.'

She shrugged and left me guessing.

And then I remembered a story once told to me by an Italian friend: she was a girl at the end of the war, living in a villa near Padua. One night she heard women screaming in the village. The screams scarred her imagination and, for years, she woke at night and heard the same hideous screaming. Long after she asked her mother about the screams and the mother said: 'Those were the Russian nurses, the ones Churchill and Roosevelt sent back to Stalin. They were packing them into trucks and they knew they were going home to die.'

The pink plastic of artificial limbs shone through the doctor's stockings. Both her legs were off at the knees. Perhaps the amputation saved her life.

'You, who have been to Russia,' she asked, 'would they let me back? The Communists I do not mind. I would do anything to go back.'

'Things have changed,' I said, 'and there is now the detente.'

She wanted to believe it was true. Then, with the particular sadness that suppresses tears, she said: 'The detente is for the Americans, not for us. No. It would not be safe for me to go.'

A mile outside the settlement there was another exile:

31

SHE WAS waiting for me, a white face behind a dusty window. She smiled, her painted mouth unfurling as a red flag caught in a sudden breeze. Her hair was dyed dark-auburn. Her legs were a mesopotamia of varicose veins. She still had the tatters of an extraordinary beauty.

She had been making pastry and the grey dough clung to her hands. Her blood-red nails were cracked and chipped.

'*J'aime bien la cuisine*,' she said. '*C'est une des seules choses que je peux faire maintenant.*'

Her French was halting and slow. Her face lit up as she remembered the idioms of her childhood. She took up a coloured photograph of her city and began to recall the names of quays, streets, parks, fountains, and avenues. Together we strolled around pre-war Geneva.

Long ago she sang in operettas and cafés concerts. She came to Argentina, the land of opportunity and the tango in the early 1930s. She showed me copies of her own song, *Novia Pálida*, *The Pale Bride*. The tempo was slow waltz. On the green cover was her picture, taken in 1932, leaning over the white rail of a ship, in a sailor suit with a wide white collar, smiling a diffident smile.

At some negative turning point she had married a moon-faced Swede. They joined two failures in one and drifted towards the end of the world. Caught by chance in this eddy, they built the perfect cottage of his native Malmö, with its intelligent windows and vertical battens painted red with iron-oxide.

The Swede died fifteen years ago and she had never left Río Pico. Their son was a trucker. He wore chequered shirts and a red handkerchief at the neck, but when he relaxed, his face collapsed in Nordic sadness.

Her two rooms led one into the other. A pair of plastic curtains divided the space. She had painted them in trompe l'oeil to resemble the crimson velvet of theatre draperies, tied back with tassels of gold.

'I can still paint a little,' she said.

She had covered every inch of wall with murals, some in paint, some in coloured crayons.

A yellow sun rolled over the pampa and into the room. It played over the sails of yachts drifting on a summer's day; on cafés hung with Japanese lanterns; on the Château de Chillon, mountain chalets and the Île des Peupliers.

She had carved little wooden faces of angels, painted them with rosy cheeks and set them round the cornice. On one wall was a small picture in oils, a sunny landscape cleft by a black gulch. At the bottom were skulls and bones and, above, hung a ricketty bridge. Halfway across stood a little girl with a white frightened face and red hair streaming in the wind. She was tottering to fall but a golden angel hovered above and offered her his hand.

'I like this painting,' she said. 'It is my guardian angel. My Angel, who has always saved me.'

A copy of *The Pale Bride* lay open on the music stand of the piano. Black gaps yawned where the ivory had come off. I noticed that not all her fingernails were painted. Some were red. Some she had left blank. Perhaps she did not have enough nail-paint to complete both hands.

I left the soprano and went to call on the Germans:

32

THE WIND blew the smell of rain down the valley ahead of the rain itself, the smell of wet earth and aromatic plants. The old woman pulled in her washing and fetched the cane chairs off the terrace. The old man, Anton Hahn, put on boots and a waterproof and went into the garden to check that all the catchments were clear. The peon came over from the barn with an empty bottle and the woman filled it with apple *chicha*. He was drunk already. Two red oxen stood yoked to a cart, bracing themselves for the storm.

The old man walked round his vegetable garden and his flower garden bright with annuals. Having seen that they would get the full benefit of the rain, he came inside the house. Apart from its metal roof nothing distinguished it from the houses of a South German village, the half-timbering infilled with white plaster, the grey shutters, the wicket fence, scrubbed floors, painted panelling, the chandelier of antler tines and lithographs of the Rhineland.

Anton Hahn took off his tweed cap and hung it on an antler. He took off his boots and canvas gaiters and put on rope-soled slippers. His head was flat on top and his face creased and red. A little girl with a pigtail came into the kitchen.

'Do you wish your pipe, *Onkel*?'

'*Bitte.*' And she brought a big meerschaum and filled it with tobacco from a blue and white jar.

The old man poured himself a tankard of *chicha*. As the rain

slammed on the roof, he talked about the Colonia Nueva
Alemania. His uncles settled here in 1905 and he had followed
after the Great War.

'What could I do? The Fatherland was in a bad condition.
Before the war, no family could have enough sons. One was a
soldier. One was a carpenter, and two stayed on the farm. But
after 1918 Germany was full of refugees from the Bolsheviks.
Even the villages were full.'

His brother lived on the family farm on the borders of Bavaria
and Wurttemberg. They wrote letters once a month but had not
met since 1923.

'The war was the biggest mistake in history,' Anton Hahn said.
He was obsessed by the war. 'Two peoples of the Superior Race
ruining each other. Together England and Germany could have
ruled the world. Now even Patagonia is returning to the *indigenas*.
This is a pity.'

He went on lamenting the decline of the West and, at one
point, dropped the name Ludwig.

'Mad Ludwig?'

'The King? Mad? You call the King mad? In my house?
No!'

I had to think fast.

'Some people call him mad,' I said, 'but, of course, he was a
great genius.'

Anton Hahn was hard to pacify. He stood up and lifted his
tankard.

'You will join me,' he said.

I stood.

'To the King! To the last genius of Europe! With him died the
greatness of my race!'

The old man offered me dinner, but I refused, having eaten
with the soprano two hours before.

'You will not leave my house until you have eaten with us.
After that you may go where you will.'

So I ate his ham and pickles and sun-coloured eggs and drank
his apple *chicha* which went to my head. Then I asked him about
Wilson and Evans.

'They were gentlemen,' he said. 'They were friends of my
family and my uncles buried them. My cousin knows the story.'

The old woman was tall and thin and her yellowing skin fell from her face in folds. Her hair was white and cut in a fringe across her eyebrows.

'Yes. I remember Wilson and Evans. I had four years at the time.'

It was a hot, windless day in early summer. The Frontier Police, eighty of them, had been hunting the outlaws up and down the Cordillera. The Police were criminals themselves, mostly Paraguayos; you had to be white or Christian to join. Everyone in Río Pico liked the North Americans. Her mother, Doña Guillermina, dressed Wilson's hand, right here in the kitchen. They could easily have gone over into Chile. How could they know the Indian would betray them?

'I remember them bringing in the bodies,' she said. 'The *Fronterizas* brought them down on an ox-cart. They were here, outside the gate. They had swelled up in the heat and the smell was terrible. My mother sent me to my room so I shouldn't see. Then the officer cut the heads off and came up the steps, here, carrying them by the hair. And he asked my mother for preserving alcohol. You see, this *Agencia* in New York was paying five thousand dollars a head. They wanted to send the heads up there and get the money. This made my father very angry. He shouted them to give over the heads and the bodies and he buried them.'

The storm was passing. Columns of grey water fell on the far side of the valley. Along the length of the apple orchard was a line of blue lupins. Wherever there were Germans there were blue lupins.

By the corral a rough wood cross stuck out of a small mound. The arching stems of a pampas rose sprung up as if fertilized by the bodies. I watched a grey harrier soaring and diving, and the sweep of grass and the thunderheads turning crimson.

The old man had come out and was standing behind me.

'No one would want to drop an atom bomb on Patagonia,' he said.

33

WHO WERE Wilson and Evans? Anything is possible in the murk of outlaw history, but there are a few clues:

On January 29th 1910, Police Commissioner Milton Roberts wrote to Pinkerton's in New York with descriptions of Llwyd ApIwan's murderers. Evans was about 35. Height 5ft 7in. Thick set. Colour of hair red but probably false. Wilson was younger, about 25. Height around 5ft 11in. Slight build. Fair hair. Tanned. Nose short and straight. Walks with the right foot turned out. (Remember also that Wilson was the crack shot, not Evans.)

Roberts added that Wilson had been a companion of Duffy (Harvey Logan), in Patagonia and in Montana where they had done a train robbery. This can only be the Wagner Train Hold-up on June 3rd 1901. The composition of the gang was: Harvey Logan, Butch Cassidy, Harry Longabaugh, Ben Kilpatrick 'The Tall Texan', with O. C. Hanks and Jim Thornhill in charge of horses.

Roberts's letter assumes that Evans and Wilson and Ryan and Place were four separate individuals. But his descriptions tally exactly with those for Cassidy and the Kid, except in the matter of age. This is not an insuperable problem. The Welsh policeman never saw the outlaws face to face. And I found, in Patagonia, that people had the habit of underestimating age by ten to fifteen years.

Yet the grave at Río Pico is impossible to square with Lula Betenson's account of her brother's return unless the following is true: Butch Cassidy is said to have told friends in Utah that the Sundance Kid was gunned down in South America, but that he escaped and travelled with an Indian boy on a kind of Huck Finn idyll. Recently I had a letter from Señor Francisco Juárez in Buenos Aires, which appeared to support this conjecture. He went to Río Pico after my visit and was told that Evans had got away from the *Fronterizas*, and that the man buried beside Wilson was an English member of the gang.

34

I LEFT Río Pico and came to a Scottish sheep-station. The notice on the gate read 'Estancia Lochinver — 1.444 kilometres'. The gate was in excellent trim. On the post was a painted top-knot in the form of a thistle.

I walked the 1.444 kilometres and reached a house of cor-rugated iron, with twin gables and a high pitched roof, built in a style more suitable for granite. The Scotsman stood on the steps, a big, gristly man with white hair and black eyebrows. He had been rounding up sheep all day. Three thousand animals grazed in his paddock. He was expecting the shearers in the morning.

'But ye can't trust 'em to come when they say. Ye can't even talk to people in this country. Ye can't tell 'em they did a bad job or they'll pack and leave. Ye tell 'em anything's wrong and they'll cut the beasts to ribbons. Aye, it's a butchery, not a shearing that they do.'

His father had been a crofter on the island of Lewis and came out when the big sheep companies were opening up. The family did well, bought land, learned a little Spanish, and kept Scotland in their hearts.

He wore the kilt and piped at Caledonian Balls. He had one set of pipes sent from Scotland and another he made himself in the long Patagonian winter. In the house there were views of Scotland, photographs of the British Royal Family, and Karsh's picture of Winston Churchill.

'And ye know who he was, don't ye?'

A tin of Mackintosh's toffees was placed reverently under the Queen.

His wife had been stone deaf since her car collided with a train. She had not learned to lip-read and you had to scribble questions on a pad. He was her second husband and they had been married twenty years. She liked the refinements of English life. She liked using a silver toast-rack. She liked nice linen and fresh chintzes and polished brass. She did not like Patagonia. She hated the winter and missed having flowers.

'I've a terrible time getting things to grow. Lupins do well, but my carnations never survive the cold, and mostly I make do with annuals—godetias, clarkias, larkspurs and marigolds—but you can never tell how they're going to do. This year the sweet peas are a disaster, and I do so love them for vases. Flowers do improve the home, I think.'

'Aagh!' he muttered. 'I care none for her damn flowers.'

'What's that you said, dear? He's overworked, you know. Bad heart! He shouldn't be riding round the camp all day. *I'm* the one who should be rounding up sheep. He *hates* horses. When I lived in Buenos Aires I always loved to ride.'

'Bah! She knows bugger all about it. She rides round some fancy estancia and thinks she can round up sheep.'

'What are you saying, dear?'

'She's right in one thing, though. I never liked the horse. But ye can't get anyone to ride for ye now. This was a fine country once. Ye paid 'em and they worked. Now I've got the boy and he'll be off any minute, and I've got the old peon, but he's eighty-three and I have to strap him to his horse.'

The Scotsman had lived forty years in the valley. He had the reputation of being very tight-fisted. One year, when the price of wool was up, he and his wife went to Scotland. They stayed in first-class hotels and were a week on Lewis. There he became familiar with the things his mother spoke of—gulls, herring boats, heather, peat—and he had felt the call.

Now he wanted to leave Patagonia and retire to Lewis. She wanted to leave, but not necessarily to Lewis. She was in better health than he. He did not know how to get out. The price of wool was falling and the Perónistas were after the land.

Next morning we stood outside the house and looked along the line of telegraph poles, watching for the shearers' truck. In place of a lawn was a flat expanse of packed dirt, and, in the middle, a wire-netting cage.

'And what do you keep in there?' I asked.

'Aagh! The bugger died on me.'

Curled in the bottom of the cage lay the dried-up skeleton of a thistle.

35

GOING DOWN to Comodoro Rivadavia I passed through a desert of black stones and came to Sarmiento. It was another dusty grid of metal buildings, lying on a strip of arable land between the fizzling turquoise Lake Musters and the slime-green Lake Colhué-Huapi.

I walked out of town to the petrified forest. Wind pumps whirled insanely. A steel-blue heron lay paralysed under an electric cable. A dribble of blood ran along its beak. The tongue was missing. The trunks of extinct monkey-puzzles were broken clean as if in a sawmill.

A lot of Boers lived round Sarmiento, and met up at the Hotel Orroz for lunch. Their names were Venter, Visser, Vorster, Kruger, Norval, Eloff, Botha and de Bruyn—all descendants of hard-line Afrikaners who emigrated to Patagonia in 1903, sickened by the Union Jack. They lived in fear of the Lord, celebrated Dingaan's Day and took oaths on the Dutch Reformed Bible. They did not marry outsiders and their daughters had to go to the kitchen if a Latin entered the house. Many went back to South Africa when Dr Malan came to power.

But the town's most distinguished citizen was the Lithuanian, Casimir Slapelič. Fifty years ago he found the dinosaur in the barranca. Now, toothless, hairless and in his middle eighties, he was one of the oldest flying pilots in the world. Each morning he put on his white canvas flying-suit, pottered down to the Aero Club in his Moskva and hurled himself and his antique monoplane to the gales. The risk merely increased his appetite for life.

The wind had polished his nose and coloured it pale lilac. I found him at lunch ladling the bortsch into the ivory orb of his head. He had made his room cheerful, in the Baltic way, with flowered curtains, geraniums, diplomas for stunt flying and a signed photograph of Neil Armstrong. All his books were in Lithuanian, the aristocrat of Indo-European languages, and concerned his country's plans for independence.

His wife had died and he had adopted a young Indian couple,

out of kindness and for company. The girl sat against the white wall, suckling her baby, devouring visitors with mica-shining eyes.

Casimir Slapelič was a prodigy. Once he had tried to be a bird man. Now he would like to go to the Moon.

'But I will fly you in the plane,' he said.

'Perhaps,' I said.

'I will fly you over the Painted Desert.'

It was blowing half a hurricane. Driving in the Moskva I noticed that his legs, bowed to a pair of perfect arcs, had little control over the foot-pedals.

'We'd better not go in the plane,' I said.

'Then I shall take you to my sister. She has a collection of Indian arrow heads.'

We drove to a concrete bungalow and walked through a garden to the back door. A white phallus reared among his sister's marigolds.

'The tibia of a dinosaur,' said Casimir Slapelič.

The sister had a leathery face of great age. She was one of a tight group of Sarmiento ladies, the archaeologists. They were not proper archaeologists but collectors of antiquities. They scoured caves, killing-sites, and lake shores for the relics of ancient hunters. Each had her network of peons who brought objects in from the camp. The 'professionals' cursed them as looters.

That afternoon the Baltic exile was 'at home' to a Welsh-woman. The visitor watched her unworthy competitor unwrap her treasures from white tissue, but her envious eyes did not accord with her patronizing remarks.

Casimir Slapelič's sister knew how to feed her rival's jealousy. She displayed cards covered with black velvet mounted with arrow heads, bright as jewels, and so arranged that they looked like tropical fish. Her fingers played over their faceted surfaces. There were flat knives of pink and green flint; boleadora stones; a blue idol, and some arrows fletched with eagle feathers.

'But my collection is better,' the Welshwoman said.

'Bigger but less beautiful,' said the Lithuanian.

'I shall sell mine to the Presidenta and it will go to the National Museum.'

'If she'll buy it,' said the older woman.

Casimir Slapelič was bored. We went out into the garden.

'Dead men's things,' he said. 'I do not like.'

'Nor do I.'

'What shall we see now?'

'The Boers.'

'The Boers are difficult but we'll try.'

We drove to the east side of town where the Boers had their bungalows. Slapelič knocked on one and the whole family came out into the yard, stared with set faces at the Englishman, and didn't say a word. He called on another and the door slammed. He found the Welsh husband of a Boer woman who would talk but knew little. And then he found a fleshy Boer woman who leaned over her red garden gate and looked fierce. She also would talk, but for money and in the presence of her lawyer.

'Not very friendly,' I said.

'They are Boers,' said Casimir Slapelič.

36

At Comodoro Rivadavia I called on Father Manuel Palacios, the comprehensive genius of the South. He lived in the Salesian College, a hulk of concrete, lurking between the cliff and the sea. The storm kicked up clouds of dust, and flares from the oil rigs lit them a lurid orange.

A priest sheltered in the doorway of the chapel, chatting to two boys. He had the prettiest wreath of grey curls. Gusts ripped at his soutane and uncovered his porcelain-white legs.

'Where can I find Father Palacios?'

His unwrinkled forehead puckered. He looked concerned.

'You can't.'

'He lives here?'

'But doesn't receive visitors. He is working. Day and night he works. Besides, he is recovering from an operation. Cancer,' he whispered. 'He has so little time.'

He outlined the accomplishments of the Patagonian polymath. Father Palacios was Doctor of Theology, of Anthropological Theory and Archaeology. He was a marine biologist, zoologist, engineer, physicist, geologist, agronomist, mathematician, geneticist, and taxidermist. He spoke four European languages and six Indian ones. He was writing a general history of the Salesian Order and a treatise on biblical prophecies of the New World.

'But what to do with this writing?' the father tittered. 'What responsibility placed on our shoulders! How to protect this treasure? How to publish?'

He clicked his tongue.

'Why do you want to see him?'

'I understand he's an expert on the Indians.'

'Expert? He *is* an Indian! Well, I shall lead you to him, but I can't promise he will see you.'

Undeterred by the dust-storm, the polymath sat in a grove of tamarisks, immersed in a North American manual of applied engineering. He wore a blue beret and a baggy grey suit. The tortoise folds of his neck craned from a celluloid collar. He offered me his footstool and begged me sit at his feet. He waved his colleague to a chair that someone had rescued too late from a bonfire, and consulted a silver watch.

'I have half an hour at your disposal in which to outline the prehistory of Patagonia.'

Father Palacios flooded me with information: statistics, radio-carbon dates, migrations of men and animals, marine regressions, upheavals of the Andes or the appearance of new artefacts. Possessed of a photographic memory he could describe in detail every Indian rock-painting of the South: ' ... in the Second Petrified Forest, there is a unique representation of a mylodon ... at Río Pinturas you will find a rodeo of palaeo-llamas, the men are wearing phallic caps ... a second fresco depicts the use of a decoy as described by Pigafetta ... at Lago Posadas there is a mortal combat between a macrauchenia and a smilodon ... '

I took careful notes. The father, his soutane flapping, stood by the charred remains of the chair.

'*Qué inteligencia!*' he said. '*Oh Padre! Qué sabiduría!*'

Father Palacios smiled and continued. I noticed, though, that he was no longer talking to me. Instead, gazing to heaven, he addressed his monologue to the lowering clouds.

'O Patagonia!' he cried. 'You do not yield your secrets to fools. Experts come from Buenos Aires, from North America even. What do they know? One can but marvel at their incompetence. Not one palaeontologist has yet unearthed the bones of the unicorn.'

'The unicorn?'

'Precisely, the unicorn. The Patagonian unicorn was contemporary with the extinct megafauna of the Late Pleistocene. The last unicorns were hunted to extinction by man in the fifth or sixth millennium B.C. At Lago Posadas you will find two paintings of unicorns. One holds its horn erect as in Psalm 29: "My horn shalt thou exalt like the horn of an unicorn". The other is about to impale a hunter and stamps the pampas, as described in the Book of Job.' (In Job 38:21 it is the horse that '*paweth the valley*', while in verses 9–10 the unicorn is found unfit to haul a plough.)

The lecture melted into a dream voyage. Marquesans beached their canoes in the fjords of Southern Chile, scaled the Andes, settled by Lake Musters and merged with the indigenous population. Father Palacios described his own discovery, in Tierra del Fuego, the sculpture of a headless woman, life size and smothered in red ochre.

'*Oh Dios! Que conocimientos!*'

'And you have photographs?' I asked.

'Certainly, I have photographs,' he smiled again, 'but they are not for publication. And now let me ask you a question. Upon which continent did the human species emerge?'

'Africa.'

'False! Totally false! Here in Patagonia, sentient beings in the Tertiary witnessed the formation of the Andes. An ancestor of man lived in Tierra del Fuego before the African australopithecines. Furthermore,' he added casually, 'the last one was seen in 1928.'

'*Genio!*'

Father Palacios then outlined the story (which he has since published in a learned journal) of the Yoshil:

The Yoshil (an Indian name) was—and perhaps still is—a

tail-less protohominid, with lichenous hair of a yellowish green colour. It stood about eighty centimetres high, walked on two feet and lived in the territory of the Haush. It always went armed with a stone or short club. By day it lived in the *ñire* trees (*Notofagus antarctica*) but at night it would warm itself by the fire of a lonely hunter. The Yoshil was probably vegetarian and fed on wild fruits, fungi, and the white grubs that are the staple of the Magellanic woodpecker.

The first modern account of the Yoshil was that of the Haush hunter, Yioi:molke, who saw one while hunting cormorants at Caleta Yrigoyen in 1886; the last positive sighting was in 1928 by the hunter Pai:men. But the most distressing encounter was that of the Indian, Paka, Father Palacios's informant, some time during the Great War.

Paka was camping alone in the forest when a Yoshil appeared at the fire. He knew of its dangerous reputation, reached for his bow, but the animal bounded for safety. Paka thought he'd be murdered if he slept and lay down with his weapon at the ready. The Yoshil approached. He fired and heard a scream of pain. In the morning he found the corpse nearby. To his horror, the animal had the same features as his brother, who had recently died. He dug a tomb, uncertain if he was burying a Yoshil, or reburying his brother.

'I have decided,' Father Palacios concluded, 'to name the creature *Fuegopithecus Pakensis*. The name, of course, is provisional. The Yoshil may be the same species as the other Patagonian protohominid, *Homunculus Harringtoni*, from Chubut. Only skeletal material will clarify the issue.'

'*Dios! Qué ciencia!*'

'And now,' he said, 'I think we have finished our survey,' and buried himself in his book.

I left, gasping with wonder at the inspiration of the autodidact.

'A genius,' breathed my companion, as we brushed through the tamarisks towards the college buildings.

'Tell me, am I wrong or is the college shut?'

'Shut,' he said. 'Shut. Various problems.'

The walls were covered with scarlet fists and the pronouncements of some proletarian front.

'The boys,' he shook his head. 'The boys.'

The chapel bell clanked.

'And now I must go to Mass,' he said. 'Tell me, brother, which religion have you?'

'Protestant.'

'Different road,' he sighed. 'Same Divinity. *Adiós, Hermanō*.'

37

I NOW had two reasons to head back to the Cordillera: to see Charley Milward's old sheep-station at Valle Huemeules and to find Father Palacios's unicorn. I took a bus to Perito Moreno and got there in a dust-storm. The restaurant was owned by an Arab, who served lentils and radishes and kept a sprig of mint on the bar to remind him of a home he had not seen. I asked him about traffic going north. He shook his head.

'A few Chilean trucks, maybe, but very very few.'

The distance to Valle Huemeules was over a hundred miles but I decided to risk it. At the edge of town someone had written 'Perón=Gorilla' in blue paint on an abandoned police post. Nearby was a pile of gin bottles, a memorial to a dead trucker; his friends chucked on a bottle whenever they passed. I walked two hours, five hours, ten hours, and no truck. My notebook conveys something of the mood:

Walked all day and the next day. The road straight, grey, dusty, and trafficless. The wind relentless, heading you off. Sometimes you heard a truck, you knew for certain it was a truck, but it was the wind. Or the noise of gears changing down, but that also was the wind. Sometimes the wind sounded like an unloaded truck banging over a bridge. Even if a truck had come up behind you wouldn't have heard it. And even if you'd been downwind, the wind would have drowned the engine. The one noise you did hear was a guanaco. A noise like a baby trying to cry and sneeze at once. You saw him a hundred yards off, a single male, bigger and more graceful than a llama, with his orange coat and white upstanding tail. Guanacos are shy animals, you were told, but this one was mad for you. And when you could walk no more and laid out your sleeping bag, he was there gurgling and snivelling and keeping the same distance. In the morning he was right up close, but the shock of you getting out of your skin was too much for him. That was the end of a friendship and you watched him bounding away over a thorn bush like a galleon in a following sea.

Next day hotter and windier than before. The hot blasts knocked you back, sucked at your legs, pressed on your shoulders. The road beginning and ending in a grey mirage. You'd see a dust-devil behind and, though you knew now never to hope for a truck, you thought it was a truck. Or there'd be black specks coming closer, and you stopped, sat down and waited, but the specks walked off sideways and you realized they were sheep.

A Chilean truck did come on the afternoon of the second day. The driver was a cheerful tough, his feet smelling of cheese. He liked Pinochet and was pleased with the general situation in his country.

He took me to Lago Blanco, where the lake water was a dull creamy white, and beyond was a basin of emerald grass blocked by a line of blue mountains. This was Valle Huemeules.

Charley Milward was last here in 1919. The bar-keeper remembered his moustaches. '*Los enormes bigotes*', she said, and imitated the way he hobbled with a stick. The policeman was having his late-afternoon gin and she ordered him to drive me to the estancia. Meekly he agreed, but to show his mettle went home for a revolver.

The Estancia Valle Huemeules was painted red and white and bore the mark of efficient centralization. It was run by the Menéndez-Behety family, the sheep-farming moguls of the South, who with a French wool-buyer bought Charley out after the First World War. The manager was a German and mistrusted me on sight. I think he suspected I had a claim on the place, but he did allow me to sleep in the peons' quarters.

They were in the middle of shearing. The shearing shed had

twenty bays and as many shearers; wiry Chilenos, stripped to the waist, their pants shiny black with grease from the wool. A driveshaft, powered by a steam engine, ran the length of the gallery. There were noises of whirring pistons, slapping belts, ratcheting clippers and bleating sheep. When the boys tied the animals' legs, all the fight went out of them and they lay, dead weight, till the torture was over. Then, naked and gashed with red cuts about their udders, they bounded wildly into the air, as if jumping over an imaginary fence, or jumping to be free.

The day ended in a vicious sunset of red and purple. The supper bell rang and the shearers downed clippers and ran for the kitchen. The old cook had a sweet smile. He cut me off half a leg of lamb.

'I can't eat that much.'

'Surely you can.'

He held his hands across his stomach. It was all over for him. 'I have cancer,' he said. 'This is my last summer.'

After dark the gauchos reclined against their saddles and stretched out with the ease of well-fed carnivores. The apprentices fed poplar logs into an iron stove on which two maté kettles were boiling.

One man presided over the ritual. He filled the hot brown gourds and the green liquid frothed to the neck. The men fondled the gourds and sucked at the bitter drink, talking about maté the way other men talked about women.

They gave me a straw mattress, and I curled up on the floor and tried to sleep. The men threw craps and their conversation turned to knives. They unsheathed their own blades and compared their qualities, drumming the tips on the table. The light came from a single hurricane lamp and the shadowy blades twitched on the white wall above my head. A Chilean shearer made comic suggestions about what his knife could do to a gringo. He was very drunk.

Another man said: 'I'd better let the gringo sleep in my room.'

38

A Boer gave me a lift back south, through Perito Moreno, to Arroyo Feo, where the volcanic badlands began. He was a veterinary surgeon and he didn't think much of the other Boers.

A frill of pleated white cliffs danced round the horizon. The surface of the ground was blotched with scabs of dribbling magenta. I spent the night with a road gang, whose caravans sat inside a ring of yellow bulldozers. The men were eating greasy fritters and asked me to share them. Perón smirked over the company.

Among them was a Scot with ginger hair and the physique of a caber thrower. He peered at me with milky blue eyes, feeling out affinities of race and background with a mixture of curiosity and pain. His name was Robbie Ross.

The other men were Latins or Indian half-breeds.

'This is an Englishman,' one of them said.

'A Scotsman,' I corrected.

'*Sí, soy Escocés,*' said Robbie Ross. He had no words of English. '*Mi patria es la Inglaterra misma.*'

For him England and Scotland were an indivisible blur. He shouldered the brunt of the hard work and was target for the others' witticisms.

'*Es borracho,*' the man said. 'Is a drunk.'

Obviously the men didn't expect Robbie Ross to get mad. Obviously they had called him a drunk before. But he set his clenched fist on the table and watched his own whitening knuckles. The colour drained from his face. His lips quivered, and he lunged for the man's throat, and tried to drag him from the caravan.

The others overpowered him and he began to cry. In the night I heard him crying and in the morning he wouldn't even look at another Englishman.

39

AN OLD red Mercedes truck drove into the camp at eight and the driver stopped for coffee. He was heading for Lago Posadas with a load of bricks and took me on. Paco Ruiz was eighteen. He was a pretty boy with strong white teeth and candid brown eyes. His beard and beret helped him cultivate the Ché Guevara look. He had the beginning of a beer stomach and did not like walking.

His father was a bank clerk who had scraped up the money for the truck. Paco loved his truck and called her Rosaura. He scrubbed her and polished her and hung her cab with lace frills. Above her dashboard he fixed a statuette of the Virgin of Luján, a St Christopher and a plastic penguin that nodded with the corrugations of the road. He pinned nudes to the roof, but somehow the girls were an abstraction whereas Rosaura was a real woman.

He and Rosaura had been on the road three months. When she wore out, there'd be money for a new Rosaura and they'd drive on and on for ever. Paco Ruiz was very idealistic. He did not want to make money and was pleased when people called him a *tipo gaucho*. The other teamsters helped him and taught him how to swear. His favourite expression was *concha de cotorra* which means 'parrot-cunt'.

Paco had overloaded Rosaura, and with her slipping clutch and patched tyres, we had to grind downhill in low gear. We were halfway down a small canyon, when he flicked the gear into top and we roared to the bottom. There was a hissing sound.

'*Puta madre!* Puncture!'

The left inside tyre had burst. Paco parked Rosaura on the gravel verge, tilting inwards so the slope would take the weight off the wheel. He unfreed the spare tyre and threw down the jack. But it was the wrong jack. He had lent his own—and this was typical—to a friend with a heavier load. And this small jack lifted the wheel so high but not high enough.

So Paco shovelled a hole out under the tyre and slipped off the wheels, but as he removed the inner one, the foot of the jack started slipping through the road surface. Rosaura yawed sideways and the bricks shifted.

'*Qué macana!* What a mess!'

We waited seven hours for a truck and then could stand waiting no longer and tried again. Paco lay under the axle and worked the jack, this time packing the feet with stones. He was caked with grease and dust, red in the face, and showing signs of losing his temper. He dug a bigger hole under the axle, got the chassis jacked up so far, and even got both wheels back. But they were askew and he couldn't tighten the nuts and he started booting the wheel and screaming: '*Puta ... puta ... puta ... puta ... putana ... puta ... puta ... puta ...*'

I walked to the nearest estancia for help. The owner was a toothless Malagueño in his nineties. He had no jack and I cut back over the grey scrub. I could see the line of the road and Rosaura's red cab, but, coming up close, I saw she had keeled over further and no sign of Paco. I ran, thinking he was trapped underneath, and found him sitting away from the road, white, frightened and whimpering, feeling the bruise coming up on his shin. He had tried again and his leg had been grazed when the jack slipped off the axle. Now it really was a mess. Never kick the woman you love.

40

PACO AND I got help from the road gang and drove into Lago Posadas a day late. We stayed with a gentle, depressed Castilian, a monarchist, who had left Burgos when the King left Madrid, preferring to live in a Republic other than his own.

'The unicorn,' he said. 'The famous unicorn. I know the place. We call it Cerro de los Indios.' And he gestured out across the tamarisks of the flood-plain to a dome of reddish rock straddling the entrance to the valley. The sky was a hard thin blue and the two circling black dots were condors.

'There are many condors,' he said, 'and also pumas.'

The Cerro de los Indios was a lump of basalt, flecked red and green, smooth as patinated bronze and fracturing in linear slabs. The Indians had chosen the place with an unfaltering eye for the sacred. From the foot of the rock I looked down the turquoise line of Lakes Posadas and Purreydon stretching through a corridor of purple cliffs into Chile. On each overhang the hunters had painted the animals of the chase in red ochre. They had also painted themselves, tiny pin-men leaping about energetically. The paintings were thought to be about ten thousand years old.

Alone on its rock face, Father Palacios's unicorn exalted its horn as it was written in the Book of Psalms. It had a thick neck and tapering body.

'Can't be old,' I thought. 'Must be a bull in profile.'

But if it were old, really old, then it had to be a unicorn.

Underneath was a votive shrine with offerings—a tin of Nestlé's milk, a plaster model of a girl in bed, a nail dipped in grey paint, and some burned-out candles.

41

THE SPANIARD'S wife packed me a lunch of cold chops and I walked north through a country broken by gulches and mesas, where the most unlikely colours had been spat to the surface. In one place the rocks were alternately lilac, rose-pink and lime-green. There was a bright-yellow gorge bristling with the bones of extinct mammals. It led into a dried lake bed, ringed with purple rocks where cow skulls stuck out of a crust of flaky orange mud.

The unnatural colours gave me a headache, but I cheered up on seeing a green tree—a Lombardy poplar, the punctuation mark of man.

Beside an adobe cabin a wizened old couple were sunning themselves. The woman had covered the walls of her room with collage. Her surroundings had enflamed her imagination. The showpiece was a painted plaster head of a Japanese geisha, haloed, like a madonna, with the hairy thighs of Argentine foot-ballers. Above this was a pottery dove, emblem of the Holy

Ghost, now converted to a bird of paradise with blue plastic ribbons and dyed ostrich plumes. She had placed a photo of the Patagonian fox next to a crayon drawing of General Rosas.

The woman passed me her maté gourd. She filled my bottle with water that tasted sweet from sheep-droppings, and waved me to the path across the mountains.

In a brick-red sunset I came to the cottage of a German. He lived with a scrawny Indian boy. The two were sitting down to eat, formally, at table, on metal chairs from an ice-cream parlour. Both had identical knives and were hacking at a charred leg of lamb. Neither spoke to the other or to me. Silently the German gave me a tin plate. Silently, after dinner, he led me to the barn and pointed to a pile of sheepskins.

In the morning it was overcast and rain-clouds were streaming out of Chile. The German stretched his arm and pointed to a nick in the line of black cliffs. His wrist flopped, indicating a valley the far side. I waved and he lifted his huge brown hand to the sky, splaying his fingers wide.

I followed some horse-tracks that combed through stubbly yellow grass. At one place, the ground was strewn with white flakes, the carapace of a dead armadillo. The track zig-zagged up the mesa and went down into a brown basin littered with dead trees. At the far end was a farmhouse set in poplars.

The owner was coming out with his peons. He was a tall young man in a striped poncho. His horse was black and gleaming, and his silver trappings jingled as he rode.

'The women are in the kitchen,' he called. 'Tell them to get you some coffee.'

His wife and mother sat in a white-tiled kitchen. They gave me coffee and chocolate cake and ewe's milk cheese and spiced apple jelly. All year they sat in the kitchen, except for the ten days when they provisioned in Comodoro. I thanked the ladies and walked another eight miles. By mid-day I was looking down on the poppy-red roofs of the Estancia Paso Roballos.

Opposite, the *meseta* of Lago Buenos Aires tilted upwards to the West. Its walls rose off a jade-green river, a sheer rampart two thousand feet, layer on layer of volcanic strata, striped like a pennon of chivalry in bands of pink and green. And where the *meseta* broke off, there were four mountains, four peaks piled one on the other in a straight line: a purple hump, an orange column, a cluster of pink spires, and the cone of a dead volcano, ash-grey and streaked with snow.

The river ran down to a lake, Lago Ghio, with water a bright milky turquoise. The shores were blinding white and the cliffs also were white, or striped horizontally white and terracotta. Along the north shore were clear water lagoons of sapphire blue separated from the opaline water by a band of grass. Thousands of black-necked swans studded the surface of the lake. The shallows were pink with flamingos.

Paso Roballos really did look like a site for the Golden City and perhaps it was.

42

AROUND 1650 two Spanish sailors, both deserters and murderers, stumbled out of the forests opposite the island of Chiloé, after walking up the eastern side of the Andes from the Strait of Magellan. Perhaps to divert the Governor's attention from their crimes, they reported the existence of a city of silver-roofed palaces, whose inhabitants were white-skinned, spoke Spanish and were descendants of survivors from Pedro de Sarmiento's colony on the Strait.

The men's story revived interest in Trapalanda, the Enchanted City of the Caesars, another El Dorado hidden in the Southern Andes, and named after Sebastian Cabot's pilot, Francisco César. In 1528 he wandered up-country from the River Plate, crossed the Andes and saw a civilization where gold was in common use. Around his report there grew a legend that fired human hopes and human greed until the nineteenth century.

Several expeditions set out to find the City. Many single wanderers disappeared on the same quest. An eighteenth-century description placed it south of Latitude 45° (Paso Roballos is at Lat. 47°), a mountain fortress, situated below a volcano, perched above a beautiful lake. There was a river, the Rio Diamante, abounding in gold and precious stones. The city took two days to cross and had a single entrance defended by a drawbridge. The buildings were of dressed stone, the doors studded with jewels; the ploughshares were of silver, and the furniture of the humblest dwelling of silver and gold. There was no sickness; old people died as if sleep had come upon them. The men wore tricorn hats, blue coats and yellow capes (in Indian mythology the colours of the Supreme Being). They cultivated pepper and the leaves of their radishes were so big you could tether a horse to them.

Few travellers have ever set eyes on the City. Nor is there any one opinion about its true location: the island of Patmos, the forests of Guyana, the Gobi Desert or the north face of Mount Meru are among the suggestions. All these are desolate places. The names of the City are equally various: Uttarakuru, Avalon, The New Jerusalem, The Isles of the Blessed. Those who saw it reached their destination after terrible hardships. In the seventeenth century two Spanish murderers proved you don't have to be Ezekiel to mistake a rock face for Paradise.

43

THE TENANT of the Estancia Paso Roballos was a Canary Islander from Tenerife. He sat in a pink-washed kitchen, where a black clock hammered out the hours and his wife indifferently spooned rhubarb jam into her mouth. The house was all passage and unused rooms. In the salon a settee flaked patches of gilding to the floor. The optimistic plumbing of half a century had collapsed and reeked of ammonia.

Homesick and dreaming of lost vigour, the old man named the flowers, the trees, the farming methods and dances of his sunlit mountain in the sea.

Hailstones battered the currant bushes of the garden.

The couple's son-in-law was the gendarme, his occupation to guard the frontier and detain sheep-smugglers. He had a magnificent athlete's body, but the accordion of his forehead whined a story of immobility and repressed ambition.

His head swam with migrations and conquests. He spoke of

Vikings in the Brazilian jungle. A professor, he said, had un-earthed runic inscriptions. The people of Mars had landed in Peru and taught the Incas the arts of civilization. How else to explain their superior intelligence?

One day he would return his wife to her father. He would drive the police *camioneta* north, over the Paraná, through Brazil and Panama, and Nicaragua and Mexico, and the *chicas* of North America would fall into his arms.

He smiled bitterly at the mirage of an impossible dream.

'Why do you walk?' the old man asked. 'Can't you ride a horse? People round here hate walkers. They think they're madmen.'

'I can ride,' I said, 'but I prefer walking. One's own legs are more reliable.'

'I once knew an Italian who said that.'

His name was Garibaldi. He also hated horses and houses. He wore an Araucanian poncho and carried no bag. He would walk up to Bolivia and then orbit down to the Strait. He could cover forty miles a day and only worked when he wanted boots.

'I haven't seen him for six years,' the old man said. 'I suppose the condors have got him.'

Next morning after breakfast he pointed to a terrace high on the mountain opposite.

'That's where the fossils come from.'

The Welshwoman in Sarmiento found mylodon bones here and the mandible of a macrauchenia. I climbed up, sheltered behind a rock from the driving sleet, and ate a can of stale sardines. An ancient seabed had been thrust up here, littered with fossil oysters, wet, glinting, and many million years old.

I sat and thought of fish. I thought of *portugaises* and Maine lobsters and *loup-de-mer* and bluefish. I even thought of cod, my stomach rebelling against the diet of greasy lamb and old sardines.

Stumbling about and getting knocked flat by the blasts, I found some obsidian knives along with the armour plating of a glyptodon, Ameghino's *Propalaeohoplophorus*. I congratulated myself on a discovery of importance: no artefacts had yet been found with a glyptodon. But, later, in New York, Mr Junius Bird assured me my glyptodon had fossilized before men came to the Americas.

From Paso Roballos I walked east — or rather ran before the gale — my leather rucksack heavy with bones and stones. The sides of the track were littered with empty champagne bottles, thrown away by gauchos riding home. The names on the labels were: Duc de Saint-Simon, Castel Chandon, and Comte de Valmont.

I crossed back to the coast, arriving at Puerto Deseado, in the first days of February.

44

THE TOWN of Puerto Deseado is distinguished for a Salesian College that incorporates every architectural style from the Monastery of St Gall to a multi-storey car-park; a Gruta de Lourdes; and a railway station in the form and proportion of a big Scottish country house.

I stayed at the Estacíon de Biología Marina with a party of scientists who dug enthusiastically for sandworms and squabbled about the Latin names of seaweed. The resident ornithologist, a severe young man, was studying the migration of the Jackass Penguin. We talked late into the night, arguing whether or not we, too, have journeys mapped out in our central nervous systems; it seemed the only way to account for our insane restlessness.

Next morning we rowed to the penguin colony on an island in mid-river. This, roughly, is what the ornithologist said:

The Magellanic or Jackass Penguin winters in the South Atlantic off the coast of Brazil. On November 10th sharp, fishermen at Puerto Deseado see the advance guard swimming up-river. The birds station themselves on the islands and wait for the rest. The masses arrive on the 24th and start refurnishing their burrows. They have a taste for bright pebbles and collect a few to decorate the entrances.

Penguins are monogamous, faithful unto death. Each pair occupies a minute stretch of territory and expels outsiders. The female lays from one to three eggs. There is no division of labour between the sexes: both go fishing and take turns to nurse the young. The colony breaks up with the cold weather in the first week of April.

The young had hatched and swelled to a size larger than their parents. We watched them waddle awkwardly to the shore and wallop into the water. In the seventeenth century, the explorer Sir John Narborough stood on the same spot and described them 'standing upright like little children in white aprons in company together'.

Albatrosses and penguins are the last birds I'd want to murder.

45

ON OCTOBER 30th 1593, the ship *Desire*, of 120 tons, limping home to England, dropped anchor in the river at Port Desire, this being her fourth visit since Thomas Cavendish named the place in her, his flagship's, honour, seven years before.

The captain was now John Davis, a Devon man, the most skilled navigator of his generation. Behind him were three Arctic voyages in search of the North-West Passage. Before him were two books of seamanship and six fatal cuts of a Japanese pirate's sword.

Davis had sailed on Cavendish's Second Voyage 'intended for the South Sea'. The fleet left Plymouth on August 26th 1591, the Captain-General in the galleon *Leicester*; the other ships were the *Roebuck*, the *Desire*, the *Daintie*, and the *Black Pinnace*, the last so named for having carried the corpse of Sir Philip Sydney.

Cavendish was puffed up with early success, hating his officers and crew. On the coast of Brazil, he stopped to sack the town of Santos. A gale scattered the ships off the Patagonian coast, but they met up, as arranged, at Port Desire.

The fleet entered the Magellan Strait with the southern winter already begun. A sailor's frostbitten nose fell off when he blew it. Beyond Cape Froward, they ran into north-westerly gales and sheltered in a tight cove with the wind howling over their mastheads. Reluctantly, Cavendish agreed to revictual in Brazil and return the following spring.

On the night of May 20th, off Port Desire, the Captain-General changed tack without warning. At dawn, the *Desire* and the *Black Pinnace* were alone on the sea. Davis made for port, thinking his commander would join him as before, but Cavendish set course for Brazil and thence to St Helena. One day he lay down in his cabin and died, perhaps of apoplexy, cursing Davis for desertion: 'This villain that hath been the death of me'.

Davis disliked the man but was no traitor. The worst of the winter over, he went south again to look for the Captain-General. Gales blew the two ships in among some undiscovered islands, now known as the Falklands.

This time, they passed the Strait and out into the Pacific. In a storm off Cape Pilar, the *Desire* lost the *Pinnace*, which went down with all hands. Davis was alone at the helm, praying for a speedy end, when the sun broke through the clouds. He took bearings, fixed his position, and so regained the calmer water of the Strait.

He sailed back to Port Desire, the crew scurvied and mutinous and the lice lying in their flesh, 'clusters of lice as big as peason, yea, and some as big as beanes'. He repaired the ship as best he could. The men lived off eggs, gulls, baby seals, scurvy grass and the fish called *pejerrey*. On this diet they were restored to health.

Ten miles down the coast, there was an island, the original Penguin Island, where the sailors clubbed twenty thousand birds to death. They had no natural enemies and were unafraid of their murderers. John Davis ordered the penguins dried and salted and stowed fourteen thousand in the hold.

On November 11th a war-party of Tehuelche Indians attacked 'throwing dust in the ayre, leaping and running like brute beasts, having vizzards on their faces like dogs' faces, or else their faces are dogs' faces indeed'. Nine men died in the skirmish, among them the chief mutineers, Parker and Smith. Their deaths were seen as the just judgement of God.

The *Desire* sailed at nightfall on December 22nd and set course for Brazil where the Captain hoped to provision with cassava flour. On January 30th he made land at the Isle of Plasencia, off Rio de Janeiro. The men foraged for fruit and vegetables in gardens belonging to the Indians.

Six days later, the coopers went with a landing party to gather hoops for barrels. The day was hot and the men were bathing, unguarded, when a mob of Indians and Portuguese attacked. The Captain sent a boat crew ashore and they found the thirteen men, faces upturned to heaven, laid in a rank with a cross set by them.

John Davis saw pinnaces sailing out of Rio harbour. He made for open sea. He had no other choice. He had eight casks of water and they were fouled.

As they came up to the Equator, the penguins took their revenge. In them bred a 'loathsome worme' about an inch long. The worms ate everything, iron only excepted – clothes, bedding, boots, hats, leather lashings, and live human flesh. The worms gnawed through the ship's side and threatened to sink her. The more worms the men killed, the more they multiplied.

Around the Tropic of Cancer, the crew came down with scurvy. Their ankles swelled and their chests, and their parts swelled so horribly that 'they could neither stand nor lie nor go'.

The Captain could scarcely speak for sorrow. Again he prayed for a speedy end. He asked the men to be patient; to give thanks to God and accept his chastisement. But the men were raging mad and the ship howled with the groans and curses of the dying. Only Davis and a ship's boy were in health, of the seventy-six who left Plymouth. By the end there were five men who could move and work the ship.

And so, lost and wandering on the sea, with topsails and sprit-sails torn, the rotten hulk drifted, rather than sailed, into the harbour of Berehaven on Bantry Bay on June 11th 1593. The smell disgusted the people of that quiet fishing village.

Returning to Devon, John Davis found his wife taken up with a 'sleek paramour'. The next two years he sat at a table and composed the books that made his reputation: *The World's Hydrographical Description*, proving America to be an island; and *The Seaman's Secrets*, a manual of celestial navigation, showing the use of his own invention, the backstaff, to measure the height of heavenly bodies.

But the restlessness got him in the end. He went with the Earl of Essex to the Azores; then to the East Indies, as pilot for the Zeelanders. He died aboard the English ship, *Tyger*, in the Straits of Malacca on December 29th 1605. He had been too trusting of some Japanese pirates and made the mistake of asking them for a meal.

'The Southern Voyage of John Davis' appeared in Hakluyt's edition of 1600. Two centuries passed and another Devon man, Samuel Taylor Coleridge, set down the 625 controversial lines of *The Ancient Mariner*, with its hammering repetitions and story of crime, wandering and expiation.

John Davis and the Mariner have these in common: a voyage to the Black South, the murder of a bird or birds, the nemesis which follows, the drift through the tropics, the rotting ship, the curses of dying men. Lines 236–9 are particularly resonant of the Elizabethan voyage:

> The many men so beautiful!
> And they all dead did lie:
> And a thousand, thousand slimy things
> Lived on and so did I.

In *The Road to Xanadu*, the American scholar John Livingston Lowes traced the Mariner's victim to a 'disconsolate Black Albitross' shot by one Hatley, the mate of Captain George Shelvocke's privateer in the eighteenth century. Wordsworth had a copy of this voyage and showed it to Coleridge when the two men tried to write the poem together.

Coleridge himself was a 'night-wandering man', a stranger at his own birthplace, a drifter round rooming-houses, unable to sink roots anywhere. He had a bad case of what Baudelaire called 'The Great Malady: Horror of One's Home'. Hence his identification with other blighted wanderers: Cain, The Wandering Jew, or the horizon-struck navigators of the sixteenth century. For the Mariner was himself.

Lowes demonstrated how the voyages in Hakluyt and Purchas fuelled Coleridge's imagination. 'The mighty great roaring of ice' that John Davis witnessed on an earlier voyage off Greenland reappears in line 61: 'It cracked and growled and roared and howled.' But he did not, apparently, consider the likelihood that Davis's voyage to the Strait gave Coleridge the backbone for his poem.

46

I PASSED through three boring towns, San Julián, Santa Cruz and Río Gallegos.

As you go south down the coast, the grass gets greener, the sheep-farms richer and the British more numerous. They are the sons and grandsons of the men who cleared and fenced the land in the 1890s. Many were 'kelpers' from the Falklands, who landed with nothing but memories of Highland clearances and had nowhere else to go. They made big money in the sheep booms round the turn of the century, since their limitless supply of cheap labour allowed Patagonian wool to undercut its competition.

Today their farms are on the verge of bankruptcy but are still smartly painted up. And you can find, nestling behind wind-breaks: herbaceous borders, lawnsprayers, fruit-cages, conservatories, cucumber sandwiches, bound sets of *Country Life* and, perhaps, the visiting Archdeacon.

Patagonian sheep-farming began in 1877 when a Mr Henry Reynard, an English trader in Punta Arenas, ferried a flock from the Falklands and set it to graze on Elizabeth Island in the Strait. It multiplied prodigiously and other merchants took the hint. The leading entrepreneurs were a ruthless Asturian, José Menéndez, and his amiable Jewish son-in-law Moritz Braun. The two were rivals at first, but later combined to assemble an empire of estancias, coal-mines, freezers, department stores, merchant ships, and a salvage department.

Menéndez died in 1918, leaving a proportion of his millions to Alphonso XIII of Spain, and was buried at Punta Arenas in a reduced version of the Victor Emmanuel Monument. But the Braun and Menéndez families continued to swamp the territory through their company, known for short as *La Anónima*. They imported stud flocks from New Zealand, shepherds and their dogs from the Outer Isles, and farm-managers from the British Army, who stamped the smartness of the parade ground over the operation. The result was that the Province of Santa Cruz looked like an outpost of the Empire, administered by Spanish-speaking officials.

Almost all the peons were migrants. They came—as they still come—from the green and beautiful island of Chiloé, where the air is soft, conditions primitive and the farms overcrowded; where there is always fish to eat and nothing much to do; and the women are fierce and energetic and the men are lazy and gamble away their earnings.

The Chilotes sleep in spartan dormitories, get saddle-sores on their backsides, and fight the cold on a diet of meat and maté till they collapse of age or stomach cancer. In general they work without enthusiasm. Often, at nights, I heard them grousing about their employers: '*Es hombre despótico*', they'd say. But if you mentioned the name of Archie Tuffnell, they'd hold back and say 'Well, Mister Tuffnell is an exception.'

47

'So you want to find Mister Tuffnell,' the barman said. 'It's not easy. First there's a road that's hardly a road and then there's a track that isn't even a track.'

He was a big man in a striped suit and double-breasted waistcoat. Seals and keys jingled on his fat gold chain. His hair was *engominado*, like a tango dancer's, gleaming wings of jet-black hair, but the white was showing at the roots and he looked sick and shaky. He had been a great womanizer and his wife had just got him back.

He drew a map on a paper napkin. 'You'll see the house in some trees by a lake,' he said and wished me luck.

I found the place in the dark. Moonlight glimmered on the pearly shells of fossil oysters. There were some ducks swimming on the lake, black forms on silver ripples. I followed a thread of golden light into a clump of poplars. A dog barked. The door opened and the dog slunk past with a lump of red meat in its mouth. The woman pointed to a cabin in some willows.

'The old man lives over there,' she said.

A straight-backed gentleman in his eighties peered through steel-rimmed spectacles and grinned. His face was shiny pink and he wore khaki shorts. I apologized for the late hour and explained my business.

'Did you ever know a Captain Milward?'

'Old Mill. Course I knew Old Mill. H.M. Consul Punta Arenas de Chile. Irritable old bugger. Can't remember too much about him. Young wife. A bit solid but a good-looker. Look here, come in and let me cook you some dinner. Fancy finding this place on your own.'

Archie Tuffnell loved Patagonia and called her 'Old Pat'. He loved the solitude, the birds, the space and the dry healthy climate. He had managed a sheep-farm for a big English land company for forty years. When he had to retire, he couldn't face the coop of England, and had bought his own camp, taking with him 2,500 sheep and 'my man Gómez'.

Archie had given the house over to the Gómez family and lived alone in a prefabricated cabin. His domestic arrangements were a lesson in asceticism: a shower, a narrow bed, a desk, and two camp stools but no chairs.

'I don't want to get sunk down in an armchair. Not at my age. Might never get up.'

He had two sporting prints in the bedroom, and a sacred corner for photographs. They were sepia photographs, of confident ladies and gentlemen, grouped in front of conservatories or in hunting rig.

He was not a clever man but a wise one. He was a self-centred bachelor, who avoided complications and did little harm to anyone. His standards were Edwardian but he knew how the world changed; how to be one step ahead of change, so as not to change himself. His rules were simple: Keep liquid. Never wait for higher prices. Never use money to show off to your workers.

'They're a proud lot,' he'd say. 'You've got to keep your distance or they think you're a toady. I do it by speaking lousy Spanish on purpose. But *you*'ve got to do what they *have* to do. They don't give a hoot what you've got in the bank as long as *you* eat what they eat.'

'My man Gómez' and Archie were inseparable. All morning they pottered round the garden, weeding the spinach or planting tomato seedlings. Señora Gómez cooked lunch and, in the heat of the day, the old man took a nap, while I sat in the blue kitchen listening to Gómez on the subject of his master.

'What a miracle,' he said. 'So intelligent! So generous! So handsome! I owe everything to him.'

In the place of honour, where in some households you saw a picture of Perón or Jesus Christ or General San Martín, beamed an uncommonly large photo of Mister Tuffnell.

48

I STOOD on the shore at San Julián and tried to picture a dinner party in Drake's cabin; the silver plates with gilt borders, the music of viol and trumpet, the plebeian Admiral and his gentleman guest, the mutineer Thomas Doughty. I then borrowed a leaky rowing boat and rowed over to Gibbet Point, combing the shore for the 'great grinding stone' set over Doughty's tomb and carved with his name in Latin 'that it might be better understood by all that should come after us'. Drake had him beheaded alongside the gibbet from which Magellan hung his mutineers, Quesada and Mendoza, fifty-eight winters before. Wood preserves well in Patagonia. The coopers of the *Pelican* sawed the post and made tankards as souvenirs for the crew.

Over lunch in the hotel some sheep-farmers were plotting to block the trunk road with bales, protesting against the government of Isabel Perón which had pegged the price of wool far below its value on the international market. The hotel itself was built in mock-Tudor style with black beams nailed over corrugated sheet. The style suited San Julián's various sixteenth-century associations:

49

Bernal Díaz relates how, on seeing the jewelled cities of Mexico, the Conquistadores wondered if they had not stepped into the *Book of Amadis* or the fabric of a dream. His lines are sometimes quoted to support the assertion that history aspires to the symmetry of myth. A similar case concerns Magellan's landfall at San Julián in 1520:

From the ship they saw a giant dancing naked on the shore, 'dancing and leaping and singing, and, while singing, throwing sand and dust on his head'. As the white men approached, he raised one finger to the sky, questioning whether they had come from heaven. When led before the Captain-General, he covered his nakedness with a cape of guanaco hide.

The giant was a Tehuelche Indian, his people the race of copper-skinned hunters, whose size, strength and deafening voices belied their docile character (and may have been Swift's model for the coarse but amiable giants of Brobdingnag). Magellan's chronicler, Pigafetta, says they ran faster than horses, tipped their bows with points of silex, ate raw flesh, lived in tents and wandered up and down 'like the Gipsies'.

The story goes on that Magellan said: 'Ha! Patagon!' meaning 'Big-Foot' for the size of his moccasins, and this origin for the word 'Patagonia' is usually accepted without question. But though *pata* is 'a foot' in Spanish, the suffix *gon* is meaningless. πάταγος, however, means 'a roaring' or 'gnashing of teeth' in Greek, and since Pigafetta describes the Patagonians 'roaring like bulls', one could imagine a Greek sailor in Magellan's crew, a refugee perhaps from the Turks.

I checked the crew lists but could find no record of a Greek sailor. Then Professor Gonzáles Díaz of Buenos Aires drew my attention to *Primaleon of Greece*, a romance of chivalry, as absurd as *Amadis of Gaul* and equally addictive. It was published in Castille in 1512, seven years before Magellan sailed. I looked up the English translation of 1596 and, at the end of Book II, found reason to believe that Magellan had a copy in his cabin:

The Knight Primaleon sails to a remote island and meets a cruel and ill-favoured people, who eat raw flesh and wear skins. In the interior lives a monster called the Grand Patagon, with the 'head of a Dogge' and the feet of a hart, but gifted with human understanding and amorous of women. The islanders' chief persuades Primaleon to rid them of the terror. He rides out, fells the Patagon with a single sword thrust, and trusses him up with the leash of his two pet lions. The Patagon dyes the grass red with blood, roars 'so dreadfully that it would have terrified the very stoutest hearte', but recovers and licks his wound clean 'with his huge broade tongue'.

Primaleon then decides to ship the creature home to Polonia to add to the royal collection of curiosities. On the voyage the Patagon cringes before his new master, and on landing Queen Gridonia is on hand to inspect him. 'This is nothing but a devil,' she says. 'He gets no cherishing at my hands.' But her daughter, the Princess Zephira, strokes the monster, sings to him and teaches him her language, while he 'delights to gaze a fair lady in the face' and follows 'as gently as if he had been a spaniell'.

Wintering at San Julián, Magellan also decided to kidnap two giants for Charles V and his Queen Empress. He put a number of gewgaws in their hands and, while his men riveted iron fetters round their ankles, assured them that these too were another kind of ornament. Seeing they were trapped, the giants roared (in Richard Eden's translation) 'lyke bulls and cryed uppon their great devill Setebos to help them'. One escaped but Magellan got the other aboard and baptized him Paul.

History may aspire to symmetry but rarely achieves it: the Giant Paul died of scurvy in the Pacific and his body fed the sharks; Magellan's body lay face down in the shallows at Mactan, felled by a Filippino sword.

Ninety years would then pass before the first performance of *The Tempest* at Whitehall on November 1st 1611. Shakespeare's sources for the play are the subject of brisk debate, but we know he read the account in Pigafetta's *Voyage* of the vile trick at San Julián:

Caliban   I must obey. His art is of such pow'r
             It would control my dam's god, Setebos,
             And make a vassal of him.

Into the mouth of Caliban, Shakespeare packed all the bitterness of the New World. ('This island's mine, by Sycorax my mother, which thou tak'st from me.') He saw how the white man's language was a weapon of war ('The red plague rid you for learning me your language.'); how the Indians would grovel to any jackass who promised freedom ('I'll kiss thy foot...' ' 'I'll lick thy shoe ... 'Ban 'Ban Cacaliban has a new master — get a new man'); and he read Pigafetta more carefully than is usually noticed:

Caliban	Hast thou not dropped from Heaven?
Stephano	Out of the moon I do assure thee: I was man i' the moon when time was.

and:

Stephano	If I can recover him [Caliban], and keep him tame and get to Naples with him, he's a present for any Emperor that ever trod on neat's leather.

The question is: did Shakespeare know the book that triggered off the events at San Julián?

I believe he did. Both monsters were half human. The Grand Patagon was 'engendered by a Beaste in the woods'; Caliban a 'poisonous slave got by the Devil himself'. Both learned a foreign language. Both loved a white princess (even if Caliban did try to rape Miranda). And both were identical in one important particular: the Patagon had the 'head of a Dogge', while Trinculo says of Caliban: 'I shall laugh myself to death at this puppy-headed monster.'

The origin of the 'dog-heads' is to be found in the 'vizzards' or battle masks, such as worn by Genghiz Khan's cavalry or the Tehuelches when they attacked John Davis at Puerto Deseado. Shakespeare could have picked them out of Hakluyt. But either way Caliban has a good claim to Patagonian ancestry.

50

IN THE British Club at Río Gallegos there was chipped cream paint and not a word of English spoken. The twin black smoke-stacks of the Swift Corporation's old freezer reared above the prison yard.

On a windy sidewalk, a group of British sheep-farmers stood outside the Bank of London and South America. They had been discussing the wool slump with the manager. One family was bankrupt. Their boy, waiting in a Land-Rover, said: 'I don't mind. Means I don't have to go to boarding school.' But a man in battered tweeds hopped up and down, shouting: 'Filthy Latin yellow-bellies! Damn 'em! Damn 'em! Damn 'em!'

This branch was once the Bank of London and Tarapacá. I went in and asked the cashier about some North Americans.

'You mean the Boots Cassidy Gang,' he said.

They were here in January 1905. They went to Punta Arenas where they met a crusty retired sailor called Captain Milward and, as guest members of the British Club, taught youngsters like Archie Tuffnell a few tricks at pool. Across the Argentine border they stayed at an English estancia. They entertained the locals by dressing up as real Western outlaws and riding into Río Gallegos firing six-shooters in the air.

'*Aquí vienen los gringos locos!*' the townspeople laughed. 'Here come the mad gringos!'

As usual they said they were looking for land. They went to the bank to discuss a loan with the manager, a Mr Bishop. He asked them to lunch and they accepted. They tied him up, and his clerks, bundled 20,000 pesos into a bag and £280 sterling, and rode out of town.

'There go the mad gringos!'

Etta held the horses. I was told she lingered on, chatting to a circle of admirers, until her own men were clear. Then, pulling the pearl-handled revolver which she wore, tied to a velvet ribbon down the back of her neck, she shot the glass conductors off the telegraph line, cutting off communication with the one police post between them and the safety of the Cordillera.

Walking down the main street of Río Gallegos I saw the book-shop was selling copies of a new book, *Los Vengadores de la Patagonia Trágica* by a left-wing historian Osvaldo Bayer. Its subject was the Anarchist rebellion against the estancia-owners in 1920–1. I bought the three volumes in Buenos Aires and read them, fascinated; for this revolution in miniature seemed to explain the mechanics of all revolution.

I asked Archie Tuffnell about it and he scowled.

'Bad business. Bunch of Bolshie agitators came down and stirred up trouble. That was one thing. Then the Army came down and that was another. Shot good men. They shot good, honest, reliable men. They even shot *my* friends. It was a filthy business from start to finish.'

The leader of the revolt was called Antonio Soto.

51

PEOPLE IN the South still remember the lanky, red-headed Gallician, with the down scarcely off his cheek, and the squinting blue eyes that go with Celtic vagueness and fanaticism. He wore breeches and puttees then, and his cap at a jaunty angle. And he'd stand in the muddy street, while the wind ripped at his red flags, shouting phrases borrowed from Proudhon and Bakunin, of Property being Theft, and Destruction a creative passion.

A few Spanish immigrants even remember his earlier incarnation, as prop-boy for some travelling actors who came down from the north and played Calderón and Lope de Vega in the bare auditorium of the Círculo Espanol. And sometimes he'd take a bit part and stand, decoratively, against the whitewashed walls of an Extremaduran village, peeling from its canvas backcloth.

Others remember him coming back to Río Gallegos twelve years after the firing squads. He was still playing the Anarchist orator and wore his shirt unbuttoned to the navel. But he had a real worker's body to show off this time, scarred with the burns he got in a saltpetre mine in Chile. He stayed at the Hotel Miramar and lectured the families of men who had lain those twelve years under bleached wood crosses. That was his last visit and he played to empty houses. Only a few nodding Spaniards heard him out and the governor booted him back over the border.

But most of those who knew Antonio Soto recall a hulk of fallen muscle and an expression ranging from truculence to quiet despair. He lived in Punta Arenas then and ran a small restaurant. And if customers complained about the service he'd say: 'This is an Anarchist restaurant. Serve yourself.' Or he'd sit with other Spanish exiles and remember Spain through the thin jet streaming from his *porrón*, remembering whom to honour in Spain, and whom to hate, and reserving a special curse for the boy he once saw on the streets of his home port, El Ferrol, the smug boy, whose career was the obverse of his own and whose name was Francisco Bahamonde Franco.

Soto was the posthumous son of a naval rating who drowned in the Cuban War. At the age of ten he quarrelled with his step-father and went to live with maiden aunts in Ferrol. He was pious and puritanical and carried floats in religious processions. At seventeen he read Tolstoy's denunciation of military service and skipped to Buenos Aires to avoid his own. He drifted into the theatre and the fringes of the Anarchist Movement. There were many Anarchists in Buenos Aires and Buenos Aires is one big theatre.

He joined the Serrano-Mendoza Spanish Theatre Company and in 1919 sailed on tour for the ports of Patagonia. His coming to Río Gallegos coincided with a wool slump, wage-cuts, new taxes and new tensions between the Anglo-Saxon sheep-farmers and their men. From the far end of the earth, the Britishers watched the Red Revolution and likened themselves to Russian aristocrats stranded on the steppe. One week their newspaper, the *Magellan Times*, ran a picture of a room in a country house, its owner grovelling before a muscle man, whose naked torso was criss-crossed by cartridge belts. The caption ran: 'A nocturnal orgy of the Maximalists at the estate of Kislodovsk. 5,000 roubles or your lives!'

Soto's mentor in Río Gallegos was a Spanish lawyer and dandy, José María Borrero, a man of forty, with a face puffy from drink and a row of fountain pens in his top pocket. Borrero had started out with a doctorate in theology from Santiago de Compostella. He had ended up in the Far South, running a bi-weekly news-sheet, *La Verdad*, which sniped at the British plutocracy. His language thrilled his compatriots and they began to imitate his style: 'In this society of Judases and Pulchinellas, Borrero alone preserves the rare integrity of Man ... among these twittering pachyderms with their snapping teeth and castrated consciences.'

Borrero overwhelmed Soto with superior education, seditious talk and love. He and a fellow radical, the Judge Viñas (a man motivated only by personal vendettas) alerted him to the plight of the Chilean migrants and the iniquity of the foreign *latifundistas*. In particular they singled out two men: the Anglophile Acting-Governor, E. Corréa Falcón, and his foul-mouthed Scottish police commissioner called Ritchie. Soto made the easy switch from the theatre into politics. He got a job as a stevedore and, within weeks, was elected Secretary-General of the Workers' Union.

A new life opened up for him. On the Chilotes his voice had the effect of unstoppering the resentments of centuries. Something about his youth or messianic innocence impelled them to acts of self-sacrifice and then to violence. Perhaps they saw in in him the white saviour promised in their folklore.

He called them to stop work and they obeyed; they even flocked to join his march to celebrate the eleventh anniversary of the shooting of Francisco Ferrer, at Monjuich, Barcelona. (Soto said his Chilotes were honouring the Catalan educator as Catholics honoured the Maid of Orleans or the Mohammedans Mohammed.) Conceiving all life as a squalid economic struggle, he made no concessions to the propertied classes. He blackmailed the hotel-keepers, the merchants and sheep-farmers. He made them grovel as his price for lifting the boycott, and when they accepted his terms, he merely stepped up the pressure and the insults.

Attempts to silence him failed: nor could the jail hold him, for his faction was too strong. One night a knife flashed on an empty street, but the blade hit the watch in his waistcoat pocket and the hired killer fled. His escape only confirmed his sense of mission. He called for a General Strike, to bring down the powers that governed Santa Cruz, not noticing that the base of his support had narrowed. The local Syndicalists patched up their quarrel with the employers and jeered at Soto's wild impracticality. Soto countered that they were pimps for the brothel *La Chocolatería*.

Isolated from the moderates, Soto started the revolution on his own. His allies were some propagandists by the deed, who called themselves The Red Council. The leaders were Italian: a Tuscan deserter; a Piedmontese who had once made shepherdesses in a Dresden porcelain factory. With a band of five hundred rough riders, the Red Council swooped on estancias; looted guns, food, horses and drink; freed the Chilotes from their inhibitions; left heaps of fire-twisted metal; and dissolved again on to the steppe.

Ritchie sent a patrol to investigate but it fell into an ambush. Two policemen and a chauffeur were killed. A subaltern named Jorge Pérez Millán Témperley, an upper-class boy with a weakness for uniforms, got a bullet through his genitals. When the bandits forced him to ride with them, the pain permanently unhinged him.

On January 28th 1921 the 10th Argentine Cavalry sailed from Buenos Aires with orders from President Yrigoyen to pacify the province. The commanding officer was Lt-Col. Héctor Benigno Varela, a tiny soldier of limitless patriotism, a student of Prussian discipline, who liked his men to be men. At first Varela disgusted the foreign landowners, for his programme of pacification consisted of free pardons for all strikers who surrendered their arms. But when Soto came out of hiding and announced a total victory over Private Property, the Army and the State, the colonel sensed he had made a fool of himself and said: 'If it starts up again, I'll come back and shoot the lot.'

The pessimists were right. All along the coast that winter, strikers marched, looted, burned, picketed and prevented officials from boarding steamers. And when the spring came Soto was planning his second campaign with three new lieutenants (the Red Council had fallen into an ambush): Albino Argüelles, a Socialist official; Ramón Outerelo, a Bakuninist and ex-waiter; and a gaucho named Facón Grande for the size of his knife. Soto still believed the government was neutral and ordered each commander to seize a stretch of territory, to raid and take hostages. Secretly he was dreaming of a revolution that would spread from Patagonia and engulf the country. He was not very bright. His character was frigid and austere. At nights he went off to sleep alone. The Chilotes required a leader to share every detail of their lives and began to mistrust him.

This time Dr Borrero was conspicuous for his absence. He was having an affair with an estanciero's daughter and had taken advantage of depressed land prices to buy a place of his own. It then came out that, all along, he was on the payroll of *La Anónima*, the company of the Brauns and Menéndezes. The Anarchists noted his defection and sneered at the 'degenerates who were once socialists, drinking in cafés at the workers' expense, who today, like true Tartuffes, clamour for the murder of their old comrades'.

President Yrigoyen called for Varela a second time and allowed him to use 'extreme measures' to bring the strikers to heel. The Colonel disembarked at Punta Loyola on November 11th 1921 and began requisitioning horses. He interpreted his instructions as tacit permission for a bloodbath, but since Congress had abolished the death penalty, he and his officers had to inflate the Chilotes into 'military forces, perfectly armed and better munitioned, enemies of the country in which they live'. They claimed Chile was behind the strike and, when they caught a Russian Anarchist with a notebook full of Cyrillic characters, here plainly was the Red hand of Moscow.

The strikers melted away without a fight. They were not well armed and couldn't even use the arms they had. The Army filed reports of gunfights and arsenals captured. But the *Magellan Times* for once reported the truth: 'Various bands of rebels, finding their cause lost, have surrendered and the bad element among them shot.'

On five separate occasions, the soldiers got the strikers to surrender by promising to respect thier lives. On all five, the shooting began afterwards. They shot Outerelo and Argüelles. Varela shot Facón Grande at Jaramillo station, two days after he reported him killed in battle. They shot hundreds of men into graves they dug themselves, or shot them and heaped the bodies on bonfires of *mata negra* and the smell of burned flesh and wood resin drifted across the pampas.

The end of Soto's dream came at the Estancia La Anita, the

prize establishment of the Menéndez family. He held his hostages in the green and white house, where, from the *art-nouveau* conservatory, you can see the Moreno Glacier sliding through black forests into a grey lake. His men were in the shearing shed but they began leaving in groups when they heard about the column coming up the valley.

The hardliners, led by two Germans, wanted to pile up woolbales, to turn the shed into a blockhouse and fight to the last man. But Soto said he'd run for it, said *he* was not made for dog-meat, said he'd continue in the mountains or abroad. And the Chilotes did not want to fight. They preferred to trust the word of an Argentine officer than the promises of air.

Soto sent two men to Captain Viñas Ibarra to ask for terms. 'Terms?' he shrieked. 'Terms for what?' and sent them to make terms with Jesus Christ. He did not, however, want to expose his men to fire and dispatched a junior officer to negotiate. On December 7th the rebels saw him advancing cautiously in their direction: a chestnut horse, a man in khaki, a white flag and yellow goggles glinting in the sun. His terms: Unconditional surrender and lives respected. The men should line up next morning in the yard.

The Chilotes' decision let Soto off. That night he and some of the leaders took the best guns and horses and rode out, up and over the sierra, and came down to Puerto Natales. The Chilean carabineers, who had promised to seal the frontier, did nothing to stop him.

The Chilotes were waiting for the soldiers in three lines, in homespun clothes smelling of sheep and horse and stale urine, their felt hats drawn down low, and their rifles and ammunition piled three paces in front, and their saddles, their lariats and their knives.

They thought they were going home, thought they'd be expelled and sent back to Chile. But the soldiers herded them back into the shearing shed, and when they shot the two Germans, they knew what was going to happen. About three hundred men were in the shed that night. They lay in the sheep-pens and the light of candles flickered on the roof-beams. Some of them played cards. There was nothing to eat.

The door opened at seven. A sergeant ostentatiously distributed

picks to a work-party. The men in the shed heard them marching
off and heard the chink of steel on stone.

'They're digging graves,' they said.

The door opened again at eleven. Troops lined the yard with
rifles at the ready. The ex-hostages looked on. A Mr Harry Bond
said he wanted a corpse for every one of his thirty-seven stolen
horses. The soldiers brought the men out for justice in groups.
Justice depended on whether a sheep-farmer wanted a man back
or not. It was just like sorting sheep.

The Chilotes were papery white, their mouths lowered and their
eyes distended. The unwanted ones were led off past the sheep-
dip and round a low hill. The men in the yard heard the crackle of
shots and saw the turkey buzzards coming in over the barranca
feathering the morning wind.

About a hundred and twenty men died at La Anita. One of the
executioners said: 'They went to their deaths with a passivity
that was truly astonishing.'

With some exceptions, the British community was overjoyed
at the result. The Colonel, whom they had suspected of cowardice,
had redeemed himself beyond expectation. The *Magellan Times*
praised his 'splendid courage, running about the firing line as
though on parade ... Patagonians should take their hats off to the
10th Argentine Cavalry, these very gallant gentlemen.' At a
luncheon in Río Gallegos, the local president of the Argentine
Patriotic League spoke of 'the sweet emotion of these moments'
and his joy at being rid of the plague. Varela replied he had only
done his duty as a soldier, and the twenty British present, being
men of few Spanish words, burst into song: '*For he's a jolly good
fellow ...* '

Off-duty at San Julián, the soldiers made for the brothel *La
Catalana*, but the girls, all over thirty, screamed 'Assassins! Pigs!
We won't go with killers!' and were hauled off to jail for insulting
men in uniform and so the flag of the nation. Among the girls
was a Miss Maud Foster, 'an English subject, of good family,
with ten years' residence in the country'. *Requiescat!*

Varela did not return to a hero's welcome but to graffiti
reading 'SHOOT THE CANNIBAL OF THE SOUTH'. Congress
was in uproar; not that people cared too much for Soto and his
Chileans, but Varela had made the mistake of shooting a Socialist

official. The question was not so much what the Colonel did as who gave him orders. They pointed to Yrigoyen, who was embarrassed, appointed Varela director of a cavalry school and hoped the matter would simmer down.

On January 27th 1923 Colonel Varela was shot dead, on the corner of Fitzroy and Santa Fé, by Kurt Wilkens, a Tolstoyian Anarchist from Schleswig-Holstein. A month later, on February 26th, Wilkens was shot dead in the Prison of the Encausaderos by his warder, Jorge Pérez Millán Témperley (though how he got there nobody knew). And on Monday, February 9th 1925, Témperley was shot dead in a Buenos Aires hospital for the criminally insane by a Yugoslav midget called Lukič.

The man who gave Lukič the gun was an interesting case: Boris Vladimirovič, a Russian of pedigree, a biologist and an artist, who had lived in Switzerland and known—or claimed to have known—Lenin. The 1905 Revolution drove him to drink. He had a heart attack and left for Argentina to begin a new life. He got sucked back to the old life when he robbed a *bureau de change* to raise funds for Anarchist propaganda. A man was killed. and Vladimirovič earned twenty-five years in Ushuaia, the prison at the end of the world. Here he sang the songs of the Motherland, and for the sake of quiet, the Governor had him transferred to the capital.

On Sunday, February 8th, two Russian friends brought him the revolver in a basket of fruit. The case was hard to prove. There was no trial, but Boris Vladimirovič disappeared for ever into the House of the Dead.

Borrero died of T.B. at Santiago del Estero in 1930 after a gunfight with a journalist in which one of his sons was killed.

Antonio Soto died of cerebral thrombosis on May 11th 1963. Since the Revolution, he had lived in Chile, as miner, trucker, ciné-projectionist, fruit-vendor, farm-worker and restauranteur. I am told that in 1945 he worked in the iron foundry of a Mrs Charles Amherst Milward.

52

A͏ᴛ Río Gallegos I stayed in a cheap hotel, painted a poisonous green, that catered for migrants from Chiloé. The men
played dominoes late into the night. When I asked about the
revolution of 1920, their answers were mumbled and vague; they
had a more recent revolution to think about. Then I asked about
the sect of male witches, known on Chiloé as the *Brujería*. From
what little I knew, I felt it might explain their behaviour in 1920.

'The *Brujería*,' they smiled. 'That's only a story.' But one old
man went cold and silent at the mention of the word.

The Sect of the *Brujería* exists for the purpose of hurting
ordinary people. No one knows the exact whereabouts of its
headquarters. But there are at least two branches of its Central
Committee, one in Buenos Aires, the other in Santiago de Chile.
It is not certain which of these is the senior, or if both are
beholden to Superior Authority. Regional committees are
scattered through the provinces and take their orders, without
question, from above. Junior members are kept in ignorance of
the names of the higher functionaries.

On Chiloé the Committee is known as the Council of the Cave.
The cave lies somewhere in the forests south of Quincavi, somewhere below ground. Any visitor to it suffers thereafter from
temporary amnesia. If he happens to be literate, he loses his hands
and the ability to write.

Novices of the Sect must submit to a six-year course of in-
doctrination. Since the full syllabus is known only to the Central
Committee, the island schools have a tentative character. When an
instructor thinks his pupil is ready for admission, the Council of
the Cave assembles and puts him through a sequence of tests.

The candidate must submerge himself for forty days and forty
nights under a waterfall of the Thraiguén River, to wash off the
effects of his Christian baptism. (During this time he is allowed a
little toast.) Next, he must catch, without fumbling, a skull,
which the instructor throws from the crown of a tricorn hat. He
must kill his best friend to show he has wiped out all trace of
sentiment. He must sign a document with blood from his own

veins. And he must disinter a recently buried male Christian corpse and flay the skin from the breast. Once this is cured and dried, he sews it into a 'thieves' waistcoat'. The human grease remaining in the skin gives off a soft phosphorescence, which lights the member's nocturnal expeditions.

Full Members have the power to steal private property; to change themselves into other animals; to influence thoughts and dreams; to open doors; to drive men mad; to change the course of rivers; and to spread disease, especially some new virus that will not respond to medical treatment. In some cases the Member scars his victim lightly and allows him to buy his life back by supplying the Council of the Cave with a quantity of his own blood (to be delivered in a conch shell). If anyone is so foolish as to mock the Sect, he is put to sleep and tonsured. His hair will not grow back until he has signed a confession.

Among the technical equipment the Sect has at its disposal is the *Challanco*, a crystal stone through which the Central Committee surveys the minutest details of a man's life. No one has yet described the device with complete accuracy. Some report it as a bowl of glass; others as a large circular mirror, which emits and receives penetrating rays. The *Challanco* is known as the BOOK or the MAP. In addition to spying on all members of the hierarchy, it is thought to contain an indecipherable copy of the dogma of the Sect itself.

Only men can become members, but the Sect does use women to carry urgent messages. A woman thus employed is known as the *Voladora*. Usually a trusted member selects the most beautiful girl in his family and forces her into the role. She cannot, thereafter, return to normal life. The first stage of her initiation is a similar forty-day bath. One night, she is required to meet her instructor in a forest clearing. All she can see is a shining copper dish. The instructor gives orders but never appears. He tells her to strip and stand on tiptoe with her arms in the air. A draught of some bitter liquid makes her vomit her intestines.

'Into the dish!' he barks. 'Into the dish!'

Once freed of her insides, she is light enough to grow the wings of a bird and fly over human settlements shrieking hysterically. At dawn, she returns to the dish, redigests her intestines and recovers her human form.

The Sect owns its own ship, the *Caleuche*. She has the advantage over other vessels in that she can sail into the eye of the wind, and even submerge beneath the surface. She is painted white. Her spars are lit with innumerable coloured lights and from her deck streams the sound of intoxicating music. She is thought to carry cargo for the richest merchants, all of whom are agents for the Central Committee. The *Caleuche* has an insatiable appetite for crews and kidnaps sailors from the archipelago. Anyone with less than the rank of captain is instantly marooned on a lonely rock. Sometimes, one sees demented sailors roaming the beaches, singing the songs of the Central Committee.

The most singular creature associated with the Sect is the *Invunche* or Guardian of the Cave, a human being perverted into a monster by a special scientific process. When the Sect needs a new *Invunche*, the Council of the Cave orders a Member to steal a boy child from six months to a year old. The Deformer, a permanent resident of the Cave, starts work at once. He disjoints the arms and legs and the hands and feet. Then begins the delicate task of altering the position of the head. Day after day, and for hours at a stretch, he twists the head with a tourniquet until it has rotated through an angle of 180°, that is, until the child can look straight down the line of its own vertebrae.

There remains one last operation, for which another specialist is needed. At full moon, the child is laid on a workbench, lashed down with its head covered in a bag. The specialist cuts a deep incision under the right shoulder blade. Into the hole he inserts the right arm and sews up the wound with thread taken from the neck of a ewe. When it has healed the *Invunche* is complete.

During the process, the child is fed on human milk. After weaning, the diet is changed to young human flesh, followed by that of the adult male. When these are unobtainable, cat milk, kid and billy-goat are taken as substitutes. Once installed as Guardian of the Cave, the *Invunche* is naked and sprouts long bristly hair. It never acquires human speech, yet, over the years, it does develop a working knowledge of the Committee's procedure and can instruct novices with harsh and guttural cries.

Sometimes the Central Committee requires the presence of the *Invunche* for ceremonies of an unknown nature at an unknown place. Since the creature is immobile, a team of experts come and transport him by air.

It would be misleading to suggest that the people take the impositions of the Sect lying down. Secretly, they have declared war on the Central Committee, and have been perfecting their own intelligence and defence system. Their aim is to surprise a Member in the act of doing mischief. Caught red-handed, he is not supposed to live beyond a year. The people hope, one day, to bring their listening equipment to perfection and so penetrate the higher ranks of the Central Committee.

No one can recall the memory of a time when the Central Committee did not exist. Some have suggested that the Sect was in embryo even before the emergence of Man. It is equally plausible that Man himself became Man through fierce opposition to the Sect. We know for a fact that the *Challanco* is the Evil Eye. Perhaps the term 'Central Committee' is a synonym for Beast.

53

I CROSSED over into Fireland. On the north shore of the First Narrows, a lighthouse, striped orange and white, stood above a beach of crystalline pebbles, purple mussels and the scarlet of broken crabs. At the water's edge oyster-catchers were needling for shellfish in piles of ruby-coloured seaweed. The coast of Tierra del Fuego was an ashy stripe less than two miles away.

Some trucks were lined up outside the tin restaurant, waiting for the tide to refloat the two landing craft that ferried traffic across. Three ancient Scots stood by. Their eyes were bloodshot-pink and nursery-blue and their teeth worn to little brown pinnacles. Inside, a strong juicy woman sat on a bench, combing her hair while her companion, a trucker, laid slices of mortadella on her tongue.

The advancing tide pushed mattresses of kelp up the scarp of the beach. The gale blew out of the west. In a patch of calmer water a pair of steamer ducks burbled their monogamous conversation *tuk-tuk* ... *tuk-tuk* ... *tuk-tuk* ... I threw a pebble their way but could not disturb their absorption in each other and set their thrashing paddle-wings in motion.

The Strait of Magellan is another case of Nature imitating Art. A Nuremberg cartographer, Martin Beheim, drew the South-West Passage for Magellan to discover. His premise was entirely reasonable. South America, however peculiar, was normal compared to the Unknown Antarctic Continent, the Antichthon of the Pythagoreans, marked FOGS on mediaeval maps. In this Upside-down-land, snow fell upwards, trees grew downwards, the sun shone black, and sixteen-fingered Antipodeans danced themselves into ecstasy. WE CANNOT GO TO THEM, it was said, THEY CANNOT COME TO US. Obviously a strip of water had to divide this chimerical country from the rest of Creation.

On October 21st 1520, the Feast of St Ursula and her Eleven Thousand (shipwrecked) Virgins, the fleet rounded a headland which the Captain called Cabo Vírgenes. Yawning before them was a bay, apparently landlocked. In the night a gale blew from the north-east and swept the *Concepcion* and the *San Antonio* through the First Narrows, through the Second Narrows, and into a broad reach bearing south-west. When they saw the tidal rips, they guessed it led to the further ocean. They returned to the flagship with the news. Cheers, cannonades and pennons flying.

On the north shore a landing party found a stranded whale and a charnel-place of two hundred corpses raised on stilts. On the southern shore they did not land.

Tierra del Fuego — The Land of Fire. The fires were the camp-fires of the Fuegian Indians. In one version Magellan saw smoke only and called it Tierra del Humo, the Land of Smoke, but Charles V said there was no smoke without fire and changed the name.

The Fuegians are dead and all the fires snuffed out. Only the flares of oil rigs cast a pall over the night sky.

Until in 1619 the Dutch fleet of Schouten and LeMaire rounded the Horn — and named it, not for its shape, but after Hoorn on the Zuyder Zee, cartographers drew Tierra del Fuego as the northern cape of the Antichthon and filled it with suitable monstrosities: gorgons, mermaids and the Roc, that outsize condor which carried elephants.

Dante placed his Hill of Purgatory at the centre of the

Antichthon. In Canto 26 of *The Inferno*, Ulysses, swept on his mad track south, sights the island-mountain looming from the sea as the waves close over his ship—*infin che 'l mar fu sopra noi richiuso*—destroyed by his passion to exceed the boundaries set for man.

Fireland then is Satan's land, where flames flicker as fireflies on a summer night, and, in the narrowing circles of Hell, ice holds the shades of traitors as straws in glass.

This perhaps is why they did not land.

The tide crept up to the ferries. The sun dipped under the cloudbank, gilding its edges, and sank into the middle of the Strait. A flood of saffron light turned the waves from grease-black to viridian and the spray to a milky golden green.

> ... That this is my South-west discoverie
> *Per fretum febris*, by these streights to die ...

Donne's deathbed stanzas, his 'blowing out', through rocks and shoals into the bright beyond:

> Is the Pacifique Sea my home? Or are
> The Easterne riches? Is *Jerusalem*?
> *Anyan*, and *Magellan*, and *Gibraltare*,
> All streights, and none but streights, are wayes to them,
> Whether where *Japhet* dwelt, or *Cham*, or *Sem*.

The jaws of the ferries opened for the trucks, but none was allowed to board until passed by a Chilean army officer. He was a proud fair young man of uncommon length and old-fashioned Germanic civility. A red stripe sped down his grey trousers. His exquisite pink nails hovered over my passport, halted by a Polish visa and passed on.

The churning engines spread an iridescent film over the water. The whiff of a sheep-truck attracted flocks of seabirds—gulls, giant petrels and black-browed albatrosses—wheeling round the ferry as she crawled crabwise across the tide and short breaking seas. Taking off, the albatrosses spread themselves to the wind, their huge webs paddling the water, streaming spray until the cutting edge of their wings lifted them clear.

Instead of the Cross, the Albatross
About my neck was hung.

Nathaniel Hawthorne once saw in a museum a stuffed Great
Wandering Albatross, with its wingspan of twelve feet, and the
idea of such a bird round the Mariner's neck struck him as yet
another instance of the poem's absurdity. But Coleridge's
albatross was a much smaller bird. Here is the text, taken from
Captain Shelvocke's voyage, which gave the poem its marching
papers:

> The heavens were perpetually hid from us by gloomy
> distant clouds ... one would think it impossible that *any*
> living thing could subsist in so rigid a climate and indeed we
> ... had not the sight of one fish of any kind, nor seabirds,
> except a disconsolate Black *Albitross*, hovering near as if he
> had lost himself ... till Hatley (my second captain) observing
> in one of his melancholy fits, that this bird was always hover-
> ing near us, imagin'd from his colour that it might be some
> ill-omen ... and after some fruitless attempts shot the
> Albitross, not doubting, perhaps, that we should have a fair
> wind after it.

There are two contenders and I saw them both on Tierra del
Fuego: the Sooty Albatross, a shy bird, smoke-grey all over and
known to sailors as the Stinkpot or Prophet; or, less likely, the
Black-browed Albatross or Mollymauk, fearless and attached to
human company.

Halfway across the Strait, V-formations of black and white
cormorants flashed past, and a school of black and white dolphins
danced in the golden sea.

The day before I had met the nuns of the Santa María Auxiliadora Convent on their Saturday coach outing to the penguin
colony on Cabo Vírgenes. A bus-load of virgins. Eleven
thousand virgins. About a million penguins. Black and white.
Black and white. Black and white.

54

Two oil engineers drove me to Río Grande, the one town on the east side of the island. In the old days it flourished with the English meat trade. Now, temporarily it was given over to Israel.

A party of young kosher butchers had flown from Tel-Aviv to perform the rites of Leviticus. Their skill with the knife made them friends among the workers, but their behaviour scandalized the management on two counts: their patriarchal methods of slaughter clogged the production line; after the day's work they swam naked in the river, washing the blood from their hard, white, stringy bodies.

In driving rain I walked along the shore to the College of the Salesian Fathers. It began life as a Mission (or prison) for the Indians, and since their disappearance they ran it as an agricultural school.

The Fathers were expert taxidermists and connoisseurs of frilly pelargoniums. A priest in steel-rimmed spectacles was in charge of the museum, and asked me to sit while he knifed out the eye of a young guanaco. His bloodied hands contrasted vividly with his bloodless upper arm. He had been lacquering an outsize spider-crab and the smell of acetate filled the room. Ranged round the walls was an aviary of stuffed birds. Their red-painted throats screeched at their preserver with terrible silence.

A young priest from Verona came with the key. The museum was housed in the old Mission Church. The Indians of Tierra del Fuego were the Ona and the Haush, who were foot hunters; and the Alakaluf and the Yaghan (or Yámana) who were canoe hunters. All were tireless wanderers and owned no more than they could carry. Their bones and equipment decayed on glass shelves—bows, quivers, harpoons, baskets, guanaco capes— set alongside the material advances brought by a God, who taught them to disbelieve the spirits of moss and stones and set them to petit-point, crochet and copy-book exercises (examples of which were on display).

The priest was a placid young man with droopy eyelids. He passed his time watching how low a barometer could sink and digging Ona campsites for artefacts. He took me to some green swellings along the shore. Lancing one of these with a spade, he uncovered a purple pie of mussels, ashes and bones.

'Look,' he cried, 'the mandible of an Ona dog.'

The museum housed a stuffed specimen of this ancient, wiry, sharp-muzzled breed, now smothered by the genes of Highland sheepdogs.

55

A MAN I met in Río Grande passed me on to his cousins who farmed close to the Chilean border.

Outside the town the Estancia José Menéndez lay on a grey-green hill. Paint peeling, it looked like a cruise ship gone aground. Above the door of the shearing shed were the words JOSÉ MENÉNDEZ in gold and above them the well-modelled head of a prize ram. The smell of mutton fat drifted from the peons' kitchen.

Beyond the buildings the dirt road twisted over and round the folds in the pampas. Banks of yarrow grew along the fence. I reached some peons' quarters in the half-light. Two sheepdogs yelped but an old Chileno called them off and signalled me in. An iron stove was blazing and an old woman was pegging her laundry on a wire. The room was bare and scrubbed clean. On the walls were pictures of Hitler and General Rosas pasted up long ago and browned over with smoke resin. The old man sat me in his canvas chair and blearily answered yes and no to questions.

The woman went into the kitchen and came back with a plate of stew. She set it on the table with a knife and fork, slowly and deliberately, one, two, one, two. I thanked her and she turned her face to the wall.

A young gaucho in bombachas came in carrying an embossed leather saddle. He went to his room and set it on a stand at the foot of his bed. His back filled the doorway and he began polishing. So now there were two noises, the crackling of the fire and the gaucho rubbing his saddle.

The old man got up and looked from the window. A horseman was cantering up the turf verge of the road.

'Esteban,' he called through to the woman.

The rider bridled his horse to the fence and strode in. The woman had already set his plate down. He was a tall man, red in the face. As he ate, he talked about the wool-slump, and the province of Corrientes where he was born, and Germany where his father was born before him.

'You English?' he asked. 'Once many English here. Owners, managers, *capataces*. Civilized people. Germany and England — Civilization! The rest — *Barbaridad!* This estancia. Manager always English. Indian kill sheep. English kill Indian. Ha!'

We then talked about a Mr Alexander MacLennan who was manager of the estancia in 1899 and was better known as the Red Pig.

56

IN THE 1890s a crude version of Darwin's theory, which had once germinated in Patagonia, returned to Patagonia and appeared to encourage the hunting of Indians. A slogan: 'The Survival of the Fittest', a Winchester and a cartridge belt gave some European bodies the illusion of superiority over the far fitter bodies of the natives.

The Onas of Tierra del Fuego had hunted guanaco since Kaux, their ancestor, split the island into thirty-nine territories, one for each family. The families squabbled, it is true, but usually over women; they did not think of extending their boundaries.

Then the Whites came with a new guanaco, the sheep, and a new frontier, barbed wire. At first the Indians enjoyed the taste of roast lamb, but soon learned to fear the bigger, brown guanaco and its rider that spat invisible death.

The Onas' sheep rustling threatened the companies' dividends (in Buenos Aires the explorer Julius Popper spoke of their 'alarming Communist tendencies') and the accepted solution was to round them up and civilize them in the Mission—where they died of infected clothing and the despair of captivity. But Alexander MacLennan despised slow torture: it offended his sporting instincts.

As a boy he had exchanged the wet slates of Scotland for the boundless horizons of the British Empire. He had grown into a strong man, with a flat face reddened by whisky and the tropics, pale red hair and eyes that flashed both blue and green. He was one of Kitchener's sergeants at Omdurman. He saw two Niles, a domed tomb, patched jibbahs and the 'fuzzy-wuzzies', desert men who anointed their hair with goat grease and lay under cavalry charges, ripping the horses' guts with short hooked knives. Perhaps he knew then that wild nomads are untamable.

He left the army and was recruited by José Menéndez's agents. His methods succeeded where those of his predecessor failed. His dogs, horses and peons adored him. He was not among the farm-managers who offered £1 sterling for every Indian ear: he preferred to do the killing himself. He hated to see any animal in pain.

The Onas had traitors in their camps. One day a renegade came with a grudge against his own kind, and told MacLennan that a party of Indians was heading for the seal colony on Cabo de Peñas, south of Río Grande. The hunters butchered the seals in a landlocked cove. From the cliffs the Red Pig and his men watched the beach run red with blood and the rising tide force them within range. They bagged at least fourteen head that day.

'A humanitarian act!' the Red Pig said, 'if one has the guts to do it.'

But the Onas did have one swift and daring marksman called Täapelt, who specialized in picking off white murderers with cold selective justice. Täapelt stalked the Red Pig and found him out man-hunting one day with the local Chief of Police. One arrow pierced the policeman's neck. The other sank into the Scotsman's shoulder, but he recovered and had the arrow head mounted as a tie-pin.

The Red Pig found his nemesis in the liquor of his own country. Drunk by day and night, the Menéndez family sacked

him. He and his wife Bertha retired to a bungalow in Punta
Arenas. He died of delirium tremens in his mid-forties.

57

'B UT THE Indians *did* get the Red Pig, you know.'
       The speaker was one of two English spinster ladies I met
later in Chile. Both were in their seventies. Their father had been
manager of a meat-works in Patagonia and they were on holiday
in the South looking up old friends. They lived in a flat in
Santiago. They were nice ladies and they spoke with nice ladylike
accents.

Both wore a lot of make-up. They had plucked their eyebrows
and painted them in higher up. The elder sister was blonde,
bright gold to be exact, and white at the roots. Her lips were a
scarlet bow and her eyelids were green. The younger one was
brunette. Her hair, eyebrows, suit, handbag, and spotted silk
cravat were a matching shade of chocolate; even her lips were a
kind of reddish brown.

They were taking tea with a friend and the sun came in off the
sea, filling the room and shining on their lined and painted faces.

'Oh, we knew the Red Pig well,' the blonde one said, 'when we
were gels in Punta Arenas. He and Bertha lived in a funny little
house round the corner. The end was terrible. Terrible! Kept
seeing Indians in his sleep. Bows and arrows, you know. And
screaming for blood! One night he woke and the Indians were
all round the bed and he cried: "Don't kill me! Don't kill me!"
and he ran out of the house. Well, Bertha followed down the
street but she couldn't keep up, and he ran right on into the
forest. They lost him for days. And then a peon found him in a
pasture with some cows. Naked! On all fours! And eating grass!
And he was bellowing like a bull because he thought he *was* a
bull. And that was the *end* of course.'

58

THE GERMAN Esteban gave me a spare cot for the night and then we saw the headlights of a car. It was a taxi, taking a peon to the estancia I was aiming for. They left me at the front gate.

'Well, at least the visitor speaks English.'

The voice came round the door of a sitting-room where a log fire was blazing.

Miss Nita Starling was a small, agile Englishwoman, with short white hair, narrow wrists and an extremely determined expression. The owners of the estancia had invited her to help with the garden. Now they did not want her to go. Working in all weathers, she had made new borders and a rockery. She had unchoked the strawberries and under her care a weed-patch had become a lawn.

'I always wanted to garden in Tierra del Fuego,' she said next morning, the light rain washing down her cheeks, 'and now I can say I've done it.'

As a young woman Miss Starling was a photographer, but learned to despise the camera. 'Such a kill-joy,' she said. She then worked as a horticulturalist in a well-known nursery garden in Southern England. Her special interest was in flowering shrubs. Flowering shrubs were her escape from a rather drab life, looking after her bed-ridden mother, and she began to lose herself in their lives. She pitied them, planted out unnaturally in nursery beds, or potted up under glass. She liked to think of them growing wild, on mountains and in forests, and in her imagination she travelled to the places on the labels.

When Miss Starling's mother died, she sold the bungalow and its contents. She bought a lightweight suitcase and gave away the clothes she would never wear. She packed the suitcase and walked it round the neighbourhood, trying it out for lightness. Miss Starling did not believe in porters. She did pack one long dress for evening wear.

'You never know where you'll end up,' she said.

For seven years she had travelled and hoped to travel till she dropped. The flowering shrubs were now her companions. She knew when and where they would be coming into flower. She never flew in aeroplanes, and paid her way teaching English or with the odd gardening job.

She had seen the South African veld aflame with flowers; and the lilies and madrone forests of Oregon; the pine woods of British Columbia; and the miraculous unhybridized flora of Western Australia, cut off by desert and sea. The Australians had such funny names for their plants: Kangaroo Paw, Dinosaur Plant, Gerardtown Wax Plant and Billy Black Boy.

She had seen the cherries and Zen gardens of Kyoto and the autumn colour in Hokkaido. She loved Japan and the Japanese. She stayed in youth hostels that were lovely and clean. In one hostel she had a boyfriend young enough to be her son. She gave him extra English lessons, and, besides, the young liked older people in Japan.

In Hong Kong Miss Starling had boarded with a woman called Mrs Wood.

'A dreadful woman,' Miss Starling said. 'Tried to pretend she was English.'

Mrs Wood had an old Chinese servant called Ah-hing. Ah-hing was under the impression that she was working for an English-woman, but could not understand why, if she were English, she would treat her that way.

'But I told her the truth,' Miss Starling said. ' "Ah-hing," I said, "your employer is not English at all. She's a Russian Jewess." And Ah-hing was upset because all the bad treatment was now explained.'

Miss Starling had an adventure staying with Mrs Wood. One night she was fumbling for her latchkey when a China-boy put a knife to her throat and asked for her handbag.

'And you gave it him,' I said.

'I did no such thing. I bit his arm. I could tell he was more frightened than me. Not what you'd call a professional mugger, see. But there's one thing I'll always regret. I so nearly got his knife off him. I'd have loved it for a souvenir.'

Miss Starling was on her way to the azaleas in Nepal 'not this May but the one after'. She was looking forward to her first

North American Fall. She quite liked Tierra del Fuego. She had walked in forests of *notofagus antarctica.* They used to sell it in the nursery.

'It is beautiful,' she said, looking from the farm at the black line where the grass ended and the trees began. 'But I wouldn't want to come back.'

'Neither would I,' I said.

59

I WENT on to the southernmost town in the world. Ushuaia began with a prefabricated mission house put up in 1869 by the Rev. W. H. Stirling alongside the shacks of the Yaghan Indians. For sixteen years Anglicanism, vegetable gardens and the Indians flourished. Then the Argentine Navy came and the Indians died of measles and pneumonia.

The settlement graduated from navy base to convict station. The Inspector of Prisons designed a masterpiece of cut stone and concrete more secure than the jails of Siberia. Its blank grey walls, pierced by the narrowest slits, lie to the east of the town. It is now used as a barracks.

Mornings in Ushuaia began in flat calm. Across the Beagle Channel you saw the jagged outline of Hoste Island opposite and the Murray Narrows, leading down to the Horn archipelago. By mid-day the water was boiling and slavering and the far shore blocked by a wall of vapour.

The blue-faced inhabitants of this apparently childless town glared at strangers unkindly. The men worked in a crab-cannery or in the navy yards, kept busy by a niggling cold war with Chile. The last house before the barracks was the brothel. Skull-white cabbages grew in the garden. A woman with a rouged face was emptying her rubbish as I passed. She wore a black Chinese shawl embroidered with aniline pink peonies. She said '¿Qué tal?' and smiled the only honest, cheerful smile I saw in Ushuaia. Obviously her situation suited her.

The guard refused me admission to the barracks. I wanted to

see the old prison yard. I had read about Ushuaia's most celebrated convict.

60

T HE STORY of the Anarchists is the tail end of the same old quarrel: of Abel, the wanderer, with Cain, the hoarder of property. Secretly, I suspect Abel of taunting Cain with 'Death to the Bourgeoisie!' It is fitting that the subject of this story was a Jew.

May Day of 1909 was cold and sunny in Buenos Aires. In the early afternoon, files of men in flat caps began filling the Plaza Lorea. Soon the square pulsed with scarlet flags and rang with shouts.

Swirling along with the crowd was Simón Radowitzky, a red-haired boy from Kiev. He was small but brawny from working in railway yards. He had the beginnings of a moustache and his ears were big. Over his skin hung the pallor of the ghetto — 'unpleasantly white', the police dossier said. A square jutting chin and low forehead spoke of limited intelligence and boundless convictions.

The cobbles underfoot, the breath of the crowd, the stuccoed buildings and sidewalk trees; the guns, horses and police helmets, carried Radowitzky back to his city and the Revolution of 1905. Gravelly voices mixed with Italian and Spanish. The cry went up 'Death to the Cossacks!' And the rioters, loosing control, smashed shop-windows and unhitched horses from their cabs.

Simón Radowitzky had been in a Tsarist jail. He had been in Argentina three months. He lived with other Russian Jewish Anarchists in a tenement. He drank in their hot talk and planned selective action.

Across the Avenida de Mayo, a cordon of cavalry and a single automobile checked the advance of the crowd. In the car was the Chief of Police, Colonel Ramón Falcón, eagle-eyed, impassive. The front-rankers spotted their enemy and shouted obscenities. Calmly, he calculated their numbers and withdrew.

Patagonian Railways

Jaramillo Station

The Tomb at Río Pico

A German House at Rio Pico

The Dodge, Gaimán, Chubut

Driving to the Bethel in the Dodge

Welsh Farmer, Chubut

The Bethel, Gaimán, Chubut

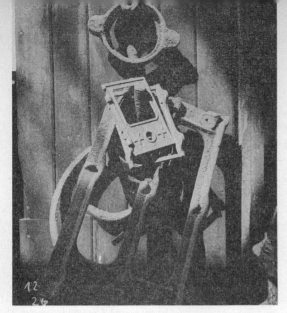

Charley Milward's Foundry, Punta Arenas

Charley Milward's House, Punta Arenas

Punta Arenas

The Moreno Glacier

The Moreno Glacier

The Cave of Hands

The Mylodon Cave

There followed a flurry of shots and a rush of horses, in which three men died and forty were wounded. (Journalists counted thirty-six puddles of blood.) The police claimed self-defence and also unearthed seditious leaflets written in Hebrew, which they used to pin the disturbance on the plague of Russian nihilists, whom a slack immigration policy had allowed to pollute the country. In Argentina the words 'Russian' and 'Jew' were synonymous.

The second act took place later the same winter. Scornful of armed guards, Colonel Falcón was driving from the funeral of his friend, the Director of State Prisons. With him was his young secretary, Alberto Lartigau, who was learning to be a man. At a corner of the Avenida Quintana, Simón Radowitzky in a dark suit was waiting with a parcel. With perfect timing he tilted it into the car, jumped back to dodge the explosion and ran towards a construction site.

He was unlucky. Some bystanders raised two policemen. A bullet caught him under the right nipple and he dropped, gritting his teeth under the blows. '*Viva la Anarquía!*' he yelled, halt-ingly, at his captors. 'I am nothing but for each of you I have a bomb.'

Colonel Falcón, a mess of broken limbs and arteries, was conscious enough to identify himself. 'It is nothing,' he said. 'Attend to the boy first.' In hospital he died of shock and loss of blood. Lartigau survived an amputation until evening. From all over the country, police delegations came for the funeral.

'Simón Radowitzky belongs to that class of helots who vegetate on the steppes of Russia, dragging out a wretched existence in the harshest of climates and the misery of their own inferior condition.' The Public Prosecutor also pointed to certain somatic peculiarities as proof of a criminal personality. A man of conscience and humanity, he asked for the death sentence, but the Judge could not pass it until he had cleared up the matter of the assassin's age.

At this point Moses Radowitzky, rabbi and old-clothes merchant, surfaced with his cousin's birth certificate. When the crabbed characters were deciphered, the court learned that the prisoner was eighteen years and seven months old, too young for the firing squad, but not for life imprisonment. Every year, around the date of the crime, the Judge ordered twenty days solitary confinement on a bread and water diet.

Simón Radowitzky disappeared into labyrinths of rats and reinforced concrete. Two years later he was transferred to Ushuaia. (The jail in the capital was unsafe.) One night sixty-two prisoners were stripped naked for medical inspection and fettered with hoops of iron. Reflectors on the quay lit the procession up the gang-plank of a naval transport. The voyage began in calm and ended in the gales of Patagonia. The convicts shared their berth with the ship's coal-bunker, and, on landing, they were black with coal dust and their ankles were ulcerated by the iron hoops.

A certain taste for degradation and the wild hopes of his race carried Radowitzky through the years of swill and potatoes. Some family photographs were his only possessions. He greeted each new indignity with a smile and discovered in himself the power to lead men. The prisoners loved him, came to him with their problems and he led their hunger strikes.

His power, once recognized, made the prison officials hate him more. The warders had standing orders to swing a lantern in his face, every half-hour as he slept. In 1918, the Deputy Governor, Gregorio Palacios, desiring his white flesh and wishing to degrade its owner yet further, buggered him. Three guards held him down and buggered him in turn. They beat his head and ripped his back with cuts and welts.

Radowitzky's friends in the capital got wind of this business and published their version under the title *La Sodoma Fuegina*. The Russian Revolution was in full swing. Graffiti reading 'Freedom for Radowitzky!' were smeared all over Buenos Aires. Some of the more enterprising Anarchists were planning to spring their favourite martyr from jail.

The only man for the job was Pascualino Rispoli, the 'last pirate of Tierra del Fuego', a Neapolitan who had tracked his renegade father to the Bar Alhambra in Punta Arenas and stayed. Pascualino had a small cutter, officially for hunting seals and sea-otters, privately for smuggling and stripping wrecks. He sailed in all weathers, dumped loose-lipped crews overboard, lost regularly at cards and was open to any kind of commission.

Sometime in October 1918, two Argentine Anarchists hired

Pascualino for the jail-break. The cutter anchored off Ushuaia on November 4th. At dawn, three days later, Radowitzky, in the uniform of a prison guard accomplice, walked through the prison gate. A dinghy ferried him aboard, and before the alarm went up, she was swallowed up in the maze of channels where, four years earlier, the German cruiser *Dresden* had eluded the British Navy.

The Neapolitan wanted to provision the fugitive and drop him on one of the outer islands until the hue-and-cry died down. But Radowitzky's urban soul recoiled from the sinister rain-forests and he insisted on being taken to Punta Arenas.

Meanwhile, the Chilean Navy agreed to co-operate with the Argentine police. Their tug *Yáñez* overtook the cutter on her last reach home, but not before Pascualino had made his passenger swim ashore for the safety of the trees. Finding nothing, but suspecting all, the officers took some of the crew to Punta Arenas, where the police made them squeal. The *Yáñez* steamed back down the coast and caught Pascualino in the act of transferring Radowitzky ashore with a load of barrels. The fugitive lay motionless in the water, under the lee of the cutter, but there was no escape. A force of carabineers had circled the place. Exhausted and freezing, he gave himself up and was shipped back to Ushuaia.

Twelve years passed. Then, in 1930, President Yrigoyen released Radowitzky as a gesture to the working class. One night in May, the ex-convict stood on the deck of a military transport and watched for the lights of Buenos Aires, but he was not allowed to land. His guards transferred him to the Montevideo ferry. Secretly Yrigoyen had promised his police chiefs to expel him from Argentine soil.

Without papers, without money, and dressed in some ill-fitting clothes got from a Turk in Ushuaia, 'the victim of the bourgeoisie' walked down the steamer gang-plank to the cheers of an Anarchist crowd. The reception committee hoped for the words and gestures of a firebrand, and were disappointed by the puzzled, mild-mannered man, with beetling brows and a face streaked with livid veins, who smiled vaguely and didn't know where to put his hands.

His new friends embraced him and hustled him off in a taxi.

He tried to answer their questions but kept harking back to his friends in Ushuaia. Separation from them, he said, was more than he could bear. When asked about his sufferings, he was tongue-tied and fumbled for a piece of paper from which he read a text thanking Dr Yrigoyen in the name of the International Proletariat. When he said he wanted to go back to Russia, the Anarchists laughed. The man hadn't even heard of the Kronstadt Massacre.

Once free, Radowitzky sank back into obscurity and nervous exhaustion. His friends used him to run messages to comrades in Brazil. He fell foul of the Uruguayan police and was put under house arrest, but, having no house, found home again in jail.

In 1936 he sailed for Spain. Three years later he was among the columns of broken men plodding over the Pyrenees into France. He went to Mexico. A poet got him a clerk's job in the Uruguayan consulate. He wrote articles for mimeographed reviews of small circulation and shared his pension with a woman, perhaps the only one he ever knew. Sometimes he visited his family in the United States, where they were making good.

Simón Radowitzky died of a heart attack in 1956.

61

THE YEAR the nations of Europe settled the course of the nineteenth century on the plain of Waterloo, a boy was born on the Murray Narrows, who would make a modest contribution to settling the course of the twentieth.

His birthplace was an arbour of green saplings, sods and rancid seal-skins. His mother cut his umbilical cord with a sharp mussel-shell and rammed his head against her copper-coloured teat. For two years the teat was the centre of his universe. He went everywhere with the teat: fishing, berrying, canoeing, visiting cousins, or learning the names—as complex and precise as Linnaean Latin—of everything that swam or sprouted, crawled or flew.

One day the teat tasted horrible, for his mother had smeared it with rancid blubber. She told him to play with boys his own age, now he could chew a steak of seal. His father then took over his education and taught him to garrotte cormorants, club penguins, stab crabs and harpoon seals. The boy learned about Watauineiwa, the Old Man in the Sky who changed not and resented change; and about Yetaita, the Power of Darkness, a hairy monster who pounced on the slothful and could be shaken off by dancing. And he learned the stories which wander at all times in the minds of all men—of the amorous seal, of the Creation of Fire, or the Giant with an Achilles heel, or of the humming bird who freed the pent-up waters.

The boy grew up fearless and loyal to the customs of his tribe. Season followed season: egg-time, baby-gulls-flying, beach-leaves-reddening, Sun-Man-hiding. Blue sea-anemones heralded the coming of spring; ibises meant equinoctial gales. Men were born and men died. The people had little sense of ongoing time.

The morning of May 11th 1830 was clear and sharp. (For the Fuegians, the date was a combination of bare branches and sea-otters returning.) Under the snow line the hills were blue and the forests purple and russet-brown. Black swells broke in white lines along the shore. The boy was out fishing with his uncle when they sighted the Apparition.

For years the People of the South had murmured about the visits of a monster. At first they assumed it was a kind of whale, but closer acquaintance revealed a gigantic canoe with wings, full of pink creatures with hair sprouting ominously from their faces. These, however, had proved at least half-human, since they knew something of the rules of barter. Friends up the coast had swapped a dog for a most useful knife made of a hard, cold, glittering stone.

Heedless of danger, the boy persuaded the uncle to paddle up to the pink man's canoe. A tall person in costume beckoned him and he leapt aboard. The pink man handed the uncle a disc that shimmered like the moon and the canoe spread a white wing and flew down the channel towards the source of pearl buttons.

The kidnapper was Captain Robert FitzRoy, R.N., Chief Officer of H.M.S. *Beagle*, now winding up her first survey of southern waters. All down the coast of Patagonia he had seen, in the beds of fossil oysters, a confirmation of his belief in the

Universal Deluge. It followed that all men were the Children of Adam; all were equally capable of improvement. For this reason he was delighted with this bright-eyed addition to his collection of three natives. The crew called him Jemmy Button.

The next phase of the boy's career is clearly documented. With two other Fuegians (a fourth died of smallpox at Plymouth), he travelled to London, saw a stone lion on the steps of Northumberland House, and settled down to boarding-school at Walthamstow, where he learned English, gardening, carpentry, and the plainer truths of Christianity. He also learned to preen before mirrors and fuss over his gloves. Before leaving, he had an audience with William IV and Queen Adelaide; and, if we believe Mark Twain, his colleague York Minster went to a Court Ball at St James's in the costume of his country—and emptied the ballroom in two minutes.

We would know less of the Fuegians' return were it not for the naturalist on the *Beagle*'s second voyage, the pleasant, snub-nosed young man with unrivalled powers of observation and a copy of Lyell's *Geology* in his luggage. Darwin quite liked Jemmy Button, but the wild Fuegians appalled him. He read (but ignored) the description by Drake's chaplain of a 'comely and harmless people' whose canoes were of fine proportion 'in the sight and use whereof princes might seem to be delighted'. Instead he lapsed into that common failing of naturalists: to marvel at the intricate perfection of other creatures and recoil from the squalor of man. Darwin thought the Fuegians 'the most abject and miserable creatures' he anywhere beheld. They resembled the devils in 'plays like *Der Freischutz*' and were as fascinated by his white skin as an orang-outang in a zoo. He sneered at their canoe; he sneered at their language ('scarcely deserves to be called articulate') and confessed he could hardly make himself believe they were 'fellow creatures and inhabitants of the same world'.

As the *Beagle* coasted towards his home at Wulaia, Jemmy Button stood on deck and pointed to his tribe's enemies standing in groups on the shore. 'Yapoos!' he shouted. 'Monkeys—Dirty —Fools—Not Men', perhaps assisting Darwin to his biggest idea. For the mere sight of the Fuegians helped trigger off the theory that Man had evolved from an ape-like species and that some men had evolved further than others. When Jemmy

Button reverted to savagery almost overnight, he proved the point.

FitzRoy and Darwin returned to England in October 1836 and began editing their diaries for publication. (Five years of sharing the same mess-table had hardened both men to diametrically opposed views.) FitzRoy, no less than Darwin, was perplexed by these savages 'the colour of devonshire cattle' bobbing about Cape Horn in bark canoes. If they too had descended from Noah, how and why did they travel thus far from Mount Ararat? And, as an appendix to his *Narrative*, he published a theory of migration that appears to anticipate Freud's mythical events within the Primal Horde:

Somewhere, under canvas, in Asia Minor, the sons of Shem and Japheth loved some black slave girls, of the cursed line of Ham and Cush, and fathered the race of reddish mulattos, who would people Asia and the Americas. Naturally, the fathers preferred their legitimate offspring to half-castes, and the latter, chafing at their bondage, walked out. Their craving for freedom stimulated emigration in all directions 'and eventually perpetuated that passion for wandering which we see today in the Arab, the migratory Malay, the roving Tartar, and the ever-restless South American Indian'.

FitzRoy believed that the emigrants stepped out clothed and literate, but that foreign climates brutalized them and killed off their livestock. They forgot how to write, took to skins when their clothes wore out, and, at this far end of the world, retained the canoe and some spears, but had degenerated into greasy, matt-haired 'satires upon mankind' whose teeth were 'flat-topped like those of a horse'.

Among the books in FitzRoy's cabin on the *Beagle* was Captain James Weddell's *Voyage towards the South Pole* in the brig *Jane* and the cutter *Beaufoy*. In the summer of 1822–3, the two vessels sailed south from Cape Horn to hunt for fur seals. They passed through fields of pack ice (one flow was covered with black earth), and on February 8th, at Latitude 74° 15', farther south than anyone had sailed before, they saw whales, birds of the blue petrel kind, and leagues of open sea. 'NOT A PARTICLE OF ICE OF ANY DESCRIPTION WAS TO BE SEEN.'

Weddell wrote on his chart: 'Sea of George IV—Navigable',

leaving the impression that the sea got warmer as one neared the
Pole. He then sailed northward to look for some phantom
islands, the Auroras. Calling in at the South Shetlands one of his
sailors saw a 'Non-describable Animal' with a red face of human
form and green hair hanging from its shoulders. Then at Hermit
Island, next to the Horn, he ran in with canoe-loads of Fuegians
who, at one point, threatened to overrun the ship. He read them
a chapter of the Bible and they listened with solemn faces: one
man held his ear to the book believing that it spoke. He also
jotted down some words of their vocabulary:

> Sayam means Water
> Abaish — Woman
> Shevoo — Approbation
> Nosh   — Displeasure

and he concluded that the language was Hebrew, though how it
had got to Tierra del Fuego was, he admitted, 'a question of
interest to philologists'. His final paragraph commended the
savages to the philanthropy of his countrymen and probably set
FitzRoy off.

At the precise moment that Darwin and FitzRoy were settling
down to their narratives, a copy of Captain Weddell's book
turned up in Richmond, Virginia, and lay on the desk of the
Editor of the *Southern Literary Messenger*, Edgar Allen Poe, who
was writing a different kind of narrative. Poe, like Coleridge
whom he idolized, was another night-wandering man, obsessed
by the Far South and by voyages of annihilation and rebirth — an
enthusiasm he would pass on to Baudelaire. He had recently
become acquainted with the theory of J. C. Symmes, an ex-
cavalry officer from St Louis, who claimed in 1818 that both
Poles were hollow and temperate.

In Poe's *Narrative of Arthur Gordon Pym*, the hero is rescued
from shipwreck by a Captain Guy, of the English sealer *Jane Guy*.
(A real Captain Guy figures in Weddell's text.) They sail on south
in search of the Auroras, pass through the same ice-fields, sight a
'singular looking animal' with silky white hair and red teeth, and
land on a warm island called Tsalal, where everything is black.
The Tsalalians are jet black and woolly haired and, since Poe was
a good Virginian nigger-hater, they represent the ultimate in

bestiality and low cunning. Their headmen are called Yampoos (after Lemuel Gulliver's Yahoos and parallel to Jemmy Button's Yapoos) and the name of their paramount chief is Too-Wit.

Outwardly Too-Wit is friendly, but secretly he is plotting murder. The Tsalalian canoes surround the *Jane Guy* and the savages plunder and tear the crew to pieces. Only Pym and a companion escape from the island, but their canoe is sucked south towards a vortex of destruction. As they plunge into the cataract, they sight—like Ulysses sighting the Mountain of Purgatory—a colossal shrouded figure. 'And the hue of the skin of the figure was of the perfect whiteness of snow.' This figure resurfaces in Rimbaud's poem 'Being Beauteous'.

Poe's Tsalalians are an amalgam of the Tasmanian Black-fellows (from Captain Cook) and the Southern Blacks (from his childhood), but Captain Weddell's Fuegians are part of it. For the Tsalalians are also descendants of Ham, the swarthy, and their language is Hebrew (Tsalal—'to be dark', Too-Wit—'to be dirty'). Neither Poe nor Darwin read each other: that both should have used the same ingredients for a similar purpose is another example of the synchronic workings of the intelligence.

The later career of Jemmy Button did nothing to redeem his people's reputation. In 1855, the Patagonian Mission Society's schooner *Allen Gardiner* anchored in the Murray Narrows and hoisted the Union Jack. On impulse her captain, Parker Snow, shouted 'Jemmy Button' and a shout rang back across the water: 'Yes! Yes! James Button! James Button!' A stout man paddled up, asked for clothes, and 'looking like a baboon dressed for the occasion' took tea in the captain's cabin as if twenty-one years had melted away.

Another four years would pass before Jemmy staged a massacre that could have been written for him by Poe. On November 6th 1869, Morning Service in the first Anglican Church at Wulaia was interrupted by a mob of Fuegians who clubbed and stoned the eight white worshippers to death. Only Alfred Coles, the ship's cook who was making lunch aboard the schooner, escaped. At the official enquiry, he swore that Jemmy planned the killing out of anger at the miserable presents sent him from England, and that afterwards he had slept in the captain's cabin.

Jemmy lived into the 1870s to see a proper mission established at Ushuaia and see the first of his people die of epidemics. About the time Marshal von Moltke was justifying Prussian militarism on Darwinian principles, the man who helped form them sank back on a pile of seal-skins and tried to sleep. His women were wailing and preparing to forget him. We cannot know what he remembered as he passed from the world—a copper-coloured teat? The stomach of a man called Majesty? Or a man-eating lion on the steps of Northumberland House?

I left Ushuaia as from an unwanted tomb and crossed over to Puerto Williams, the Chilean naval base on Navarino Island:

62

'ASK FOR Grandpa Felipe,' the lieutenant said. 'He's the only pure-blood left.'

The last of the Yaghans lived in a row of plank shanties at the far end of the base. The authorities settled them here, so they should be close to a doctor. It was drizzling. Snow smears came down close to the shore. It was high summer. Behind the settlement the trees disappeared in the clouds. The water was smooth and black and across the channel were the ribbed grey cliffs of Gable Island.

The old man said I could come in. The hut was full of smoke and my eyes smarted. He sat in a pile of fish crates, crab pots, baskets and boat gear. He was hardly taller than wide and his legs were bowed. He wore a greasy cap and had the flat leathery face of a Mongol, and black unmoving eyes that registered no emotion or expression.

Only his hands moved. They were fine hands, agile and netted with dark-grey veins. He earned a little money making canoes to sell to the tourists. He made them of bark and withes and sewed them with sheep sinew. In the old days, fathers made these canoes for their sons. Now there were no sons and still very few tourists. I watched him whittle a miniature harpoon shaft and bind on to it a tiny bone harpoon.

'Once I made big harpoons.' He broke the silence. 'I made

them of whale's bone. On all the beaches there were bones of whales. But they have gone now. I made the harpoons from a bone inside the head.'

'From the jaw?'

'Not from the jaw. From inside the head. In the whale's skull there is a *canalita* and two bones along it. The strongest harpoons came from there. Harpoons made from the jaw were not so strong.

'You are English.' He looked at me for the first time and seemed to be trying to smile.

'How did you know?'

'I know my people. Once I knew many English. There were two English sailors, Charlie and Jackie. They were tall and fair and they were my friends. We spoke English in school. We forgot our language. Mister Lawrence knew our language better than we did. He taught us to speak our own language.'

Grandpa Felipe was born in the Anglican Mission, and was probably related to Jemmy Button. As a boy he watched his people die. He watched all of his children die, except one daughter, and his wife die.

'Why did she die? She died in her sleep with her arms folded. And I did not know why.'

And he had been ill, he said. Ill all his life. A body without strength. Never able to work.

'It was the epidemics. The epidemics came and we watched our people die. Mister Lawrence wrote words on stone when they died. We did not know about epidemics. How could we know? We had good health then. We never had epidemics before.'

Boarding the boat back to Ushuaia was a big man with a blotchy red face, upturned moustaches, and the syrupy eyes of an Ottoman pasha. He wore an astrakhan hat. He had come from Santiago to see about a plant for processing krill. The whales had gone but there was still plenty of krill. I talked about Grandpa Felipe and mentioned Charlie and Jackie.

'He probably ate them,' the fat man said.

63

FROM USHUAIA it was a thirty-five-mile walk along the Beagle Channel to the Bridges's estancia at Harberton.

For the first few miles the forest came down to the shore and you looked down through branches at the dark green water and the purple streamers of kelp rising up and wavering with the tide. Further on the hills drew back and there were pastures of springy grass, dotted with daisies and mushrooms.

All along the tide-mark was a crust of sea-white driftwood, and sometimes a ship-timber or a whale vertebra. The rocks were floury white from guano. There were cormorants on them and kelp geese, flashing black and white as they took off. Offshore there were grebes and steamer ducks and, out in the strait, sooty albatrosses wheeling effortlessly, like knives flying.

It was dark when I limped into the Argentine Navy post at Almanza. Two ratings were stranded there. They spent their days looking through binoculars at the Chileans; but their radio was broken and they could not report what they saw. One came from Buenos Aires and told scatological jokes. The other was a Chaco Indian, who said nothing but sat hunched up looking into the embers of the fire.

Coming into Harberton from the land side, you could mistake it for a big estate in the Scottish Highlands, with its sheep fences, sturdy gates and peat-brown trout streams. The Rev. Thomas Bridges's settlement was strung out along the west shore of Harberton Inlet, shielded from the gales by a low hill. His Yaghan friends chose the site and he named it after his wife's Devonshire village.

The house, imported long ago from England, was of corrugated iron, painted white, with green windows and a soft red roof. Inside, it retained the solid mahogany furniture, the plumbing and the upright presence of a Victorian parsonage.

Clarita Goodall, the missionary's granddaughter, was alone in the house. As a girl she had sat on Captain Milward's knee and listened to his sea-stories. She gave me a copy of Thomas Bridges's *Yaghan Dictionary* and I sat on the veranda reading.

The flowers of an English garden seemed to glow with an inner brilliance. A path led through a wicket gate arched with a whale jaw. Woodsmoke drifted over the black water and, on the far shore, geese were calling.

64

THOMAS BRIDGES was a small, straight man, who believed in God's providence and was unafraid of risk. An orphan, he was adopted by George Packenham Despard, a Nottinghamshire clergyman and Secretary of the Patagonian Mission Society, who took him to the Falklands. He was living there when Jemmy Button murdered the missionaries. Later, he continued their work and, with the odd visit to England, lived on in Tierra del Fuego. But by 1886, with the Indians dying off, he realized the Mission's days were numbered, and, with a family of seven to support and no prospects in England, he asked President Roca for title to the land at Harberton. The move damned him in the eyes of the self-righteous.

The young Thomas Bridges had had the ear and patience to sit with an Indian called George Okkoko and master the language Darwin sneered at. To his surprise, he uncovered a complexity of construction and a vocabulary no one had suspected in a 'primitive' people. At eighteen, he decided to form a dictionary which would help him 'tell them, to my satisfaction and their conviction of the love of Jesus'. This gigantic operation was scarcely complete at his death in 1898. He had listed about 32,000 words without having begun to exhaust their reserves of expression.

The *Dictionary* survived the Indians to become their monument. I have handled Bridges's original manuscript in the British Museum and like to think of the clergyman, red-eyed into the night, with the wind howling over the house, filling the book of blue-marbled end-papers with his spidery handwriting. We know he despaired of finding in that labyrinth of the particular, words to express the intangible concepts of the Gospel. We also know he was intolerant of the Indians' superstition and never tried to understand it: the murder of his colleagues was too close. The Indians spotted this strain of intolerance and hid their deepest beliefs.

Bridges's dilemma is common enough. Finding in 'primitive' languages a dearth of words for moral ideas, many people assumed these ideas did not exist. But the concepts of 'good' or 'beautiful', so essential to Western thought, are meaningless unless they are rooted to things. The first speakers of language took the raw material of their surroundings and pressed it into metaphor to suggest abstract ideas. The Yaghan tongue—and by inference all language—proceeds as a system of navigation. Named things are fixed points, aligned or compared, which allow the speaker to plot the next move. Had Bridges uncovered the range of Yaghan metaphor, his work would never have come to completion. Yet sufficient survives for us to resurrect the clarity of their intellect.

What shall we think of a people who defined 'monotony' as 'an absence of male friends?' Or, for 'depression', used the word that described the vulnerable phase in a crab's seasonal cycle, when it has sloughed off its old shell and waits for another to grow? Or who derived 'lazy' from the Jackass Penguin? Or 'adulterous' from the hobby, a small hawk that flits here and there, hovering motionless over its next victim?

Here are just a few of their synonyms:

> Sleet—Fish scales
> A shoal of sprats—Slimy mucus
> A tangle of trees that have fallen blocking the
> path forward—A hiccough
> Fuel—Something burned—Cancer
> Mussels out of season—Shrivelled skin—Old age

Some of their linkings were beyond me:

> The fur seal—The relatives of a murdered man

Others seemed obscure and then came clear:

> A thaw (of snow)—A scar—Teaching.

The thought process is as follows:

Snow covers the ground as a scab covers a wound. It melts in patches and leaves a smooth, flattened surface (the scar). The thaw announces the arrival of spring weather. In spring the people start moving and lessons begin.

Another example:
A bog—A mortal wound (or mortally wounded)

The bogs of Tierra del Fuego are lumpy mattresses of moss, oozing with water. Their colour is a dull yellow with reddish smears, the colour of an open wound suppurating with pus and blood. The bogs cover valley floors, laid out flat as a wounded man.

Verbs take first place in this language. The Yaghans had a dramatic verb to capture every twitch of the muscles, every possible action of nature or man. The verb *īya* means 'to moor your canoe to a streamer of kelp'; *ōkon* 'to sleep in a floating canoe' (and quite different from sleeping in a hut, on the beach or with your wife); *ukōmona* 'to hurl your spear into a shoal of fish without aiming for a particular one'; *wejna* 'to be loose or easily moved as a broken bone or the blade of a knife'—'to wander about, or roam, as a homeless or lost child'—'to be attached yet loose, as an eye or bone in its socket'—'to swing, move or travel'—or simply 'to exist or be'.

Compared to the verbs, other parts of speech droop in the wings. Nouns hang suspended from their verbal roots. The word for 'skeleton' comes from 'to gnaw thoroughly'. *Aiapi* is 'to bring a special kind of spear and put it in a canoe ready for hunting'; *aiapux* is the hunted animal and so 'the sea otter'.

The Yaghans were born wanderers though they rarely wandered far. The ethnographer Father Martin Gusinde wrote: 'They resemble fidgety birds of passage, who feel happy and inwardly calm only when they are on the move'; and their language reveals a mariner's obsession with time and space. For, although they did not count to five, they defined the cardinal points with minute distinctions and read seasonal changes as an accurate chronometer.

Four examples:

Iñan	—	Season of the young crabs (when the parents carry their young).
Cūiũa	—	Season when the young let go (from a verb 'to stop biting').
Hakūreum	—	Bark loose and sap rising.
Čekana	—	Canoe building season and time of the snipe-calls. (The '*ček-ček*' sound imitates the snipe and the noise as the canoe-builder rips sheets of beech-bark from the trunk.)

Thomas Bridges coined the word 'Yaghan' after a place called Yagha: the Indians called themselves *Yámana*. Used as a verb *yámana* means 'to live, breathe, be happy, recover from sickness or be sane'. As a noun it means 'people' as opposed to animals. A hand with the suffix—*yámana* was a human hand, a hand offered in friendship, as opposed to a death-dealing claw.

The layers of metaphorical associations that made up their mental soil shackled the Indians to their homeland with ties that could not be broken. A tribe's territory, however uncomfortable, was always a paradise that could never be improved on. By contrast the outside world was Hell and its inhabitants no better than beasts.

Perhaps, that November, Jemmy Button mistook the missionaries as envoys of the Power of Darkness. Perhaps, when later he showed remorse, he remembered that pink men also were human.

65

IN HIS autobiography *The Uttermost Part of the Earth*, Lucas Bridges tells how his father's manuscript was filched by Frederick A. Cook, a glib American doctor on the Belgian Antarctic Expedition of 1898–9, who tried to pass it off as his own work. Cook was the mythomane traveller from Rip van Winkle country who began with a milk-round and claimed the first ascent of Mount McKinley and to have beaten Robert Peary to the North Pole. He died at New Rochelle in 1940, after serving a sentence for selling forged oil shares.

The manuscript of the dictionary got lost in Germany during the Second World War, but was recovered by Sir Leonard Woolley, the excavator of Ur, and presented by the family to the British Museum.

Lucas Bridges was the first White to make friends with the Onas. They trusted him alone when men like the Red Pig were butchering their kin. *The Uttermost Part of the Earth* was one of my favourite books as a boy. In it he describes looking down from Mount Spión Kop on the sacred Lake Kami, and how, later, the Indians helped him hack a trail linking Harberton with the family's other farm at Viamonte.

I had always wanted to walk the track.

66

BUT CLARITA GOODALL did not want me to go. The distance to Lake Kami was about twenty-five miles but the rivers were in spate and the bridges had fallen.

'You could break a leg,' she said, 'or get lost and we'd have to send a search party. We used to ride it in a day, but you can't get a horse through now.'

And all because of the beavers. A governor of the island brought the beavers from Canada and now their dams choked the valleys where once the going was clear. But still I wanted to walk the track.

And in the morning early she woke me. I heard her making tea in the kitchen. She gave me slabs of bread and blackcurrant jam. She filled my thermos with coffee. She took sticks soaked in kerosene and put them in a watertight bag: so if I fell in the river I should at least have fire. She said: 'Do be careful!' and stood in the doorway, in the half-light, in a long pink housecoat, waving slowly with a calm sad smile.

A film of mist hung over the inlet. A family of red-fronted geese rippled the water, and at the first gate more geese stood by a puddle. I passed along the track that led up into the mountains. Ahead was Harberton Mountain, black with trees, and a hazy sun coming over its shoulder. This side of the river was rolling grass country, burned out of the forest and spiked with charred trees.

The track rose and fell. Platforms of logs were laid in corrugations in the hollows. Beyond the last fence was a black pool ringed with dead trees and from there the path wound uphill in among the first big timber.

I heard the river before I saw it, roaring at the bottom of a gorge. The track snaked down the cliff. In a clearing were Lucas Bridges's old sheep pens now rotting away. The bridge was gone, but a hundred yards upstream the river opened out and slid over slippery brown stones. I cut two saplings and trimmed them. I took off my boots and trousers and eased out into the water, testing each footfall with the left stick, steadying myself with the right. At the deepest point the stream swirled round my buttocks. I dried off in a patch of sunlight on the far bank. My feet were red from cold. A torrent duck flew upstream. I recognized its striped head and thin whirring wings.

The track soon lost itself in the forest. I checked the compass and struck north towards the second river. It was a river no longer, but a swamp of yellow peat moss. Along its edge, young trees had been felled with sharp oblique cuts, as if with the swipe of a machete. This was beaver country. This is what beavers did to a river.

I walked three hours and came up to the shoulder of Mount Spión Kop. On ahead was the valley of the Valdez River, a half-cylinder running north twelve miles to the thin blue line of Lake Kami.

A shadow passed over the sun, a whoosh and the sound of wind ripping through pinions. Two condors had dived on me. I saw the red of their eyes as they swept past, banking below the col and showing the grey of their backs. They glided in an arc to the head of the valley and rose again, circling in the upthrust, where the wind pushed against the cliffs, till they were two specks in a milky sky.

The specks increased in size. They were coming back. They came back heading into the wind, unswerving as raiders on target, the ruff of white feathers ringing their black heads, the wings unflinching and the tails splayed downwards as air-brakes and their talons lowered and spread wide. They dived on me four times and then we both lost interest.

In the afternoon I *did* fall into the river. Crossing a beaver dam I trod on a log that felt firm but was floating. It pitched me head first into black mud and I had a hard time getting out. Now I had to reach the road before night.

The track showed up again, yawning a straight corridor through the dark wood. I followed the fresh spoor of a guanaco. Sometimes I saw him up ahead, bobbing over fallen trunks, and then I came up close. He was a single male, his coat all muddied and his front gashed with scars. He had been in a fight and lost. Now he also was a sterile wanderer.

And then the trees cleared and the river wound sluggishly through cattle pastures. Following their tracks I must have crossed the river twenty times. At one crossing I saw boot-marks and suddenly felt light and happy, thinking I would now reach the road or a peon's hut, and then I lost them and the river sluiced down a schist-sided gorge. I struck out across the forest but the light was failing and it was unsafe to clamber over dead trees in the dark.

I spread my sleeping-bag on a level space. I unwrapped the sticks and piled up one half with moss and twigs. The fire flared up. Even damp branches caught and the flames lit the green curtains of lichen hanging from the trees. Inside the sleeping-bag it was damp and warm. Rainclouds were covering the moon.

And then I heard the sound of an engine and sat up. The glare of headlights showed through the trees. I was ten minutes from the road, but too sleepy to care, so I slept. I even slept through a rainstorm.

Next afternoon, washed and fed, I sat in the parlour Viamonte, too stiff to move. For two days I lay on the sofa reading. The family had gone camping all except Uncle Beatle. We talked about flying saucers. The other day he had seen a presence in the dining-room, hovering round a portrait.

From Viamonte I crossed the Chilean half of the island to Porvenir and took the ferry to Punta Arenas.

67

IN THE Plaza de Armas a ceremony was in progress. It was one hundred years since Don José Menéndez set foot in Punta Arenas and a well-heeled party of his descendants had come south to unveil his memorial. The women wore black dresses, pearls, furs and patent shoes. The men had the drawn look that comes of protecting an over-extended acreage. Their Chilean lands had vanished in land reform. As yet they clung to their Argentine latifundias, but the good old days of English managers and docile peons were gone.

Don José's bronze head was bald as a bomb. The bust had once adorned the family's estancia at San Gregorio, but under the Allende regime the peons shoved it in an outhouse. Its reconsecration on the plaza symbolized the return of free enterprise, but the family were unlikely to get anything back. Insincere eulogies tolled like funeral bells.

The wind sighed through the municipal araucarias. Ranked round the square were the cathedral, the hotel and the palazzos of the old plutocracy, now mostly officers' clubs. A statue of Magellan pranced over a pair of fallen Indians, which the sculptor had modelled on 'The Dying Gaul'.

The top brass had lent their presence to the occasion. A band drowned the wind in Sousa marches, as the Intendente, a red-faced General of the Air-Force, prepared to unveil the memorial. The Spanish chargé d'affaires stared with the glassy eyes of absolute conviction. The American ambassador looked affable. And the crowd, which always turned out for a brass band, shambled round the ceremony with expressions of stone. Punta Arenas was a Leftist town. These were the people who elected Salvador Allende their deputy.

A block away was the *palais* which Moritz Braun imported piece-meal from Europe when he married Don José's daughter in 1902, its mansard roofs poking above a shroud of black cypresses. Somehow the house had weathered the confiscations and, in a setting of hygienic marble statues and buttoned sofas, the domestic serenity of the Edwardian era survived.

The servants were preparing the dining-room for the evening's reception. The afternoon sun squeezed through velvet draperies and bounced off a runway of white damask, reflecting light over walls of Cordoba leather and a painting of amorous geese by Picasso's father, Ruiz Blasco.

After the ceremony the older generation relaxed in the winter-garden, attended by a maid in black and white, who served scones and pale tea. The conversation turned to Indians. The 'Englishman' of the family said: 'All this business of Indian killing is being a bit overstretched. You see, these Indians were a pretty low sort of Indian. I mean they weren't like the Aztecs or the Incas. No civilization or anything. On the whole they were a pretty poor lot.'

68

THE SALESIAN FATHERS in Punta Arenas had a bigger museum than the one at Río Grande. The prize exhibit was a glass showcase containing the photo of a young, intolerant-looking Italian priest, the cured skin of a sea-otter and an account of how the two came together:

On September 9th 1889 three Alakalufs of the *canales* came to Father Pistone and offered him the otter skin, now conserved in the museum. While the Father examined it, one Indian swung a machete and dealt him a terrible blow on the left maxilla. The other two immediately set on him. The Father struggled with these examples of *Homo Silvestris* but his wound was grave. After some days in agony, he died.

The killers had lived in the Mission for seven months, well-loved and cared for by the Salesians as adopted sons. But atavism, ambition and jealousy drove them to crime. Once they had done the deed, they fled. Some time after they returned, and, in contact with Our Religion, they became civilized and were good Christians.

Life-sized painted plaster effigies of the Indians stood in mahogany showcases. The sculptor had given them ape-like features
which contrasted with the glucose serenity of the Madonna from
the Mission Chapel on Dawson Island. The saddest exhibit was
two copy-book exercises and photos of the bright-looking boys
who wrote them:

THE SAVIOUR WAS IN THIS PLACE AND I DID NOT
   KNOW IT
IN THE SWEAT OF THY BROW SHALT THOU EAT BREAD.

So, the Salesians had noticed the significance of Genesis 3:19.
The Golden Age ended when men stopped hunting, settled in
houses and began the daily grind.

69

THE 'ENGLISHMAN' took me to the races. It was the sunniest
day of summer. The Strait was a flat, calm blue and we could
see the double white crown of Mount Sarmiento. The stands had
a coat of fresh white paint and were full of generals and admirals
and young officers.

The 'Englishman' wore suede boots and a tweed cap.

'Day at the races, eh? Nothing like a good race-meeting.
Come along with me now. Come along. Come into the V.I.P.'s
box.'

'I'm not dressed properly.'

'I *know* you're not dressed properly. Never mind. They're
quite broad-minded. Come along. Must introduce you to the
Intendente.'

But the Intendente took no notice. He was busy talking to the
owner of *Highland Flier* and *Highland Princess*. So we talked to a
naval captain who stared out to sea.

'Ever hear the one about the Queen of Spain,' the 'Englishman'
asked, trying to liven up the conversation. 'Never heard the one
about the Queen of Spain? I'll try and remember it:

A moment of pleasure
Nine months of pain
Three months of leisure
Then at it again.'

'You are speaking of the Spanish Royal Family?' The Captain inclined his head.

The 'Englishman' said he had read history at Oxford.

70

THE OLD lady poured tea from a silver teapot and watched the storm blot out Dawson Island. Three chains of gold nuggets were festooned round her neck: she used to pay her peons to wash them from her streams. Soon the storm would break on this side of the Strait.

'Oh, it was beautifully done,' she said. 'Of course, we heard rumours before, but nothing happened. And then we saw the planes circling the city. There was a bit of shooting in the morning and by afternoon they had all the Marxists rounded up. It was beautifully done.'

Her farm had been one of the showplaces of Magallanes. Her father had an estate in the Highlands as well. They'd stay for the grouse and stalking and sail at the end of October.

In 1973 the Government gave her two weeks to quit. Two weeks on property they'd had for seventy years. The letter came on the 2nd. Just a few ill-mannered lines to say she'd to be out by the 15th. She'd never worked as she worked in those two weeks. She stripped the house. Of everything. She took out everything. Even the light-switches. Even the marble surrounds for the baths. She'd had them sent out from home. But the men weren't going to have them. They were going to get nothing from her.

They stabbed her in the back, of course. The worst was a man she'd had for thirty years. Always helpful. Oh yes, always polite. She looked after him when he was sick and he only started to get uppity when the Marxists came in. He tried to stop the others loading cattle. Cattle she'd already sold, so *they* should have more for themselves. Then he turned off the heating oil, her oil, the oil she'd paid for.

It was terrible. They stole her dog and trained him to kill people. All that winter they were making knives. Waiting, just waiting for orders to kill them in their beds. And what did they do when they got the place? Ruined it! Burst pipes! Sheep in the vegetable garden! And in the flower garden! *They* had no use for vegetables. Wouldn't know what to do with them.

They'd complain they had no milk. Said they got T.B. *because* she gave them no milk. So she gave them milk, *which* they poured down the drain. They hated fresh milk. Only liked tinned milk! And what did they do when they got the dairy herd? Turned it into *bifes*! Ate the lot! They couldn't be bothered to milk the cows. Half the time they were too drunk to stand up.

And the bull ... Oh! the bull! You didn't know whether to laugh or cry about the bull. The Ministry bought this prize bull in New Zealand. No need for it! Plenty of good bulls next door in Argentina. But they couldn't buy an Argentine bull, not without losing face. So they flew the bull from New Zealand to Santiago, flew it to Punta Arenas, where it was presented, with Lord knows what in the way of speeches, to the so-called model farm. And how long did the bull last? How long before they ate it? Three days! Destroy and destroy. That's all they wanted. So there'd be nothing left.

She moved her furniture from the farm to the city, to the house she'd had for fifty years. The prettiest house in Punta Arenas, and of course, *they* wanted that too. Mr Bronsovič, the Party Boss, came three times. Nothing to stop him. No respect for private property in those days. Said the Party wanted it for its head-quarters and she said: 'Over my dead body!'

The second time he came with his wife, nosing in all her cupboards and even trying out the bed. And the last time he stood in the drawing-room with his Red thugs and said: 'It's all so English. And to think she lives here alone. Aren't you frightened living here all alone?'

Yes. She wasn't going to say it to him. She was frightened. So she sold the house to a Chilean friend. For nothing, of course. The peso was worth nothing. But *they* wouldn't get it. Not yet.

Not from her, anyway. And guess what Mrs Bronsovič did when she heard the place was sold. She sent a message: 'How much did she want for her chintz-covered suite?'

They arrested Bronsovič in his shop that morning. They marched him home, shaved his head and packed him off to Dawson Island. Then some of his friends went to the Intendente to try and get him out. 'You surprise me,' the Intendente said. 'Can you recognize his handwriting?' They said yes, and he showed them their own names on Bronsovič's death list and they then said: 'He'd better stay where he is.'

The storm broke. Chutes of rain battered the flower-filled garden. The new house was small but warm. It had fitted green carpets and Chippendale furniture.

'I'm not going away,' she said. 'I belong here. They'd have to kill me first. Besides, where would I go?'

71

At Casilla 182, Punta Arenas, an iron gate painted green, with crossed Ms twined about with Pre-Raphaelite lilies, led into a shadowy garden where still grew the plants of my grandmother's generation: the blood-red roses, the yellow-spattered laurels. The house had high-pitched gables and gothic windows. On the street side was a square tower, and at the back an octagonal one. The neighbours used to say: 'Old Milward can't decide if it's a church or a castle,' or 'I suppose he thinks he'll go to heaven quicker in a place like that.'

The house belonged to a doctor and his wife showed me into a hallway of solid Anglican gloom. From the tower room I looked out over the city: at the white spire of St James's Church; at metal houses painted the colour of a Slav handkerchief; at bank buildings and warehouses by the docks. The sun slunk in from the west and caught the scarlet bow of the car ferry. Beyond were the black hump of Dawson Island and the cliffs running down to Cape Froward.

My cousin Charley kept a telescope up in the tower, and as an old sick man he'd focus out into the Strait. Or he'd sit at a desk stirring his memory to recapture the ecstasy of going down to the sea in ships:

72

ON A blustery autumn day in 1870 a steam launch cast off from the landing stage at Rock Ferry on the Mersey and chugged towards H.M.S. *Conway*, the old ship-of-the-line, then moored in the channel as a training ship for the Merchant Marine. The two passengers were a boy of twelve and a gaunt but kindly clergyman, his face lined from mission work in India. The boy was 'a small, well-built lad, ugly of countenance, but not repulsive looking', his snub nose the result of interpreting the expression 'Put your nose to the grindstone' literally.

The Reverend Henry Milward had decided that no amount of slippering would temper his son's wildness and was sending him to sea.

'Promise me one thing,' he said, as the black and white gun-ports came up close. 'Promise me you'll never steal.'

'I promise.'

He kept his promise and his father was right to extract it: his own brother was a little light-fingered.

Charley ran up the rigging and waved goodbye, but the ship's bully, a boy called Daly, blocked his way down from the cross-trees and made him hand over his jack-knife and silver pencil case. Charley never forgot the tattoo on Daly's arm.

Two years later, his basic training was over, he joined the firm of Balfour, Williamson and went to sea. His first ship, the *Rokeby Hall*, took coal and railroad track to the West Coast of America and came back with Chilean nitrate. He left two accounts of his apprentice voyages. One is a log-book, in which the entries are short, seamanlike, and often in shaky hand-writing: 'Took on 640 bags of nitrate of soda.' 'Bardsey Island abeam.' 'Seaman Reynolds hurled against the wheel. Laid up.'

Or (his only comment on rounding the Horn) 'Changed course to NNE from SE'.

The other is the unpublished collection of sea-stories he wrote as an old man in Punta Arenas. Some of the yarns are a bit disordered and repetitive. Perhaps he was too ill to finish, or perhaps others discouraged him. But *I* think they are wonderful.

He put down on paper all he could remember, of ships and men, at sea or in port; the train journeys; the dismal ports of Northern England—'Liverpool or Middlesbrough are not places to raise your spirits to a high pitch'; the wet cobbles, the bed bugs in flophouses, and the crews coming aboard drunk. And then out in the tropics, riding the bowsprit, the sails slack and the white bow wave cutting the dark sea; or up aloft on a pitching yard-arm, with green water smashing over the deck, dragging in canvas that was wet through or frozen stiff; or waking one night in a norther off Valparaíso, the ship on her beam ends and his friend saying: 'Go to sleep, Ugly, you little fool, and you won't feel the drowning', and then thirty-six hours on the pumps and the cheers of the men as the pumps sucked dry.

Food was his overriding obsession. He wrote down 'the peas like marbles in coloured water'; 'the weevily biscuits, first weevily then maggoty'; and the salt beef 'more like mahogany than meat'. He wrote the names of the dishes the boys made themselves, from biscuit, peas, molasses and salt pork—Dandyfunk, Crackerhash, Dogsbody and Slumgullion—and the boils that came on after when they ate too much. Gratefully he remembered the friends who gave him an extra feed—an old steward or a German pastrycook in a Chilean port. He remembered how the boys raided the skipper's locker and came back with pillowcases of tinned lobster, tongue, salmon and jam; how he couldn't eat them because of his promise; how he cried when the skipper found the theft and stopped their Christmas pudding; how the cook slipped them the plum duff all the same; and how, when the Captain surprised them, he stuffed his slice under his shirt and ran up the main yard and blistered his tummy.

He wrote down the yarns of San Francisco's Barbary Coast; the boarding-house masters who fed hungry sailors and delivered them, drugged, aboard crew-starved ships. Sammy Wynn was the worst of these men. He got three cadets to desert from an Austrian man-of-war but, when the reward proved higher than his blood-money, shipped them back to court martial and the death sentence.

There were the easy Californian girls; the rough justice of the magistrates' courts; or the Beale Street Gang, who drained Spanish wine out of barrels into a boat while Charley ate pumpkin pie with the watchman on the wharf; or the King of the Hoodlums who raided the ship in white tie and tails, and the silver watch Charley got for seeing this gentleman off ship.

He remembered Ah-sing, the Chinese laundryman, who spat starch from his mouth; and the Chinese crew, decked out in gorgeous silks, burning joss-sticks, bowing to the sun while flying-tackle whizzed round their heads. There were the Chilean nitrate ports; pisco vendors; shanties of whale ribs and gunny bags; and the mule trains snaking down the cliff and the odd mule slipping and falling six hundred feet to the beach below.

There was Able-Seaman Lambert, beaten black and blue for winning at poker. There were the rats that *did* leave a doomed ship; swimming races among sharks; and the time the boys hooked an eighteen-foot monster on their best shark hook: the mate wouldn't let it aboard because of some new paint, so they triced it to the stern and Charley went down on a rope's end and cut its heart out: 'I have since ridden many curious animals, but I never found anything so hard to stick to.'

The last bale of wool at Melbourne; the last sack of rice at Rangoon; the last bag of nitrate at Iquique—he put them down. And the ship easing out of harbour, and all the men singing in chorus the shanty 'Homeward Bound!' And the Captain calling: 'Steward! Grog for all hands!'—the old Geordie skipper, dressed in black and white check trousers and a green frock-coat, with a soft white hat for sea and a hard white hat for port. Charley got him down too.

Here is a story from his apprentice years.

73

WE WERE close to the Horn, running with all plain sail set to a spanking breeze on the starboard quarter. It was a Sunday morning. I was walking up and down the main hatch with Chips the Carpenter and he said: 'The girls at home are pulling with both hands.'

It's an old sailor's idea that every ship has a rope with one end made fast to her bows and the other held by the loved ones at home. And when the ship has a fair wind sailors say the girls are pulling hard on the rope. But when the wind is foul, some say there's a knot or a kink in the rope, which won't go through the block; and others say the girls are sparking round with the soldier chaps and have forgotten their sailor laddies.

Just then four bells struck. It was 10 a.m. and my turn to relieve the wheel. I had hardly got the middle spoke to my satisfaction, when the breeze backed northward a couple of points, so that the squaresails took some wind out of the fore- and aft-canvas. The carpenter was still walking up and down when the ship rolled heavily to port. There was no wind in the main royal staysail and the sheet hung slack in a bight on the deck. The carpenter lost his balance in the roll and, by mistake, laid his foot on the staysail sheet. With the next roll to windward, the sail filled again and tightened the sheet like a fiddle-string and caught Chips between the legs and dropped him in the sea.

I saw him go. I left the wheel a second and threw him a life-buoy. We put the helm down and threw the ship into the wind, letting the top-gallant and royal halyards fly. While some hands cleared the accident boat, the rest began to get in the kites (as the small sails are called), and in less than ten minutes the boat was on her way to pick up the carpenter, whom we could see swimming strongly.

At the cry 'Man Overboard!' the whole of the 'watch below' had come on deck. First into the accident boat was the apprentice Walter Paton. The Second Mate, Mr Spence, knew Paton couldn't swim much and told him to get out, and Philip Eddy, another apprentice, jumped into his place. Walter was not to be put off, though, and got in over the bows. The boat was in the water before Mr Spence saw him, and I heard a few remarks as they passed under the stern of the ship. Then we lost sight of them in the heavy sea that was running.

The boat left the ship at 10.15, all the crew with their lifebelts on. We were busy for some time getting the ship shortened down. The Captain was aloft on the mizzen cross-trees watching the boat. They had a long pull to windward and it was not till 11.30 that they were close to us coming back. But we couldn't see if they had the carpenter or not.

The Captain gave the order to 'Up Helm' for the purpose of wearing ship, to bring the boat's davits on the lee side and so hoist it aboard, and we all saw Mr Spence stand up and wave his arms. Whether to say they'd got the carpenter, or whether he thought we hadn't seen them, will never be known. But in that one fatal second, his attention was off the boat, and she broached to and capsized. She was close to us, not more than two cables, and we saw them all swimming in the water.

We put the helm down again and brought the ship into the wind. We hurried to get out the second boat, but in a sailing ship this is a very different matter from getting out the first. One boat was always ready, but the others were all bottom up on the skids; and not only bottom up, but stuffed full of gear. The Captain's fowls were in one. All the cabbages for the voyage were in another, and firebuckets and stands were stowed there to prevent them being washed overboard.

The men turned over the port boat first. But just as they had her over, a big wave struck the ship and two of them slipped, and she came down heavily and was staved in the bilge. Meanwhile I was watching the men in the water with glasses. I saw some helping others on to the bottom of the overturned boat. Then I saw Eddy and one of the Able-Seamen leave and swim towards the ship. They swam so close we could see who they were without glasses. But we were drifting faster than they could swim and they had to go back.

After turning over the starboard boat, we had to put a tackle on the main royal backstay to lift it over the side. And I don't know whether the man who put the strop on the backstay was incapable or hurried, but, time after time, the strop slipped and each time the boat came down. And the ship was drifting, drifting to leeward, and we lost sight of the boat and the poor fellows clinging to the keel. But we knew where it was by the flights of birds wheeling round the spot—albatrosses, mollymauks, sooty petrels, stinkpots—all circling round and round.

The second boat, with Mr Flynn in charge, got away, but it was nearly 1 p.m. when she passed under the stern. She had a longer pull to windward and the men were hindered by their lifebelts. And she had a much longer pull back as the ship was drifting to leeward all the time.

We lost sight of her after twenty minutes and there began a weary wait for us, knowing five of our comrades were doing their level best to cling to the upturned keel. The Captain put the ship on one tack and then another, but finally decided to remain hove to and not lose ground. So we lay there straining our eyes for the return of the boat.

At 3.30 we saw her coming back. She came in under the stern but the wind and sea had risen and it was some time before she dared come alongside. By then we had realized the worst and locked the tackles on in silence and hoisted the boat inboard. Two or three of the men were bleeding about the head, those whose caps and sou' westers were not fastened. When the ship was back on course, we were able to ask questions and the gist of what we heard was this:

They had found the boat. They had brought back the lifebuoy I threw to the carpenter, and three of the five lifebelts, and had seen the other two in the sea, but not a sign of anyone. Then the birds attacked and they had to fight them off with stretchers. They swooped on their heads and took their caps off, and the men who were bleeding were struck by the cruel beaks of the albatrosses. When they examined the lifebelts and found all the strings untied, they knew what had happened. The birds had gone for the men in the water and gone for their eyes. And the poor chaps had willingly untied the strings and sunk when they saw that no help came, for they couldn't fight the birds with any hope of winning. The lifebuoy proved they had rescued the carpenter before the second accident occurred. It made us all the sadder to know that they had accomplished this mission.

After six and a half hours they relieved me from the wheel. It was the longest trick I ever experienced. I went down to the half-deck to get something to eat, but when I saw Walter's and Philip's bedclothes turned down and their pants lying on their chests, and their boots on the floor, just as they had left them at the cry 'Man Overboard!', I lost control of myself, thought no more of being hungry and could do nothing but sob. Later the Skipper told the Third Mate to take me away and let me sleep in his cabin.

'It's enough to drive the boy mad, in there with all those empty bunks.'

74

IN 1877 Charley signed on as Second Mate on the *Childers*, a full-masted barque bound for Portland, Oregon. She was a lousy ship. The Captain foul-mouthed his mother; the crew mutinied; and the Aberdonian Mate came at Charley with an axe. One trip was enough. He left, joined the New Zealand Shipping Company and stayed twenty years, graduating from cargo to passenger ships and from sail to steam.

One evening in the late 1880s he was in the first steam room of the Aldgate Turkish Baths, alongside a big black-bearded man, who sat snoozing in a canvas chair. The face meant nothing but the tattoo on the arm had to be Daly's. Charley sneaked behind, capsized the chair and left the scarlet imprint of his hand on the man's back. Daly howled and chased Charley naked through the baths till the assistants overpowered them both. Charley managed to smooth the incident over and soon got talking about the 'dear old *Conway*'. They left the baths together, went to a theatre and dined at the Criterion.

'Verily,' Charley wrote, 'we are as ships that pass in the night.'

Slowly—for he was not brilliant and his tongue did not always endear him to his superiors—he rose up the ranks of the service. In 1888 he was 2nd Officer on a mail steamer with a big freezing compartment. When she called in at Rio, the Emperor Dom Pedro II asked the agents if he could come aboard:

'On arriving at the top of the ladder, the Emperor held out his imperial hand to be kissed by the various Portuguese and Brazilians present and then handed it to his secretary to be wiped. After each kiss the secretary produced a fresh handkerchief and wiped the hand before it was presented to the next kisser, no doubt a highly salubrious measure ... But the Captain was unaccustomed to "kiss hands". He seized it with a warm grasp and shook it most heartily, saying: "I have great pleasure in welcoming Your Majesty aboard my ship." To say the Emperor was surprised is to put it mildly. Probably his hand hadn't been shaken like that since he was a boy. He looked at it as much as to say: "Well, old chap, you were lucky to get out of that one", and passed it to his secretary to be wiped.'

Charley took the Emperor down to the freezer and showed him his first deep-frozen pheasant. Dom Pedro said to his secretary: 'We must have a freezer in Rio at once'; but before he got it, Charley said, he was deposed by 'that awful ingrate, General Fonseca'.

75

CHARLEY LOVED amateur theatricals, and, on rising to the rank of Chief Officer, gave orders for plays, charades, tableaux, potato races—anything to relieve the boredom of ten weeks at sea.

Some of the entertainments were rather unusual:

'I was Chief officer of R.M.S. *Tongariro* and when we called in at Capetown there came aboard a Professor with three Bushman Pygmies from the Kalahari Desert—an old couple and their son. They were very small, the tallest and youngest being about 4ft 6in. I don't know if they had names already but we called them Andrew Roundabout the Elder, Mrs Roundabout, and Young Andrew Roundabout.

'The old pair were very old indeed. The doctor declared that, from the white ring round the pupil of his eye, the man must be over a hundred. He himself claimed to be 115, but this was a matter of conjecture. They couldn't speak one word of Dutch, or at least only Young Andrew could; the parents spoke no language anyone could understand.

'The old man was a curious one to look at. He hadn't a hair on his head and his face was wizened and wrinkled like a monkey's. But he had his wife and son in complete subjection, so we guessed he'd been a bit of a Tartar in his time.

'We asked the Professor to give a lecture on them, and he informed us they would dance first. We were all anxious to attend, and by 8.30 the saloon was well-filled with ladies and gentlemen in evening dress, and the Captain and officers in mess uniforms. The performance began with the old man twanging his bowstring and Mrs Roundabout and Young Andrew hopping about in a most grotesque fashion. Soon Old Roundabout got excited and banged and thumped the string in double-quick time; then he unstrung the bow and using it as a whip, started lashing his wife and son till they fairly skipped round. We imagined they hadn't danced fast enough for his liking. But after a minute or two the Professor stopped them and began.

'He exhibited a lot of skulls of the various races – Europeans, Asiatics, American Indians, Chinese, Negroes, Australian Blacks and finally the skulls of Bushmen. He said that, by measurements and size of brainpan, the Bushmen Pygmies were *not* the lowest of the human race by many points and that the lowest were the Australian Blacks.

'The lecture was very interesting, but I noticed Old Roundabout looking very uneasy. Then he slipped under the table and crawled among the audience's legs to the door. Once outside, he took to his legs and ran. I fetched him back but he struggled violently. I put him in his seat and had a lot of bother getting him to stay there.

'Afterwards I asked Young Andrew, through an interpreter: "What did your father mean by running out of the lecture?" And this is what he said:

' "My father has been to plenty of these meetings. He knew quite well when the 'killing time' was coming. He was sure it was very near when he ran. He ran because he was the oldest person there. So, of course, he would be the first to be killed." '

76

IN 1890 Charley married a New Zealand girl, Jenetta Ruther-ford, and between voyages fathered two boys and a girl. She was a tragic figure, worn down by loneliness and the English climate. Her husband's attitude to marriage perhaps corresponded to the quotation I found in his scrap-book under the title *This Freedom*:

It is the man's part to sow and ride away; conception is the woman's office and that which she receives she tends to cherish and incorporate within her. Of her body that function is her glory; of her mind it is the millstone. A man rides away, a tent-dweller, an arab with a horse and the plains about him. Woman is a dweller in a city with a wall, a house-dweller, storing her possessions about her, abiding with them, not to be sundered from them.

By 1896 Jenetta's health could take England no longer and she moved to Cape Town with the children. She died there on March 3rd 1897, of tuberculosis of the hip. Charley took the children back to live with his unmarried sister in Shrewsbury.

77

SIX MONTHS later he got his first command. She was the *Mataura*, a single-screw cargo-passenger ship of 7,584 tons newly built on the Clyde. She carried 20,000 bales of wool and the

same number of frozen carcasses. She ran a few sails aloft to
steady her roll to make steerage in a crisis, but she had no
radio.

The outbound voyage was uneventful and the company
boisterous. His passengers were the New Zealand Shooting
Team returning from the Kolapura Cup. On the night of their
arrival in Wellington, the Mayor gave a soirée in the Drill Hall.
Charley had diarrhoea, had lost his evening clothes and sat
unnoticed at the back until his passengers called for a speech.

'My Lords, Gentlemen,' he said. 'I am grateful to have been
the means under Providence of bringing these brave New
Zealand warriors to their hearths and homes,' and sat down.

Nobody clapped but a tiny, wizened Frenchman, who said:
'Capitaine, you 'ave make the best speech of the evening.'

'Only if brevity be the soul of wit,' said Charley.

The Frenchman, whose name was Henri Grien, came aboard
in the morning and asked for a free passage home in return for a
half share in the patent diving dress he hoped to sell to the
British Admiralty. He said it worked on the principle of the
copper steam-hose. Anyone could go down to sixty fathoms in
perfect safety, though the Danish diver, who first tried it out off
Sydney Heads, was hauled up dead.

'Why didn't you go down yourself?'

'Fool,' said Henri. 'If I go down in suit and he goes wrong,
who is to say what is matter with?'

Charley signed him on, not so much for the suit, but as a
source of entertainment.

''Ave been in communication with the spirit world,' Henri
announced one morning. 'This ship will sink but all crew will
be save.'

'Quite so, Henri. Thank you.'

About this time Charley had another communication from a
woman onshore, who also dreamed the ship would go down.

Half an hour before sailing, his friend, Captain Croucher of the
S.S. *Waikato*, came aboard and asked for a man to complete his
articles.

'I must have a man. Give me anything in trousers and I'll
make him do.'

'You can take that if you like,' Charley pointed to the Frenchman swabbing the floor of his cabin. 'Henri, pack your bag and get aboard the *Waikato*.'

'No.'

'Did you understand? You're going home on the *Waikato*?'

'No.'

Charley took him by the neck, ran him down the ladder, kicked him up the pants and had his baggage thrown on to the wharf. Henri ran for a warrant for assault, but the magistrate was at lunch and he ran back. As the *Mataura* backed out of Queen's Wharf, he got abreast of the bridge and, mounting a bollard, shouted:

'Capitaine, remember, there is trouble to eastward.'

Charley saw some loose coal lying on deck and called to the Bosun: 'Have a shot, Bosun. See if you can knock him off his perch.'

The Bosun let fly a lump and 'fairly knocked him off', but Henri ran and stood on the corner bollard, yelling:

'Remember, there is trouble to eastward.'

'Have another shot, Bosun.'

But the Bosun missed and the last they saw of him was a tiny figure waving its arms, still standing on the bollard.

78

ON THE following Sunday, Captain, passengers and crew were ending Divine Service in the Saloon. The Chief Engineer was playing the last hymn, when there was a bang and a shudder and the engine stopped in half a revolution. Many were thrown flat.

Charley rushed to the bridge where the Chief Engineer soon joined him.

'She's completely ... She'll never go again.'

'That's nonsense. She's got to go again.'

But the Chief shrugged and retired to his cabin for a drink. Charley relieved him of his functions and went down to inspect the damage. The engine room was a 'frightful mess'; the pumps driven off the crosshead; the rocking levers and piston rods bent; and the pump's spears and links all broken. There must have been some fault in the design, and even at the Board of Trade Enquiry, no one was quite sure what happened. Apparently the circulating water hadn't escaped and the pump had come down on a solid body of water 'which as everyone knows is not compressible'.

The Second Engineer was less of a fatalist and succeeded in straightening some of the twisted metal and getting the engine to tick over. Charley rigged up some squaresails and, for three weeks, the *Mataura* limped along at four knots with the Roaring Forties behind her.

The ship had orders to round the Horn, but if the engine packed up there, she'd be swept on into the South Atlantic. So Charley decided to risk the worst lee shore in the world and make the western entrance of the Strait of Magellan. Once inside Cape Pilar, the northern tip of Desolation Island, he had a good chance of saving the ship.

At 8 a.m. on January 12th he called for the Chief Engineer, who had resumed his job. He explained they were on a lee shore and asked if he wanted to tighten the pump chains. The Chief said: 'No. She'll go another twenty-four hours as far as I can see.'

At 11.45 in a full north-westerly gale with driving mist and rain, Charley sighted the Judges' Rocks about half a mile distant. The ship was twelve miles south of her calculated position. He headed her up into the teeth of the wind to clear the Outer Apostle Rock lying off the Cape. But the gale buffeted her back and, as the rock drew up close, he took bearings and doubted if he'd weather it.

At 2 p.m. the Chief came on deck and said: 'The chains are wearing loose. We'll have to stop.'

'We can't stop,' Charley yelled.

'She may go twenty minutes but no more.'

Charley called his officers: 'If she'll go twenty minutes, she may go thirty. And if I make a fair wind by going inside the Outer Apostle, we'll round the Cape before the engines give out. I know it's dangerous, but any rock with less than twenty-six feet must break in this sea and there is no break.'

He bore away and went inside. Ten minutes later the ship's stern came down crash on a small pinnacle of rock. He felt the plates tearing off her and knew she was hurt badly. He blew the whistle to close watertight bulkheads, but the Chief had mislaid the spanner to close the tunnel doors. Water flooded the engine room and soon the fires were out.

The coast of Desolation Island is nicked with short fjords. Through binoculars Charley saw a break in the cliffs, which he took for the Sealers' Cove marked on his chart. The sails still gave him some steerage way and he made for the entrance. As the bay opened up, he saw an arm of sheltered water with a shingle beach at the end. 'I'll run her in there,' he thought, 'and save her yet.' But the stern was all awash, the ship didn't respond to the helm, she yawed sideways and stuck against the side of the passage.

The bay was not Sealers' Cove but another (on modern charts it appears as Mataura Cove and the rock as Milward Rock). They took to the boats and pulled into the inner harbour, sleeping in them that night with the gale roaring above. At dawn the Chief Officer led a party to get provisions from the wreck, but they came back empty-handed. Charley had to go himself and returned with 11 sheep, 200 rabbits and 5 cwt of flour.

'How did you manage it, Sir?' the Chief Officer asked.

'Well, Sir,' Charley said, 'the reason you couldn't manage it is that you, Sir, are a coward.' Thereafter relations were strained between the Captain and his officers.

In the morning they rowed out to sea, but the gale was yet blowing and the men blistered their hands and they saw they would not round the Cape that day. Back at Mataura Cove, they began boiling the sheep and rabbits in galvanized buckets. Checking through the stores with the Chief Steward, Charley found two cases of jam which the ship's boys had slipped in.

'What in God's name d'you think's the use of jam in circumstances such as ours?'

'But what could be better than jam, Sir?'

'Steward,' muttered Charley, 'I suppose you'd better make jam rolls.'

It was raining so hard they had to cover him with a tarpaulin or the dough would have been too thin.

Two of the passengers were ladies, who had lost their box in the wreck, so Charley rigged them out with his own lambswool drawers and Guernsey frocks. Next morning the boats tried to round the Cape a second time but failed. At a council of war, Charley said he'd give it one more try and then head south along the coast of Desolation Island and enter the Strait by the Abra Channel. The officers said it was suicidal.

Again the weather was foul and he signalled with the lady's petticoat that he was going south. He reefed his lug and ran before the storm between the Judges' Rocks and the shore. The officers did not follow and the surgeon, in Charley's boat, reported them capsize one by one. Charley left them to their fate and went on, the boat shipping water up to the thwarts.

Under the lee of Child's Island they stopped at a sheltered beach, since Charley had promised the ladies a cup of tea at the first convenient spot. But when the men went ashore for fire-wood, the wind veered and breakers began rolling into the bay. Captain and crew had to strip and shove the boat out to sea: 'Oh! It was cold. And the sight of all hands naked was enough to make a cat laugh. We were red as lobsters and our teeth chattering.'

The ladies hid under a tarpaulin in the bottom of the boat while the men dried off, rubbing up against each other, naked, with a sail in between. Suddenly a cry came up from under-neath: 'Stop! Someone's sitting on mother's head and she can't breathe.'

By noon of next day, they were inside the Strait. They thanked Almighty God for their deliverance and settled down to a luncheon of soup, tinned salmon, boiled lamb and rabbit, boiled jam rolls 'which were a trifle filling' and coffee. In the afternoon they saw a Yankee schooner beating up the Strait. Her skipper offered to take the ladies to San Francisco, but they turned him down. Charley set two blankets as a spinnaker and the boat spanked down the channel towards Cape Froward.

On rounding the Cape, the wind was foul again and all hands took turns at the oars, rowing up the last reach to Punta Arenas. In the afternoon of the third day, the S.S. *Hyson* of the China Mutual Company picked them up. They docked at 6.30 p.m. Charley put the passengers in the Hotel Kosmos; told the German manager to give them anything they wanted with money no object; arranged for the Chilean Navy to send the tug *Yáñez* to look for the men; and argued till midnight with the salvage merchants but failed to come to terms.

Back at the hotel he barged in on the ladies.

'I've come to congratulate you on your safety,' he said.

But the ladies didn't stir.

'Aren't you going to shake hands?'

Slowly, out from under the bedclothes came a single hand. Charley was suspicious and gave it a tug. He wrote in his diary:

Behold! A bare arm followed. The landlord had done nothing for them and they had simply taken off their wet clothes and crawled in between the sheets.

'Please, Captain,' said the older lady. 'Please don't make trouble. We're warm and comfortable now.'

'I most certainly am going to make trouble.'

He knew where the manager slept and woke him roughly:

'How dare you send those poor ladies to bed with no nightgear?'

'Get out. I am in bed mit mine vife. How dare *you*? Get out at vonce!'

'I don't care where you are or who you're with. But if you don't obey me instantly, I can tell you where you'll both be in a few seconds. I am putting my foot in this door. I shall count up to thirty, and if no nightclothes are passed out, it will be my painful duty to strip you and your wife of yours. One, two, three, four ... '

Charley had counted twenty-five when the manager came to his senses and handed two ladies' nightgowns round the door. He took them in triumph to his passengers and retired for the best sleep of his life.

By morning the salvage merchants had reduced their terms to 80 per cent with 20 per cent for Lloyd's. Charley refused and by twelve they said these terms included 5 per cent for himself.

'Agreed,' he said. 'That makes 75 per cent for you and 25 per cent for the underwriters.'

Don José Menéndez, who was the ringleader, came up and said: 'Captain, you are one bloody fool. Why you not take the 5 per cent?'

'I am working for the insurers and they will pay me.'
'All the same, Captain, I repeat what I said. And one day you will find out.'

79

THREE HUNDRED and five years before Charley failed to weather Cape Pilar, Captain John Davis squeezed past it in the *Desire*:

'The next day being the 11 of October, we saw Cabo Deseado (Cape Pilar) being the cape on the south shore (the North shore is nothing but a company of dangerous rocks and shoals). This cape being within two leagues to leeward off us, our master greatly doubted, that we could not double the same: whereupon the captain told him: You see there is no remedy, either we must double it, or before noon we must die: therefore loose your sails, and let us put it to God's mercy.

'The master being a man of good spirit, resolutely made quicke dispatche and set saile. Our sayles had not been halfe an houre aboord, but the footrope of our foresaile brake, so that nothing held but the oylet holes. The seas continually brake over the ship's poope and flew into the sayles with such violence, that wee still expected the tearing of our sayles, or oversetting of the ship, and withall to our utter discomfort, wee perceived that wee fell still more and more to leeward, so that we could not double the cape, and so near the shore that the counter-suffe (counter-surf) of the sea would rebound against the shippes side, so that wee were much dismayed by the horror of our present ende.

'Being thus at the very pinch of death, the winde and the Seas raging beyond measure, our Master veared some of the maine sheate and whether it was by that occasion, or by some current, or by the wonderfull power of God, as wee verily thinke it was, the ship quickened her way, and shot past that rock, where we thought she would have shored. Then between the cape and the poynt there was a little bay so that wee were somewhat farther from the shoare: and when we were come so farre as the cape, wee yeelded to death; yet our good God the Father of all mercies delivered us, and wee doubled the cape by about the length of our shippe, or very little more. Being shot past the cape, we presently tooke in our sayles, which only God had preserved unto us and when we were shot in between the high lands, the wind blowing trade, without an inch of sayle, we spooned before the sea, three men being not able to guide the helm, and in six hours were put five and twenty leagues with in the Streights, where wee found a sea answerable to the Ocean.'

From *The Voyages and Works of John Davis*, ed. Albert Hastings Markham, 1880, pp. 115–16.

80

CHARLEY'S MEN did not drown. Their masts had carried away but the boats did not capsize. They rowed back to Mataura Cove, rounded the cape on the first fine day, and fell in with the *Yáñez*.

Charley spent two months on Desolation Island salvaging the wreck, before sailing to England to face the official enquiry. He knew he'd be out of a job. The New Zealand Shipping Company didn't give wrecked captains a second chance. But already the weird magnetism of the South held him and his head was full of money-making schemes.

His first plan was to advertise English and American products by lining the Strait of Magellan with blue and white enamel billboards. These were not principally for the benefit of steamer passengers. He intended to write illustrated articles in the international press calling the public's attention to 'the desecration of beautiful scenery by advertising fiends'.

For this scheme he did not find a backer.

One spring morning, unannounced to anyone, Charley got out of a hansom cab at the Company's offices in Leadenhall Street. Henri, the Frenchman, was standing on the pavement.

'Well, Capitaine, was I right? Was there trouble to eastward?'

Charley took no notice and dashed up the steps.

'How long's that man been standing there?' he asked Mortimer, the head porter.

'About ten minutes, Sir.'

'I don't mean today. I mean how long's he been hanging around?'

'This morning, Sir. First time I ever saw him.'

Charley took Henri by the throat and shook him.

'How did you know I was coming to England today?'

'Same as what told me there was trouble to eastward—the Spirits.'

'I do not attempt to explain this,' Charley wrote. 'I only state what happened. I left the office after an interview with the manager that lasted a few minutes, sacked—sacked after twenty years service, on account of my engine breaking down.'

He also reported to a Mr Lawrie of the London Salvage Association and asked for £3 reimbursement for his bill at the Hotel Kosmos.

'Captain, I think you've made enough from your wreck to pay your hotel bill.'

Now he understood what José Menéndez meant.

'I nearly told the man I could have made £2,000 but I was honest. Then I saw it was useless to speak to a man like that of honesty. He wouldn't know the meaning of the word.'

81

CHARLEY SULKED in Shrewsbury that summer but in August had a letter from a Mr William Fitzgerald of *Wide World Magazine*, offering to pay his first-class rail fare to London. At the office he looked round for someone to present his card and then rapped on the door marked Editor and walked in. Henri Grien, in a smart suit, was pacing the floor, while a young man dictated to a secretary.

'Hello, Henri, and how are you?'

'I not know you.'

The young man jumped up from his desk.

'What the Devil do you mean, Sir, coming into my room without knocking and addressing this gentleman as Henri when his name is Louis de Rougemont.'

'Keep your hair on, young fellow. There was no one to bring my card in. I knocked twice. I addressed Henri Grien by his proper name. And as you yourself, Sir, asked me to come, I expected a different reception, but since you have so few manners I wish you a good morning.'

Charley made for the door but the Frenchman threw his arms round his neck and kissed him.

'Oh! It is my little Capitaine. Forgive me. I did no recognize you. You 'ave shave your beard.'

Charley was still nettled and strode out. The Frenchman followed.

'You can't go now, Mr de Rougemont,' the editor called. 'We have to prepare your speech for the British Association on Friday.'

'I don't care nothing for no speech. I am going with my little Capitaine.'

Neither of them cared for strong waters and went to an A.B.C. eating house in the Strand. For the first time Mr Fitzgerald had heard the name, Henri Grien:

82

HENRI GRIEN was the son of an irritable and slovenly Swiss peasant of Grasset on Lake Neuchâtel. At sixteen he ran away from his ancestral muck-cart into the arms of the ageing actress Fanny Kemble, who employed him as her footman and, for seven years, carried him into the world of footlights and greasepaint. His talent for acting went unnoticed and, in 1870, he followed that other destiny of theatrical failures: domestic service, as butler to Sir William Cleaver Robinson, the appointed Governor of Western Australia. The Governor's tastes were musical and poetic; among his friends was a French savant, M. Louis de Rougemont, the author of a treatise on virginity.

Henri left the governor and assumed the career of a drifter. He was cook on a pearling schooner and was wrecked. He was hotel dishwasher, and street-photographer in a gold-rush town. In 1882, he married a beautiful young wife who gave him four children. He became a landscape painter, working from photographs, a salesman of apocryphal mining shares, and waiter in a Sydney restaurant. One of his customers was the explorer of the Cambridge Gulf region, whose diaries Henri borrowed and copied out. Next he experimented with the diving suit that asphyxiated the Dane.

He skipped from Australia, away from the police and his wife's maintenance order, and in Wellington, New Zealand, took up with some spiritualists who found him an excellent medium. He told his life story to a journalist, who said it would make a bestseller as fiction, but Henri would not hear of this; by now dream and reality had fused into one. One summer evening he borrowed a black tie and wormed his way into the Drill Hall, where he met Captain Charles Amherst Milward.

He did come to England aboard the *Waikato* —and seems to have cursed her as well. (Shortly after, her propeller shaft broke off the Cape of Good Hope, and she was sucked south by the Agulhas Current, drifting for four months, the longest steamer drift on record. Conrad used it for his story *Falk*.) In the late spring he appeared at *Wide World*, dressed shabbily, but with a letter from a Conservative M.P. which said: 'This man has a story which, if true, will stagger the world.'

Henri told Fitzgerald he was the son of a rich Parisian merchant called de Rougemont. As a boy his mother took him to Switzerland, where he developed an aptitude for geology and trick wrestling. To avoid returning to a military career in France, he went travelling in the East; sailed with a Dutch pearler from Batavia, and was the only survivor when their schooner sank. Stranded on a coral reef, de Rougemont rode turtles for amusement, built a house of pearl shells, and made a canoe (which, like Robinson Crusoe's, was too heavy to haul to the beach).

After a number of trials, he reached the Australian mainland at Cambridge Gulf, married a coal-black woman called Yamba, and lived thirty years among the Aborigines, eating yams, snakes and witchety grubs (but never human flesh); sharing their treks, hunts, battles and corroborees. His skill in wrestling made him a tribal hero and he rose to the rank of chief. Only when Yamba died did he strike out for White civilization. At Kimberley he ran in with some gold-miners.

Mr Fitzgerald prided himself on his nose for a fake. He heard de Rougemont tell his story 'as a man might describe a bus ride' and was convinced of its veracity. That summer a team of journalists and stenographers hacked it together for publication. The key witness, Captain Milward, held his tongue: he knew what happened last time he crossed Henri Grien.

The first instalment of *The Adventures of Louis de Rougemont* appeared in July and there was an immediate run on the magazine. The book was in press. Cables flew round the world arguing the price of syndication. Hostesses pressed invitations on the Frenchman. Madame Tussaud's pressed a wax mask over his face, and the British Association for the Advancement of Science invited him to give two lectures to its annual congress at Bristol.

At the first lecture the audience was bored. He tried to liven up the second with cannibalistic details of his married life with Yamba, but the same day saw the eclipse of his reputation. The *Daily Chronicle*, sensing a scoop, carried a leader calling de Rougemont a fraud. More denunciations followed and a chorus of academics joined in. Throughout the autumn, as the British Empire rose to its zenith, the de Rougemont fraud held the headlines with the Battle of Omdurman, the Fashoda Incident, and the reopening of the Dreyfus Case. The *Daily Chronicle* found his old mother at Grasset, and on October 21st a Mrs Henri Grien of Newtown, Sydney, identified de Rougemont as the man who owed her maintenance of twenty shillings and five pence a week.

The traveller withstood the attacks with unblushing calm and resumed the theatrical career of Henri Grien. The London Hippodrome imported some turtles and rigged up a rubber tank on stage, but either the climate or the rider had a discouraging effect on them, for they were overcome with drowsiness. He then took his show *The Greatest Liar on Earth* to Durban and Melbourne. The audiences howled him to silence.

On June 9th 1921 Louis Redmond, as he was now called, died in the Infirmary of the Kensington Workhouse.

83

As the journalists were debunking de Rougemont, Charley sailed back to Punta Arenas. The wildness was not yet burned out in him.

The course of his second career is clouded by time and distance. I have had to reconstruct it from faded sepia photographs, purple carbons, a few relics and memories in the very old. The first impressions are of an energetic pioneer, confident in his new handlebar moustache; hunting elephant seals in South Georgia; salvaging for Lloyd's; helping a German gold-panner dynamite the Mylodon Cave; or striding round the foundry with his German partner, Herr Lion, inspecting the water turbines or the lathes they imported from Dortmund and Göppingen. Lion was a methodical man, who ran the place while Charley chatted up clients. Panama was not yet cut through and the business was good.

The second set of images are of the British Empire's southernmost Consul, a senior citizen of Punta Arenas and director of its bank. He was making money all right (but never quite enough), stiffening with lumbago and 'wearying for news' of home. Old members of the British Club still remember him. And I sat in the tall rooms, painted an under-sea green and hung with sporting prints and lithographs of Edward VII. Listening to the chink of whisky glasses and billiard balls, I could picture him on one of the buttoned wash-leather sofas, stretching out his bad leg and talking of the sea.

Among his letters from these years I found one to my grandfather hoping the *Titanic* disaster hadn't put him off yachting; a note to the Hon. Walter Rothschild about a shipment of Darwin's Rheas; and a report, on consular notepaper, to the employer of a dead Scot: 'He has been a disgrace to the name of Britisher ever since he came here ... He used his basin as a W.C. His room was an insult to any animal and his box contained fifteen empty whisky bottles. I am sorry but the truth is best.'

A mood of despair gradually creeps into these letters. None of his schemes ever quite turned out as planned. He drilled for oil in Tierra del Fuego, but the drill broke. The land at Valle

Huemeules promised big returns, but there were sheep-thieves, pumas, squatters and an unscrupulous land-shark: 'We are having the devil of a hitch with our land in the Argentine. The Government has given it away to a Jew who has kindly sworn that all my sheep and buildings are his.' Rather than lose all, he asked the Brauns and Menéndezes for help and they soon whittled his share down to 15 per cent.

In 1913 he brought his son out, fresh from school in England, as part of his scheme for toughening him up. Harry Milward stuck out one long snowbound winter at Valle Huemeules, loathed the farm, the farm-manager, and at this point his father. Not surprising with letters that ended: 'Now goodbye, my lad, and don't forget that God, although you are so very far from any means of grace, still he is just as near you there as here. Your ever loving father ... ' The rest of Harry's career was predictable. He went to the war, joined a fast set, married three times and ended up in England, the secretary of a golf club.

In Charley's album I found photos of the new house under construction, a Victorian parsonage translated to the Strait of Magellan. He gave half the plot for St James's Anglican Church and was its warden and principal benefactor. Proudly he unpacked the font given by Queen Alexandra. Proudly he welcomed the Bishop of the Falklands for the consecration. But the church was yet another source of trouble. He accused the vicar of choosing obscure hymns so as to show off his own voice solo. The congregation, he insisted, had a right to '*Abide with Me*' or '*Oft in Danger, Oft in Woe*'. The Rev. Cater whispered round that Captain Milward was a secret drinker.

The war caught him off his guard, in a Buenos Aires hospital, having an intestinal operation. But the war was soon upon him. Admiral Craddock's visiting card, still pinned to the green baize board in the British Club, is a reminder that the southernmost Consul was the last civilian to see him alive. Charley dined aboard the *Good Hope* two hours before the British fleet sailed for its disastrous encounter with the Germans off Coronel. In a memorandum he records the Admiral's gallant but weary acceptance of Churchill's orders: 'I am going to look for von Spee and if I find him, my number is hoisted.'

Charley hated the war: 'So many people cutting each other

throats and not knowing why.' He wasn't going to stoop to war hysteria. Nor would he break with his German partner. 'Lion is not one of the war-party,' he wrote, 'but a dear, good, honest white man.' The British community hated him for this and put it round that the Consul was politically unreliable. An anonymous letter appeared in the *Buenos Aires Herald*, referring to 'the British Consulate, as its consul is pleased to call it'.

Another relic of the war years is a gold watch presented for loyal services by the British Admiralty. After Admiral Sturdee sank von Spee's squadron off the Falklands, the cruiser *Dresden* got away and hid at the western end of the Beagle Channel, camouflaged by trees and provisioned by Germans from Punta Arenas. (British residents noticed the dwindling number of dogs in the town and joked about the doggy flavour of the German crew's sausages.) Charley found out where she was and cabled London. But, instead of acting on his advice, the Navy did the exact opposite.

The reason was simple: the 'true Britishers' had convinced the Admiralty that the Consul was a German agent and managed to get him sacked. Only when they realized their mistake did Charley get an apology. The watch was to compensate for the calumnies heaped upon him. It took a long time coming. 'I'll be in my grave,' he wrote, 'before I hear anything about that watch.'

The third exhibit from this time is a coloured print by Cecil Aldin, of dogs at a feeding bowl. It conjures up the image of Sir Ernest Shackleton, pacing round Charley's living-room, haranguing the newspaper editor, Mr Charles Riesco, about the plight of his men trapped on Elephant Island. From the article in the *Magellan Times*—'the deep set grey eyes' 'greatness equated by modesty' 'the best of our race' etc.—you would never guess what happened:

Charley was pretending to doze off in a wing chair while the explorer waved his revolver about to emphasize important points. The first bullet whizzed past Charley's ear and hit the wall. He got up, disarmed his guest and put the weapon on the mantelpiece. Shackleton was quite shaken, apologized and mumbled about the last bullet in the chamber. Charley sat down again, but Shackleton's flow was inseparable from his gun. The second bullet missed again, but hit the print. The hole is in the lower right margin.

Meanwhile the ex-consul's life had taken a new direction. He had met a young Scotswoman called Isabel, who had got stranded, penniless, in Punta Arenas, after working on an estancia in Santa Cruz. Charley looked after her and paid her fare back to Scotland. He was lonely again once she had gone. They wrote to each other: one of his letters contained a proposal.

Belle came back and they started a family. In 1919 Charley calculated his assets at £30,000, enough to retire on and provide for all his children. He sold the Fundición Milward to a Frenchman, M. Lescornez, and his partner Señor Cortéz, agreeing they should defer payments until business recovered from the post-war slump. The family packed, sailed for England, and bought a country house, 'The Elms', near Paignton.

Charley the Sailor home from sea. Charley the Pioneer with the restlessness gone; pottering round his garden; taking prizes at the Taunton Flower Show; growing old with his young wife in the English countryside; teaching the boy or playing with his two daughters, one showing signs of beauty, the other of his forthright personality—I am sad to report that this harmonious and symmetrical picture was not to be.

Panama was now cut through. Punta Arenas was again on the way to nowhere. Wool slumped. There was revolution in Santa Cruz. And the foundry failed.

Encouraged by two or more of the 'true Britishers', acting out of spite, the new owners milked the business, ran up debts, signed cheques in the Milward name, and ran.

Charley was ruined.

He kissed the children. He kissed Belle. He said goodbye for ever to the green fields of England. He bought a ticket to Punta Arenas, one way, third class. Friends in the first-class saw him gazing sorrowfully at the sea. They offered to pay the difference, but he had his pride. No deck games for him this voyage. He preferred to bunk with shepherds.

Belle sold 'The Elms' and followed, and for six years they picked up the pieces. Photos show a stooping old man in a homburg with huge whiskers and wounded eyes. He would hobble down to the foundry and growl at the men and laugh when they laughed. Belle kept the books; she would carry on for nearly forty years. Without her thrift they would have gone under, and, one by one, they paid off the debts.

I have one last image of Charley, dated around 1928, sitting in the tower with his telescope, straining to catch the last of the steamer that carried the boy to school in England. As she headed up eastward and was swallowed into the night, he said: 'I'll never see the lad again.'

84

I WAS in Punta Arenas on a Sunday and went to Matins at St James's. I sat in Charley's pew, knowing it was his by the brass ferrule screwed on for his walking stick. An American Baptist minister took the service. His sermon explained the technical difficulties of building the Verranzano Narrows Bridge, veered off among 'Bridges to God', and ended with a thundering call: 'Ye shall be that Bridge!' He asked us to pray for Pinochet but we were uncertain of the spirit in which our prayers were offered. In the congregation was an old Highland shepherd called Black Bob MacDonald who had worked for the Red Pig. 'Grand man!' he said.

I also met an American lady ornithologist, down here to study the fighting behaviour of Darwin's Rheas. She said the two males locked necks and whirled round in circles: the one who got dizzy first was the loser.

85

AN ENGLISHMAN suggested I take the air-taxi over to Porvenir on Tierra del Fuego and visit the old farm of one of Charley's contemporaries.

Mr Hobbs's cottage lay on the flat land between a flamingo lake and an arm of the Strait. It looked like a gentleman's shooting lodge, of clapboard painted a soft ochre, with white bay windows and a terracotta roof. White rambler roses tumbled over windbreaks enclosing the tiny garden. Some favourite English flowers lingered on long after the English had gone.

A Yugoslav widow had owned the place since land reform. She had put a peon in the house and let it go down. But the pitchpine floors were there and the curving banisters, and shreds of William Morris wallpaper adhered to the upper landing.

Mr Hobbs, from photos, was a thick-set man with wavy hair and a candid pink English face. He called his farm Gente Grande, 'the Big People' after the Onas who hunted here when he came. Even today the farm bore the mark of his taste for fine craftsmanship—the dog-kennels, the finials on the sheep-pens, even the pig-sty, which was painted the same colour as the house. It can't have changed much since Charley was here in 1900.

About a month before his visit, the Chilean man-of-war *Errazuriz* was surveying the north coast of Tierra del Fuego and sent a boat crew ashore. Two sailors got separated from the rest and were killed and stripped by the Indians.

A search-party went out next morning, but it was several days before they found the mutilated remains of the men. The Captain sent a force to punish the murderers, but the Onas, who knew what to expect, had bolted for the mountains.

'Tell me, Hobbs,' Charley said. 'What do you propose to do about the Indians? Now they've killed two sailors, they'll get too big for their boots and someone else'll suffer. Your homestead's handy, and what with your wife and children and nurses and servants, I think you'll be next to be honoured with their attentions.'

'I don't quite know what to do,' Hobbs said. 'The Government's so horribly nasty nowadays if you kill an Indian, even in self-defence. I'll have to wait and see what can be done.'

Charlie went back to the island a few months later and Hobbs asked him to look at some pigs he'd imported from England. On top of the sty was a fairly fresh human skull.

'You remember when the Indians killed the men from the *Errazuriz*,' Hobbs said.

'I do. I even asked you what you were going to do about it.'

'I said I'd wait and see. Well, now it's done and that is the result.'

Charley begged him tell the story, but he clamped up. Two nights later, they were in the smoking-room after dinner, when Hobbs began, suddenly: 'You were asking about the Indians. There isn't much to tell really. They began coming nearer the house. At first they stole one sheep at a time, and then they got bolder and took thirty and forty. Then one of my shepherds barely escaped by galloping his horse. So I decided it was time to do something.

'I sent out spies to report their strength and the exact place of their camp-site. I heard there were thirteen men, plus women and children. One day, when the women were not there, I gathered up my tame Indians, eight in all, and said: "We're going guanaco shooting." I armed them with old guns and revolvers. We started out a good party, but gradually I ordered my own men home, so when we drew near the Ona camp, we were only Indians, myself and one man.

'We sighted the Ona camp and I told my tame Indians to ask the wild ones where the guanaco were. But when they saw my lot coming with firearms, they let fly with arrows. The tame Indians, greeted in this manner, retaliated with rifles and killed a man. After that, of course, there was no quarter. The wild men were beaten and among the dead was the man who killed the sailors from the *Errazuriz*. That's his skull on the pig-sty.

'I, as district magistrate, had to file a report to the Government. I wrote that the tame Indians had been fighting wild ones. There had been some deaths, among them the wanted murderer.'

86

THE PILOT of the air-taxi introduced me to a Yugoslav who
flew freight to Dawson Island. He took me along. I wanted
to see the concentration camp where ministers of the Allende
regime were held, but the soldiers confined me to the aeroplane.

Charley had a story of the earlier prison on the island:

'The Salesian Fathers established a mission on Dawson Island
and asked the Chilean Government to send them any Indian
who was caught. The Fathers soon collected a great many
Indians and taught them the rudiments of civilization. This did
not suit the Indians in any way, and though they had food and
shanties to live in, they craved for their old wandering life.

'By the time I am speaking of, epidemics had reduced their
number to about forty. They had been giving a lot of trouble,
trying to escape, being mutinous, and refusing to work. Then,
suddenly, they became obedient and quiet. These signs did not
escape the Fathers, who noticed that the men were always tired
in the morning and would drop off to sleep in working hours.
They laid traps for them and found that the Indians went out into
the forest after having been placed in their huts at night. They
tried to follow, but an Indian always knew it, and would simply
roam in the woods for hours before returning to the settlement.

'This went on for several months and the Fathers got no
nearer the mystery. At last, one of them was returning from a
distant part of the island and lost his way. As night came on, he
lay down to rest—and heard voices through the trees. He crept
towards them and realized he had found the missing Indians. He
lay there all night, and when the Indians went back to resume their
day's labour, he came out of hiding. He found, hidden under
branches, a beautifully constructed canoe, dug out of a solid
tree trunk. They had made it so thin it was not too heavy to
handle, even though it was of immense size. The Indians were
tugging it to the beach about four hundred yards away, and the
Father found they had cleared a track almost to the water's edge.

'He went back to the Mission with the news. The Fathers held
a Council of War and decided to keep a sharp watch out and visit

the canoe from time to time to see how they were getting along. The days passed, as the unsuspicious Indians dragged their craft to the beach. It was a long job; for the summer nights were short and they could only shift it a few yards each night.

'The priests guessed that the Indians would wait till after Christmas Day, since they were promised extra rations. So while they were enjoying the Christmas festivities at the Mission, the Fathers sent two men with a cross-saw and newspapers. They cut the canoe through the middle, placing the newspaper on the ground to catch the sawdust, so the poor brutes would know nothing till all their provisions were aboard.

'The great night came, after weary months of waiting. They all gathered at the canoe and tried to drag it to the water—and it came away in two halves.

'That was the meanest trick I ever heard on these poor Indians, to find their canoe useless instead of carrying them away from their hated prison. It wouldn't have been half so bad if the Fathers had destroyed it when they first found it. But to allow the work to go on till the canoe was provisioned and hauled down to the beach, struck me as the very height of cruelty.

'I asked what the Indians did about it. I was told they went back to their shanties and carried on as if nothing had happened.'

87

I HAD one thing more to do in Patagonia: to find a replacement for the lost piece of skin.

The town of Puerto Natales was in sunshine, but purple clouds were piling up on the far side of Last Hope Sound. The roofs of the houses were scabby with rust and clattered in the wind. Rowan trees grew in the gardens and the red fire of their berries made the leaves seem black. Most of the gardens were choked with docks and cow parsley.

Raindrops smacked on the pavement. Old women, black specks along the wide street, scuttled for cover. I sheltered in a shop smelling of cats and the sea. The owner sat knitting socks of oiled wool. About her were strings of smoked mussels, cabbages, bricks of dried sea-lettuce, and trusses of kelp, coiled up like the pipes of a tuba.

Puerto Natales was a Red town ever since the meat-works opened up. The English built the meat-works during the First World War, four miles along the bay, where deep water ran inshore. They built a railway to bring the men to work; and when the place ran down, the citizens painted the engine and put it in the plaza—an ambiguous memorial.

The killing season used to last three months. The Chilotes had their first taste of mechanized slaughter at the killing season. It was something like their idea of Hell: so much blood and the floor red and steaming; so many animals kicking and then stiff; so many white-skinned carcasses and spilled-out guts, the tripes, brains, hearts, lungs, livers, tongues. It drove the men a little mad.

In the killing season of 1919, some Maximalists came up from Punta Arenas. They told how their Russian brothers had killed the management and now lived happily. One day in January the English Assistant Manager contracted two men for a painting job and refused to pay because the work was bad. They shot him through the chest that afternoon and then the rest of them ran amok. They commandeered the railway, told the driver to get up more steam, but there was no more steam and they shot him too. They lynched three carabineers and looted stores and burned them.

The Governor of Magallanes sent a ship with troops and a judge. They took twenty-eight ringleaders away and work went on in the meat-works, just as it was before the Maximalists came.

In the Hotel Colonial, I asked the owner's wife about the riot.

'It's too long ago,' she said.

'Then do you remember a man called Antonio Soto? He was the leader of the strike in Argentina, but he used to work here at the *Ciné Libertad*.'

'Soto? I don't know that name. Soto? No. You mean José Macías. He was in the strike. With the leaders too.'

'He lives here?'

'He did live here.'

'Can I find him?'

'He just shot himself.'

88

JOSÉ MACÍAS shot himself in his barber's shop, facing the mirror in his own barber's chair.

The last person to see him alive was a schoolgirl, who, at eight-thirty, had been walking up the Calle Bories, in a black dress and wide white collar, her shadow crinkling beside her along the corrugated housefronts. She looked at the windows of the house, painted a particularly arctic shade of blue, and saw — as she saw each morning — the barber eyeing her from behind the white blind. Shuddering, she hurried on.

At noon, the barber's cook, Conchita Marín, left her house on the ragged edge of town and walked up the Calle Baqueano to get her employer's lunch. She bought some vegetables in the corner shop and called in at the *Restaurant Rosa de Francia*, where she bought two empanadas for herself. When she saw the white blind drawn she knew that something was wrong.

The barber was a man of regular habits and would have told her if he intended to go out. She knocked but knew there would be no reply. She called on the neighbours but they hadn't seen the barber either.

Conchita Marín set down her basket. She wormed her way through the palings into the garden, opened the faulty catch of the kitchen window and climbed into the house.

Using an old Winchester, the barber had put a bullet through his right temple. With reflexes still functioning he had fired a second shot which missed and hit a calendar of the local glacier. The chair swivelled to the left and the body slumped sideways to the floor. His fish-eyes gaped glassily at the ceiling. A pool of blood lay on the blue linoleum. Blood had clotted on his steely Indian-stiff hair.

Macías prepared for death with his habitual attention to detail. He shaved, and trimmed his moustache. He drank his maté and emptied the green sludge into the garbage pail. He polished his shoes and put on his best Buenos Aires suit of striped worsted.

The front room was bare and white. Flanking the plate-glass mirror were two cabinets of pale wood containing pomades and brilliantines. On the shelf above the basin, he arranged shaving brushes, scissors and razors. Two flasks of hair spray faced each other, their nozzles pointing inwards, their red rubber puffers apart.

The impact of the shot ruined the symmetry of his last composition.

Macías had the reputation of being tight-fisted, but of being correct in all his dealings. He left no will and very little money, yet he owned three houses with tenants in them; they had no complaints against their landlord. He was nervous about his health, was a bigoted vegetarian, and dosed himself with herb teas. He rose early and had the habit of tidying the street before anyone was about. His neighbours called him 'El Argentino', for his aloofness, the sharp cut of his clothes, his maté drinking, and for the once impetuous elegance of his tango.

Originally he came from the south of Chiloé, but left the island as a boy. He apprenticed himself to a gang of sheep-shearers, who worked the estancias of Patagonia. He got caught up in the peons' revolt in 1921, was apparently close to the leaders and escaped with them into Chile. Settling in Puerto Natales, he started up as a barber, which was similar to shearing sheep but better class. He married and had a daughter, but his wife left for a bigamous union with a mechanic in Valparaíso. Over the years he forsook the Revolution and became a Jehovah's Witness.

He shot himself on a Monday. The Sunday crowds had seen him out bicycling, for health they said, the old man in a beret and flapping raincoat, bent against the wind, zig-zagging street by street, then peddling out along the bay till he was swallowed up in the immensity of the landscape.

The townspeople had three main theories about the suicide: either his persecution mania had got the better of him since the Junta's coup; or he had calculated the End of the World for Sunday and shot himself in the anticlimax of Monday morning. The third theory explained the death in terms of arteriosclerosis. There were people who heard him say: 'I'll finish it before it finishes me.'

Conchita Marín was a careless, spirited and heavy-breasted woman with two sons and no husband. Her lovers had fish-scales on their jerseys and came in fresh from the sea. The morning I

called on her, she had on a pink jumper, jingly earrings and an
uncommon amount of green eye-paint. A few plastic curlers were
trying to establish order in her tangle of black hair.

Yes, she was fond of the barber. He was very correct and very
reserved. And also very strange! An intellectual, she said.
'Imagine, he used to lie on his back in the garden and gaze at
the stars.'

She pointed to a drawing in coloured crayons.

'Señor Macías made this drawing for me. Here is the Sun. Red.
Here is the Moon. Yellow. Here is the Earth. Green. And this is
the famous *cometa* ... '

She pointed to an orange streak zooming in from the top corner
of the paper.

'Let me read what it says ... *Cometa* ... *Ko* ... *hou* ... *tek*. Well,
Señor Macías said this cometa was coming from God to kill us
for our sins. But then it went away.'

'Did he have any political connections?' I asked.

'He was a Socialist. I think he was a Socialist.'

'Did he have any Socialist friends?'

'No friends. But he read Socialist books. *Many* books! He read
them to me in the kitchen. But I did not understand.'

'What were the books?'

'I cannot remember. I could not listen when he read. But I
remember one name ... Wait! A famous writer. A writer from
the North. Very Socialist!'

'Ex-President Allende?'

'No. No. No. Señor Macías did not like this Señor Allende at
all. He said he was a *maricón*. He said all the government were
maricones. *Maricones* in the Government! Imagine! No. The name
of this writer began with an M ... Marx! Could it be Marx?'

'It could be Marx.'

'It *was* Marx! *Bueno*, Señor Macías said that everything this
Señor Marx wrote in his book was true, but others changed what
he said. He said it was a perversion, a perversion of the truth.'

Conchita Marín was pleased with herself for having remembered the name of Señor Marx.

'Would you like to see Señor Macías's testament?' she asked,
and produced a colour print of a long-haired dachshund, which
the barber had captioned: 'THE ONE AND ONLY FRIEND OF

MAN (the one who bears him no rancour)'. On the other side I read the following:

> True missionaries assume the authority and concentration of the Apostle Paul.
> No sociology without salvation
> No political economy without the Evangelist
> No reform without redemption
> No culture without conversion
> No progress without forgiveness
> No new social order without a new birth
> No new organization without a New Creation
> No democracy without the Divine Word
> NO CIVILIZATION WITHOUT CHRIST
> ARE WE READY TO DO WHAT OUR MASTER ORDERS
> (according to his express desires?)

Yes, Conchita Marín said, the barber was sick, quite sick. He had arteriosclerosis. But there was something else, something always preying on his mind. No, he never talked about the strike in Argentina. He was very reserved. But sometimes she wondered about the scar at the base of his neck. A bullet, she said. Must have gone clean through. Imagine! He kept the scar hidden always. Always wore a stiff collar and a tie. She had seen the scar once when he was ill and he had tried to hide it.

The barber's daughter, Elsa, was a crushed spinster with sad skin and thinning hair, who lived in a house of two rooms washed the colour of cornflowers, and earned her living as a seamstress. She had seen her father once in the past year, but had not spoken to him for two. He had been an adventurer in his youth, she said. '*Sí, Señor, muy pícaro.*' As a child she remembered him singing to the guitar.

'But they were all sad songs. He was a sad man, my father. He was not educated and he was sad because he had no learning. He read many books but he did not understand.' And with a look that encompassed all his sufferings as well as her own, she pronounced him an *infeliz*.

She showed me a photograph of a man with a shock of swept-back hair, anguish-chiselled features and fearful eyes. He wore the Buenos Aires suit with pointed lapels, a high starched collar and a bow tie. When I asked about the scar, she was quite taken aback and said: 'How could she have told you that?'

The pharmacist on the plaza was one of Macías's old customers. He put me on to a peon who had known the barber in the Argentine strike. The old man lived with the widow who owned the ice-cream parlour. His eyes were cloudy with cataract; blue veins stood out on their lids. His hands were knotted with arthritis and he sat huddled over a wood stove. His protector eyed me mistrustfully, her arms pink to the elbow in ice-cream mix.

The old man was quite communicative at first. He was with the strikers who surrendered to Viñas Ibarra at Río Coyle. 'The Army had permission to kill everybody,' he said definitely, as if one couldn't expect anything else of armies. But when I asked him about the leaders and mentioned Macías's name, he became quite incoherent.

'Traitors!' he spluttered. 'Bar-keepers! Hair-dressers! Acrobats! Artists!', and began to cough and wheeze, and the woman washed her hands and arms of the ice-cream mix and came over and patted him on the back.

'Please, Señor, you must go. He is very old. It is better you do not disturb him.'

José Macías may have had no friends, but he did have customers to whom he talked. One of these was Bautista Díaz Low. Both men were the same age. Both came from the same part of Chiloé. They could reminisce about Chiloé when they tired of blasting each other with unusual information.

Bautista's ancestors were Spanish, Indian and English. His mother's grandfather was Captain William Low, the privateer and sealer, who piloted FitzRoy and Darwin through the *canales*. The great-grandson was a short square man with an amused smile, a steel-hard body and a bloody-mindedness he himself attributed to his *sangre británica*.

Seventy years of fist fights had flattened his nose. He could still drink anyone under the table, while airing his concepts of larger justice and telling even larger stories about his life. Yet photos existed to prove he had tamed an untamable stallion at the age of sixteen; had been a prize fighter and strike leader; had quarrelled with union thugs and had dodged their attempts on his life, in the course of which he had developed a theory that once you kill — or even plan to kill — you are doomed.

'The only lawful weapon is the fist. Ha! All those who plotted against me are under the ground. There is no God but Right!'

As enemy of both capitalist and worker he had retreated up the far side of Last Hope Sound and hacked his own estancia from the wilderness. There I found him, in the blue-shingled house he built with his own hands. And we sat, drinking and laughing through the night, in his eccentric emerald-green kitchen, with two peons and a sealer.

Every two weeks Bautista sailed his red cutter down to Puerto Natales to reprovision himself and stay a night or two with his wife, who preferred his bullish presence at a distance and stayed in town feeding their five sons.

'Five drunk sons! *Qué barbaridad!* What have I done to deserve five drunk sons? Their mother says they work, but I say they are drunk.'

I asked Bautista about the barber's suicide. He thumped his fist on the table.

'José Macías had been reading the Bible and the Bible is a book that makes men mad. The question is: What made him read the Bible?'

I told him what I knew about Macías's part in the strike and of the scar which evidently shamed him. I said how the leaders got away leaving the men to the firing squads and wondered if the bullet wound on his neck was somehow connected.

Bautista listened with attention and said: 'I put Macías's suicide down to women. That man was tremendously lecherous, even at his age. And jealous! He never let his women talk to anyone. Not even to other women. Well, of course, they all left him and that's why he got religious mania. But it's funny you should mention the strike. All the men I knew who came through that strike were haunted men. Perhaps old Macías shot himself as the repayment of a debt.'

I went back to Puerto Natales and checked what I already knew: before he fired the shot José Macías unbuttoned his shirt-front and bared his neck to the mirror.

89

IN THE bar of the Hotel Colonial, the schoolmaster and a retired shepherd were having their lunch-time brandies and moaning quietly about the Junta. The shepherd knew the Mylodon Cave well. He advised me to call first on Señor Eberhard, whose grandfather found the place.

I walked out of town along the bay towards the smokestacks of the meat-works. Red fishing smacks veered erratically at their moorings. A man was shovelling seaweed into a horse-cart. He made a vague gesture as if he'd seen a madman. Then a truck stopped and took me some of the way.

It was dark when I reached Puerto Consuelo. A flotilla of white coscoroba swans were swimming close inshore. The gables of a big German house showed above a planting of pines, but the windows were shuttered and the doors barred. Just then I heard a generator start up and saw a light about half a mile off.

Alsatians howled as I came into the yard; I was glad they were chained up. A tall, eagle-faced man, with white hair and patrician manners, came to the door. I explained, nervously and in Spanish, about Charley Milward and the Giant Sloth.

'So,' he said in English, 'you are of the family of the robber. Come in.'

He led me into a bare white German house of the 1920s, where there were glass-topped tables and tubular steel chairs by Mies van der Rohe. Over dinner he talked about his grandfather and we pieced the story together.

90

HERMAN EBERHARD was a virile boy of tremendous appetites. His father was a Colonel in the Prussian Army, who had gone from Rothenburg ob der Tauber to serve the Elector, and sent him to a military academy, from which, one summer morning, he walked out. He said he was going swimming in the river, left a spare set of clothes on the bank, and disappeared for five years — to a pig farm in Nebraska, a whaling station in the Aleutians, and to Pekin.

There, the German military authorities kidnapped him and shipped him home. His father had himself appointed the judge of his son's court martial and sentenced him to twenty years hard labour for desertion. Herman's friends appealed that the father was biased and got the sentence reduced to eighteen months — which he served.

He left Germany for ever and went to the Falklands where he worked as a pilot. One year, the British Embassy in Buenos Aires asked him to take the Earl of Dudley's yacht, the *Marchesa*, through the *canales* to Valparaíso. Having no sense of money, Herman said he was happy to do it for the ride, but, on leaving the yacht, Lord Dudley pressed an envelope into his hand and told him not to open it. Inside was a cheque for £1,000: in those days a lord was a lord.

The cheque was too big to squander and Eberhard became a sheep-farmer. In 1893, looking for new pasture, he rowed up Last Hope Sound with two English naval deserters, and on coming to Puerto Consuelo said: 'We could do something here.'

In February 1895, Eberhard investigated the cave which he could see yawning into the mountain at the back of his settlement. With him went his brother-in-law Ernst von Heinz, a Mr Greenshield, a Swede called Klondike Hans, and their dog. They found a human skull and a piece of skin sticking out of the floor. The skin was about four feet long and half as wide. One side was bristly and covered with salt encrustation, the other embedded with white ossicles. Mr Greenshield said it was a cowhide stuck with pebbles. Eberhard said there were no cows and thought it the skin of an unknown sea-mammal. He hung it on a tree and let the rain wash it clean of salt.

A year later, the Swedish explorer Dr Otto Nordenskjöld visited the cave and found another piece of skin — or may have snipped a bit of Eberhard's. He also found the eye-socket of a vast mammal, a claw, a human thighbone of giant size, and some stone tools. He sent the lot to Dr Einnar Lönnberg of the

Uppsala Museum, who was mystified and excited, but dared not publish without more information.

Rumours of something strange at Puerto Consuelo next attracted Dr Francisco Moreno of the La Plata Museum. He came in November 1897 and found nothing of interest except Eberhard's skin still hanging on the tree, but halved in size. The German gave it to him and he packed it off to La Plata with other material from his travels.

A month after the crate arrived, Moreno's colleague and enemy, Florentino Ameghino, the doyen of South American palaeontologists, published a sensational paper: *First Note on Mylodon Listai—a LIVING Representative of the Ancient Gravigrade Fossil Edentates of Argentina.*

But first a little of the background:

91

THE MYLODON was a Giant Ground Sloth, rather bigger than a bull, of a class unique to South America. In 1789 a Dr Bartolome de Muñoz sent from Buenos Aires the bones of its even bigger cousin, the Megatherium, to the King of Spain's cabinet of curiosities in Madrid. The King ordered a second specimen, live or dead.

The skeleton astonished naturalists of Cuvier's generation. Goethe worked it into an essay which appears to anticipate the Theory of Evolution. The zoologists had to picture an antediluvian mammal, standing fifteen feet high, which was also a magnified version of the ordinary, insect-eating sloths that hung upside-down from trees. Cuvier gave it the name Megatherium and suggested that Nature had wanted to amuse herself with 'something imperfect and grotesque'.

Darwin found the bones of a mylodon among his 'nine great quadrupeds' on the beach at Punta Alta, near Bahía Blanca, and sent them to Dr Richard Owen at the Royal College of Surgeons. Owen laughed at the idea of giant sloths up giant trees before the Flood. He reconstructed *Mylodon Darwini* as a cumbersome animal that reared up on its haunches, using its legs and tail as a tripod, and, instead of climbing up trees, clawed them down. The mylodon had a long extensible tongue, like a giraffe's, which it used to scoop up leaves and grubs.

Throughout the nineteenth century mylodon bones continued to surface in the barrancas of Patagonia. Scientists were puzzled by the innumerable lumps of bone found with the skeletons until Ameghino correctly interpreted them as an armour plating, like the plaques of an armadillo.

There was, however, a point at which the extinct beast merged with the living beast and the beast of the imagination. Indian legends and travellers' tales had convinced some zoologists that a big mammal had survived the catastrophes of the Ice Age and lingered on in the Southern Andes. There were five contenders:

a. The *Yemische*, a kind of ghoul.

b. The *Su*, or *Succuruth*, reported as early as 1558, living on the banks of Patagonian rivers. The creature had the head of a lion 'with something human about it', a short beard from ear to ear, and a tail armed with sharp bristles which served as a shelter for the young. The *Su* was a hunter but not for meat alone; for it hunted animals for their skins and warmed itself in the cold climate.

c. The *Yaquarū* or 'Water-Tiger' (often confused with the *Su*). The English Jesuit, Thomas Falkner, saw one on the Paraná in the eighteenth century. It was a vicious creature that lived in whirlpools, and when it ate a cow, the lungs and entrails floated to the surface. (It was probably a caiman.) 'Water-Tigers' also figure in George Chaworth Musters's memoir *At Home with the Patagonians*; the author describes how his Tehuelche guide refused to cross the Río Senguer for fear of 'yellow quadrupeds larger than a puma'.

d. The *Elengassen*, a monster described by a Patagonian Cacique to Dr Moreno in 1879. It had a human head and armoured carapace, and would stone strangers who approached its lair. The only way to kill it was through a chink in its belly.

e. The fifth and most convincing report of unexplained fauna was a huge animal 'resembling a Giant Pangolin' shot at in the late 1880s by Ramón Lista, then Governor of Santa Cruz.

Such was the background to Florentino Ameghino's pamphlet.

For years, he told journalists, his brother Carlos had heard the Indians tell of the *Yemische*. At first they assumed it was an aboriginal terror myth, a mere product of their incoherent theology. Now they had new and startling evidence to believe in its existence as a living mammal:

In 1895, he said, a Tehuelche called Hompen was trying to cross the Río Senguer, but the current was strong and his horse refused to enter. Dismounting, Hompen waded in to persuade it to follow. But the horse whinnied, reared, and bolted for the desert. At that instant Hompen saw the *Yemische* advancing towards him.

Coolly eyeing the beast, he threw his boleadoras and *bola perdida* 'weapons of formidable efficiency in the hands of an Indian'. He entangled it, skinned the carcass, and kept a small piece for his friend the white explorer.

Carlos sent the skin on to Florentino. The moment he handled the skin and saw the white ossicles he knew that the '*Yemische* and the Mylodon of past ages were one'. The discovery vindicated Ramón Lista's hunting story: he was renaming the animal *Neomylodon Listai* in memory of the assassinated ex-Governor.

'And the skeleton?' asked the journalist.

'My brother is looking into the matter of the skeleton. I hope to have it in my possession soon.'

No. Dr Ameghino did not think the animal could have floated from Antarctica on an iceberg.

Yes. He had asked the Minister of Public Works for a large sum of money for a mylodon hunt.

Yes. The Tehuelches hunted mylodons, often with sunken pits, hidden by leaves and branches.

No. He didn't doubt they would catch it. 'Despite its invulnerable carapace and aggressive habits, it will eventually fall prisoner to man.

No. He was not impressed by Dr Moreno's discoveries at the Eberhard Cave. If Dr Moreno knew he had a mylodon skin, why hadn't he brought it to the attention of science?

Ameghino's press conference was another international sensation. The British Museum pestered him to cut off a tiny piece. The Germans wanted a photo of the dead animal. And, throughout Argentina, there were a number of sightings: an estanciero on the Paraná lost a peon to a 'water-tiger' and heard the crack of branches and the animal swimming: 'clap ... clap ... clap ... ' and howling 'ah ... joooooo!'

Moreno got back to La Plata and took his piece of skin to London. He left it at the British Museum for safe-keeping, where it remains. In a lecture to the Royal Society on January 17th 1899 he said he had always known it was a mylodon, and that the animal was long extinct but preserved under the same conditions as moa feathers from New Zealand.

Dr Arthur Smith Woodward, Keeper of Palaeontology, only half believed this. He had handled moa feathers. In St Petersburg he had also handled pieces of Pallass's woolly rhinocerous and the deep-frozen mammoth from Yakutia. Compared to these, he said, the mylodon skin was so 'remarkably fresh' and the blood clot so red that, were it not for Dr Moreno, he would have 'no hesitation in pronouncing the animal recently killed'.

Certainly there was sufficient doubt in England for the *Daily Express* to finance the expedition of a Mr Hesketh Prichard to look for it. Prichard found no trace of the mylodon, but his book *Through the Heart of Patagonia* seems to have been an ingredient of Conan Doyle's *The Lost World*.

Meanwhile two archaeologists dug in the cave. The Swede Erland Nordenskjöld was the more methodical. He found three stratified levels: the upper contained human settlement; in the middle were the bones of some extinct fauna including the 'Dawn Horse'; but only in the bottom layer did he find remains of the mylodon.

The second excavator, Dr Hauthal of La Plata, was an impressionist who apparently didn't even understand the principles of stratigraphy. He uncovered the layer of perfectly preserved sloth dung, mixed with leaves and grass, which covers the floor to the depth of a metre. He also pointed to the wall of stones which cut off the back part of the cave. And he announced that the place was a mylodon corral. Early man had domesticated mylodons and kept them penned up for winter rations. He said he was changing the name again, from *Neomylodon Listai* to *Gryptotherium domesticum*.

Among Erland Nordenskjöld's helpers was the German gold-panner Albert Konrad. Once the archaeologists were out of the way, he rigged up a tin shanty at the cave-mouth and started dynamiting the stratigraphy to bits. Charley went up to help him and came away with yards of skin and piles of bones and claws, which, by this time, were a saleable commodity. He packed the collection off to the British Museum, and after a tremendous haggle with Dr Arthur Smith Woodward (who thought Charley was trying to up the price when he learned that Walter Rothschild was paying) sold it for £400.

My grandparents got married about this time and I imagine he must have sent a small piece as a wedding present.

Ameghino's part in the affair is most suspicious. He never came up with Hompen's piece of skin. The chances are he snooped in Moreno's crate, and saw the skin but dared not steal it. One fact is certain: his pamphlet became as rare as the beast it attempted to describe.

The modern verdict, based on radio-carbon dates, is that the mylodon was alive ten thousand years ago, but not since.

92

IN THE morning I walked with Eberhard in driving rain. He wore a fur-lined greatcoat and glared fiercely at the storm from under a Cossack hat. He said his favourite writer was Sven Hedin, the explorer of Mongolia.

Mongolia—Patagonia, Xanadu and the Mariner.

We looked at his German barns now falling in ruins. He had lost most of his land in the reform and took it with stoic resignation. As a young man he had worked as an apprentice on the *Explotadora*:

'Was run like a crack regiment in the British Army. Orders were posted up each morning in two languages and you won't guess what they were.'

'English and Spanish,' I said.

'Wrong.'

'English and German?' I was puzzled.

'Try again.'

'Spanish and ... '

'Wrong. English and Gaelic.

'General Manager of the *Explotadora*,' he continued, 'was Mr Leslie Greer. This man was a tyrant, an absolute tyrant. But he was a brilliant administrator and everyone knew where he was. Then he said NO to Directors and they sacked him. Directors wanted yes-men and they got them. So they wondered why their profits go down and they called in technicians. Technicians had superior degrees and all that and ordered managers about. Countermanded managers' orders and managers countermanded their orders, and the whole blinking edifice fell down under its own weight.

'Now I tell you story about Mr Greer: Goes up to B.A. and lunches at his club, Hurlingham or some such place. Dining-room is full but he asks two English gentlemen: "Please can I sit at your table?" "Certainly," Englishman says. "I must introduce myself," he says. "My name is Leslie Greer, General manager of the *Sociedad Explotadora de Tierra del Fuego*." "And I," this Englishman says, "I am GOD. And this here is my friend and colleague Jesus Christ." '

I asked him about the miner Albert Konrad:

'I have seen Albert Konrad with my eyes. Ja! I remember him in 1920s coming through here with mules. You must know, this Albert Konrad was most unpopular in Chile for selling out the mylodon. So he went over the border to live in Río de las Vueltas. So he was coming down to Punta Arenas with mules. And my father said: "Hey! Albert. What have you got on those mules? Stones?" "Stones no," he said. "Those stones are gold." But they were stones, ordinary stones.'

Sometime in the 1930s a gaucho riding down Río de las Vueltas passed Konrad's cabin and heard a door creaking on its hinge. The German was slumped over his Mauser. He had been dead all winter. The inside of the cabin was bursting with grey stones.

93

I WALKED the four miles from Puerto Consuelo to the Cave.
It was raining but the sun dipped under the clouds and
sparkled on the bushes. The cave-mouth gaped, four hundred
feet wide, into a cliff of grey conglomerate. Hunks had tumbled
to the floor and were piled about the entrance.

The inside was dry as the desert. The ceiling was shaggy with
white stalactites and the sides glittered with salt encrustation.
Animal tongues had licked the back wall smooth. The straight
wall of rocks dividing the cave had fallen from a fissure in the
roof. By the entrance was a small shrine to the Virgin.

I tried to picture the cave with sloths in it, but I could not erase
the fanged monster I associate with a blacked-out bedroom in
wartime England. The floor was covered with turds, sloth turds,
outsize black leathery turds, full of ill-digested grass, that looked
as if they had been shat last week.

I groped in the holes left by Albert Konrad's dynamiting,
looking for another piece of skin. I found nothing.

'Well,' I thought, 'if there's no skin, at least there's a load of
shit.'

And then, poking out of a section, I saw some strands of the
coarse reddish hair I knew so well. I eased them out, slid them
into an envelope and sat down, immensely pleased. I had
accomplished the object of this ridiculous journey. And then I
heard voices, women's voices, voices singing: 'María ... María ...
María ... '

Now I too had gone mad.

I peered over the fallen rocks and saw seven black figures
facing the shrine of the Virgin.

The Sisters of Santa María Auxiliadora were out on another of
their unusual excursions. The Mother Superior smiled and said:
'Aren't you afraid in here by yourself?'

I had intended to sleep in the cave but thought better of it, and
the nuns gave me a lift to one of the old estancias of the
Explotadora:

94

HE WAS going to die. His eyelids were swollen and so heavy he had to strain to stop them falling and covering his eyes. His nose was thin as a beak and his breath came in thick fetid bursts. His coughs retched through the corridors. The other men moved off when they heard him coming.

He took from his wallet a crumpled photograph of himself, on leave from military service, long ago, in a palm-filled garden in Valparaíso. The boy in the photo was unrecognizable in the man: the cocky smile, the wasp-waisted jacket and Oxford bags, and the sleek black hair shining in the sun.

He had worked twenty years on the estancia and now he was going to die. He remembered Mr Sandars, the manager, who died and was buried at sea. He did not like Mr Sandars. He was a hard man, a despotic man, but the place had gone down since. It was bad under the Marxists and it was worse under the Junta. He spluttered between coughs.

'The workers,' he said, 'have had to pay for this Marxist Movement, but I do not think it will last.'

I left him to die and went down to Punta Arenas to catch the ship.

95

THE HOTEL Residencial Ritz was a building of white concrete straddling half a block between the naval officers' club and the beach. The management prided itself on its spotless white damask tablecloths.

The ladies' lingerie salesman from Santiago paced up and down the hall of the hotel before the curfew lifted at five. If he had gone for his walk earlier, the guards might have shot him. He came back to breakfast with his pocket full of stones. The walls of the dining-room were a hard blue. The floor was covered with blue plastic tiles, and the tablecloths floated above it like chunks of ice.

The salesman sat down, emptied his pockets and began to play with the stones, talking to them and laughing. He ordered coffee and toast from the fat, snuffle-nosed Chilote girl who worked in the kitchen. He was a big, unhealthy man. Folds of flesh stood out on the back of his neck. He wore a beige tweed suit and a hand-knitted sweater with a roll collar.

He looked in my direction and smiled, showing a set of swollen pink gums. Then he withdrew the smile, looked down and played again with the stones.

'What glorious rosy hues the clouds have this morning!'

He had broken the silence, suddenly, in a burst.

'Permit me to ask you a question, Sir? What is the cause of this phenomenon? The cold rising, I have heard it said.'

'Perhaps,' I said.

'I have been walking on the beach and have gazed at the forms which the Creator has painted in the sky. I have seen the Chariot of Fire transformed into the arching neck of a swan. Beautiful! The hand of the Creator! One should either paint or photograph his work. But I am not a painter and I do not possess a camera.'

The girl fetched his breakfast. He cleared a space among the stones for his cup and plate.

'Are you perhaps acquainted, Sir,' he continued, 'with something of *la poesía mundial*?'

'Some,' I said.

His forehead puckered with concentration and he declaimed slow, ponderous stanzas. At the end of each he clenched his fist and set it slowly on the table. The girl had been standing with the coffee pot. She put it down, buried her face in her apron and ran laughing for the kitchen.

'What was that?'

'I don't know.'

'The *Solitudes* of Góngora,' he said and began again, straining to extract the last shred of emotion from the lines, moving his hands sideways and splaying his fingers.

'*A las cinco de la tarde.*

Eran las cinco en punto de la tarde ... '

'Lorca,' I suggested.

'Federico García Lorca,' he whispered, as if exhausted by

prayer. '*The Lament for Ignacio Sánchez Mejías*. You are my friend. I see you are not wholly ignorant of our Hispanic literature. Now what's this?'

He jerked his head back and shouted more poetry.

'I don't know.'

'The Venezualan National Anthem.'

I saw him later in the day, slump-shouldered in the drizzle, plodding the streets with his black-and-white check cap and case of lingerie samples. Models, in pink corsets and brassieres, stared from shop-windows with vacant blue plastic eyes. The underwear shops were owned by Hindus.

In the night the noise of his crêpe soles kept me awake again. He went out at five, but I heard him come back several times. At breakfast I passed the kitchen door and saw the girls helpless with giggles.

He was standing among the tablecloths, his bristly face fixed in a hopeless smile. On every table and at every place was an arrangement of stones.

'These are my friends,' he said in a hoarse, emotional voice. 'Look! Here is a whale. Wonderful! The confirmation of God's genius. A whale with a harpoon in its side. Here is the mouth and here the tail.'

'And this?'

'The head of a prehistoric animal. And here a monkey.'

'This?'

'Another prehistoric animal, probably a dinosaur. And this,' he pointed to a pitted yellowish lump, 'the head of primitive man. The eyes. You see? Here the nose. And the jaw, here. Look, even the low forehead, token of inferior intelligence.'

'Yes,' I said.

'And this,' he picked up a round grey pebble, 'this is my favourite. Turned one way, a porpoise. Upside down, the Blessed Virgin Mary. Wonderful! The imprint of God upon a humble stone!'

The Manager of the Ritz did not like being woken before nine. But other clients wanted breakfast and the tables had to be cleared. In the course of the morning, I dropped some things back to my room. They had taken him to hospital.

'*Es loco*,' the manager said. 'He is mad.'

96

THERE IS a man in Punta Arenas, dreams pine forests, hums Lieder, wakes each morning and sees the black strait. He drives to a factory that smells of the sea. All about him are scarlet crabs, crawling, then steaming. He hears the shells crack and the claws breaking, sees the sweet white flesh packed firm in metal cans. He is an efficient man, with some previous experience of the production line. Does he remember that other smell, of burning? And that other sound, of low voices singing? And the piles of hair cast away as the claws of crabs?

Walter Rauff is credited with the invention and administration of the Mobile Gas Truck.

97

AFTER WAITING a week for the ship we heard her siren sounding from behind the gymnasium (which was a concrete copy of the Parthenon) and, down at the dock, saw the stevedores manhandling crates instead of loafing round the steamship company, flat black caps against a pink wall. The whole of that week, the booking clerk had shrugged when we asked where the ship was, shrugged and picked the wen on his forehead, the ship could have gone down for all he knew or cared. But now he was scribbling out tickets, sweating, gesticulating, and barking orders. Then we filed through the green customs shed, along the rusty plates of the steamer, to the gang-plank, where the Chilotes queued up with the faces of men who had waited four hundred years.

The ship was once the S.S. *Ville de Haiphong*. The third class had the quality of an Asiatic jail and the closing bulkheads looked more for keeping back coolies than floodwater. The Chilotes bunked down in the big communal cabin with its floor scabbed with squashed roaches, smelling of mussel stew before and after they had sicked it up. The fans in the first class had been disconnected, and in the panelled saloon we drank with the personnel of a kaolin mine, whom the ship would drop, one midnight, on their white womanless island in the middle of the sea. As we eased out of port a Chilean businessman played *La Mer* on a white piano missing many of its keys.

The Captain was a chic type with unshakeable confidence in his rivets. He got better food than we did, and we saw the sly expression on the steward's face as he took the carnations off our table and served pigs' trotters and the ship started pitching and banging into three-cornered waves.

In the morning, black petrels were slicing the swells and, through the mist, we saw chutes of water coming off the cliffs. The ladies' lingerie salesman from Santiago had got out of hospital and was pacing the foredeck, chewing his lip and muttering poetry. There was a boy from the Falklands with a seal-skin hat and strange sharp teeth. ''Bout time the Argentines took us over,' he said. 'We're so bloody inbred.' And he laughed and pulled from his pocket a stone. 'Look what he gave me, a bloody stone!' As we came out into the Pacific, the businessman was still playing *La Mer*. Perhaps it was the only thing he could play.

Some Sources

Prehistoric animals in Patagonia

George Gaylord Simpson, *Attending Marvels*, New York, 1934; and the same author's papers published by the American Museum of Natural History, New York. For the history of the mylodon, I also used a collection of documents and newspaper clippings collected by Mr Tim Currant of the British Museum (Natural History).

Río Negro

W. H. Hudson, *Idle Days in Patagonia*, London, 1893.

The Kingdom of Araucania and Patagonia

Orélie-Antoine de Tounens, *Son avènement au trône et sa captivité au Chili*, Paris, 1865.
Armando Braun Menéndez, *El Reino de Araucania y Patagonia*, Buenos Aires, 5th ed., 1967.
Leo Magne, *L'extraordinaire aventure d'Antoine de Tounens*, Paris, 1950.

The Welsh

John E. Bauer, 'The Welsh in Patagonia', in *Hispanic American Review*, vol. 34, no. 4, 1954.
An account of a visit to John Evans at Trevelin appears in A. F. Tschiffeley's other book, *This Way Southward*, New York, 1940.

Butch Cassidy

Alan Swallow, ed., *The Wild Bunch*, Denver, 1966.
Lula Parker Betenson, *Butch Cassidy My Brother*, Provo, Utah, 1975.

Butch Cassidy's letter to Mrs Davis is in the Utah State Historical Society and reprinted with their permission. I could not have written this section without the help of Kerry Ross Boren, outlaw historian of Manila, Utah.

Patagonian Outlaws

Asencio Abeijón, *Memorias de un Carrero Patagónico*, 2 vols, 1973–5, Buenos Aires.

The City of the Caesars

Manuel Rojas, *La Cuidad de los Césares*, Santiago, 1936.

The Patagonian Giants

Helen Wallis, 'The Patagonian Giants', in *Byron's Circumnavigation*, Hakluyt Society, London, 1964.
R. T. Gould, 'There were Giants in those Days', in *Enigmas*, London, 1946.
For help in pinning down the origin of the word 'Patagonia' I am most grateful to Joan St George Saunders and Professor Emilio Gonzáles Díaz, of Buenos Aires.

The Revolution

Osvaldo Bayer, *Los Vengadores de la Patagonia Trágica*, 3 vols, Buenos Aires, 1972–4.
José María Borrero, *La Patagonia Trágica*, reprinted, Buenos Aires, 1967.
Contemporary copies of the *Magellan Times* printed in Punta Arenas.

Folklore of Chiloé

Narciso García Barria, *Tesoro Mitológico de Chiloé*, 1968.

Indians of Tierra del Fuego

Lucas Bridges, *The Uttermost Part of the Earth*, London, 1948.
Samuel Kirkland Lothrop, *The Indians of Tierra del Fuego*, New York, 1928.
Martin Gusinde, *The Yámana*, trans. F. Schütze, New Haven, 1961.

Edgar Allan Poe

Introduction to *The Narrative of Arthur Gordon Pym*, by Harold Beaver, Penguin Books, London, 1975.

Simón Radowitzky

Osvaldo Bayer, *Los Anarquistas Expropiadores*, Buenos Aires, 1975.

The Dictionary

Rev. Thomas Bridges, *Yámana–English Dictionary*, ed. Professor T. Hesterman, Mödling, Austria, 1933, limited edition of 300 copies.

The End of the World

Unmentioned in the text are Jules Verne's symbolic last novel *The Lighthouse at the End of the World*, and W. Olaf Stapledon's *Last and First Men*, London, 1930. In this memorable fantasy, the human species, now completely Americanized, perishes through epidemics of cannibalism and pulmonary and nervous diseases. A few stragglers, however, survive to the south of Bahía Blanca, and a new civilization springs up in the Far South under the influence of an adolescent of prodigious sexual capacity, known as The Boy who Refused to Grow Up. The Patagonian Civilization colonizes the rest of the globe, but is no less stupid than its predecessor and destroys itself with an atomic cataclysm.

Captain Charles Amherst Milward

I could not have written this book without the help of Charley Milward's daughter, Monica Barnett, of Lima. She allowed me access to her father's papers and the unpublished manuscript of his stories in her possession. This was particularly generous since she is writing her own biography in which they will appear in full. My sections 73, 75 and 86 are printed from the manuscript with minor alterations. His other stories, from sections 72 to 85, have been adapted from the original.

FOR THE BEST IN PAPERBACKS, LOOK FOR THE

In every corner of the world, on every subject under the sun, Penguin represents quality and variety—the very best in publishing today.

For complete information about books available from Penguin—including Puffins, Penguin Classics, and Arkana—and how to order them, write to us at the appropriate address below. Please note that for copyright reasons the selection of books varies from country to country.

In the United Kingdom: Please write to *Dept. JC, Penguin Books Ltd, FREEPOST, West Drayton, Middlesex UB7 0BR.*

If you have any difficulty in obtaining a title, please send your order with the correct money, plus ten percent for postage and packaging, to *P.O. Box No. 11, West Drayton, Middlesex UB7 0BR*

In the United States: Please write to *Consumer Sales, Penguin USA, P.O. Box 999, Dept. 17109, Bergenfield, New Jersey 07621-0120.* VISA and MasterCard holders call 1-800-253-6476 to order all Penguin titles

In Canada: Please write to *Penguin Books Canada Ltd, 10 Alcorn Avenue, Suite 300, Toronto, Ontario M4V 3B2*

In Australia: Please write to *Penguin Books Australia Ltd, P.O. Box 257, Ringwood, Victoria 3134*

In New Zealand: Please write to *Penguin Books (NZ) Ltd, Private Bag 102902, North Shore Mail Centre, Auckland 10*

In India: Please write to *Penguin Books India Pvt Ltd, 706 Eros Apartments, 56 Nehru Place, New Delhi 110 019*

In the Netherlands: Please write to *Penguin Books Netherlands bv, Postbus 3507, NL-1001 AH Amsterdam*

In Germany: Please write to *Penguin Books Deutschland GmbH, Metzlerstrasse 26, 60594 Frankfurt am Main*

In Spain: Please write to *Penguin Books S.A., Bravo Murillo 19, 1° B, 28015 Madrid*

In Italy: Please write to *Penguin Italia s.r.l., Via Felice Casati 20, I-20124 Milano*

In France: Please write to *Penguin France S.A., 17 rue Lejeune, F-31000 Toulouse*

In Japan: Please write to *Penguin Books Japan, Ishikiribashi Building, 2-5-4, Suido, Bunkyo-ku, Tokyo 112*

In Greece: Please write to *Penguin Hellas Ltd, Dimocritou 3, GR-106 71 Athens*

In South Africa: Please write to *Longman Penguin Southern Africa (Pty) Ltd, Private Bag X08, Bertsham 2013*